Labor
Relations
in Europe

Labor Relations in Europe

A History of Issues and Developments

Hans Slomp

Contributions in Labor Studies, Number 29

GP

GREENWOOD PRESS

New York • Westport, Connecticut • London

HD
8374
.S57
1990

Library of Congress Cataloging-in-Publication Data

Slomp, Hans
   Labor relations in Europe : a history of issues and developments /
Hans Slomp.
   p.   cm. — (Contributions in labor studies, ISSN 0886–8239 ;
no. 29)
   Includes bibliographical references.
   ISBN 0–313–26756–1 (lib. bdg. : alk. paper)
   1. Industrial relations—Europe—History. I. Title. II. Series.
HD8374.S57   1990
331'.094—dc20   89–23262

British Library Cataloguing in Publication Data is available.

Library of Congress Catalog Card Number: 89–23262
ISBN: 0–313–26756–1
ISSN: 0886–8239

First published in 1990

Greenwood Press, Inc.
88 Post Road West, Westport, Connecticut 06881

Printed in the United States of America

The paper used in this book complies with the
Permanent Paper Standard issued by the National
Information Standards Organization (Z39.48-1984).

10 9 8 7 6 5 4 3 2 1

Contents

Introduction

Studies of European labor relations have traditionally taken one of two major approaches. Descriptive nation studies and case studies of specific developments have dominated on the European continent. Their main focus has been on the labor *movement* rather than on labor *relations*. In contrast, the Anglo-Saxon approach has used a more explicit comparative and theoretical orientation. It is expressed not only in comparative surveys but also in monographs (mainly American) on labor in specific continental countries.

Discussions of neo-corporatism and the union response to the recent crisis have narrowed the gap between the two traditions. Yet, even today the traditional division of labor survives, with Anglo-Saxons developing new concepts and continental students filling in or refining the Anglo-Saxon theses. The recent boom in comparative research is still a predominantly Anglo-Saxon affair.

Of course, both traditions have their pros and cons. The continental surveys offer a wealth of inside information and insight into national developments, but they allow hardly any distinction between national idiosyncrasies and common trends. The Anglo-Saxon tradition offers comparative perspectives and frames of references, as well as concepts with which to tackle the wealth of material. However, especially when covering a large number of countries, it sometimes draws upon scattered evidence, taken from different periods. A disadvantage of both traditions is their focus on national developments, for example, on national differences. In the former approach this is inherent to the perspective; in the second it is related to attempts to show the many manifestations or faces of labor relations. As a consequence, Europe remains a patchwork of different nations with respect to labor relations, each with its own system, its own forms of bargaining and labor conflict. In contrast to other academic disciplines, such as economic and social history, and political science, this national perspective has not yet been complemented by a European view, stressing similarities and common developments.

This book is an effort to such a European view. It has been written to serve a threefold purpose. First and foremost, it is intended to be a general introduction to European labor relations for those who are unfamiliar with the subject. Such an introduction should start with a survey of European trends and issues, not with a nation-based study of British, French, or German labor relations.

Second, it contributes directly to the descriptive tradition by offering comparative material from a range of countries. Trends and events are not only part of a national labor relations system, but also of a wider European setting, as national expressions of more general developments. By doing so, this survey might facilitate the distinction between what is really specific for one country and what is just a minor variation from a European trend.

Third, by its systematic ordering of material, it contributes indirectly to theories of labor relations. This will allow a more selective use of data in theories, taken from comparable periods and similar situations. In that respect it will serve the sacred principle of *ceteris paribus* of any research. The author hopes it will also increase the number of countries discussed in comparative and theoretical studies.

That the contribution to the Anglo-Saxon approach is indirect has to do with the nature of the work at hand. This book has been written in accordance with the continental approach, which, the author feels, is the best way to serve the first purpose, an introduction to European labor relations.

The descriptive perspective has been applied rigorously. It is visible first of all in the chronological presentation. Each chapter covers a specific period, based on important changes in economic and political conditions common to most of Europe, such as crises and wars, to mention only the worst of times. The first chapter contains a short, general survey of labor during the Industrial Revolution. The second describes the major trends and issues of the nineteenth century to 1875. The third and fourth cover the turn of the century, and the remaining chapters each discuss one or two decades in the twentieth century.

Most chapters cover all of Europe, but the first and second chapters are limited to countries that were industrialized, or at least industrializing, in the mid-nineteenth century, in order to avoid extensive reference to preindustrial conditions. A second exception is the separation made between Western and Eastern Europe from 1948 until the 1980s when Eastern Europe became the scene of dramatic change. Moreover, from Chapter 3 onward a distinction is made between different models of labor relations. Within the wider scope of a European view, the models should do justice to the many forms of European labor relations.

In accordance with the continental approach, attention is devoted not just to the form, but also to the content of labor relations. The survey covers the issues of labor relations as practiced by employers or employers' associations and trade unions, rather than the issues of labor relations as an academic discipline. For example, conflict issues are a major subject, while strike rates are not. Only the first chapter has a wider focus, including a survey of the rise and nature of industrial labor (omitting labor in agriculture). Although some well-established theoretical notions have been incorporated, an explicit theoretical frame of reference or direct references to labor relations theory are lacking. Another evident deviation from most Anglo-Saxon studies is the amount of space devoted to politics. This may be due to the bias of an author who was trained as a political scientist, but another relevant factor is the intimate links in continental Europe between labor relations and national as well as international politics—links in which politics influenced labor relations and vice versa. This focus means that most attention is paid to the national level rather than to the workplace. Less attention is also devoted to explanations that relate mainly to the level of industrial branches, such as degree of competition, which constitute popular topics in the Anglo-Saxon approach.

Most of the sources used are general national surveys, and therefore, most of the text on each nation is probably more or less common knowledge in that particular nation. Therefore, footnotes have been omitted and replaced by a bibliography organized by country. When an attempt is made to argue that the revolt of the *canuts* in 1834, the great railway strikes at the turn of the century, the Great Strike of 1926, the Saltsjöbaden agreement of 1938, the rise of *Mitbestimmung* after the Second World War and the *Accord de Grenelle* of 1968, to name a few highlights, are not isolated national events, but related to similar events elsewhere in Europe, the bibliography will provide a further key to the fascinating field of European labor relations.

The responsibility for the book rests with the author, but many people were helpful in this endeavor. Theo Berben, Martin Gerritsen, Arend Geul, Peter de Goede, Albaer Hillen, Wibo Koole, Wolfgang Lecher, René Mouriaux, Paul Nobelen, Bob Reinalda, and Göran Therborn read earlier drafts or chapters of the manuscript or assisted in gathering material. Ank Michels read several drafts and helped to clarify the distinctions made in labor relations models. As the text was being expanded and reduced, students in several classes made useful suggestions. Anneli Vos typed the handwritten manuscript and retyped new drafts. Barry van Driel corrected the English. The author is grateful to them all. Particular thanks to Irene, Michiel, and Hiske, who shared the burden.

Labor
Relations
in Europe

1

The Rise of Industrial Labor

THE EMERGENCE OF INDUSTRIAL LABOR

Until the mid-nineteenth century industrial labor was mainly a transformation of two traditional types of workers: urban artisanal workers and laborers employed in their own homes under the putting-out system.

Artisans and craft workers had dominated urban economic life for centuries. They started as apprentices, became journeymen, and eventually independent masters, who combined their own manual work with the supervision over journeymen and apprentices. Handicraft production was small-scale. Most masters only had a limited amount of capital to invest and employed no more than two or three journeymen. The latter lived with the master's family until they married or passed the test for mastery and set up on their own. Masters and journeymen were organized in guilds, which prescribed not only the mode of production and the price of the product, but also the number of apprentices per master, the wages of the journeymen, and the qualifications needed to settle as an independent master. Before the Industrial Revolution, the concentration of capital and the expansion of the market had already changed the existing relations between masters and journeymen. Guilds disappeared, and in several trades masters could pass on the right to economic independence to their sons or sons-in-law. They became mere employers, no longer teaching, housing, or feeding their journeymen. The number of the latter increased, but journeyman became the terminal status. They were downgraded to skilled or specialized but dependent workers.

The Industrial Revolution mechanized the trades and reinforced their concentration, though most mechanized workshops did not exceed ten to fifteen workers. Some former masters and journeymen became industrial employers, and a great number of them clearly lost their independence. The speed of this proletarianization process depended on external forces (such as the nature of the market) and on internal conditions, like the costs of raw materials and tools as well as the nature of the skills involved. If conditions were favorable, it was possible to keep the trade closed and obtain or retain a privileged position in an exclusive trade. If not, artisans and journeymen became industrial craft workers or home workers, dependent on middlemen or on the mills. In general, the artisans in the luxury trades in national capital cities occupied the strongest position. These cities remained centers of artisanal work conducted in small workshops without mechanized motive power. However, Parisian tailors were particularly hard-hit because they could hardly ever purchase their own—expensive—cloth. The same applied to building workers, such as masons and roofers. They could purchase their own tools, but not the materials they had to work on.

Traditional artisanal production was not always continued as craft work or mechanized artisanal work. Often it was replaced by putting-out to a rural cottage industry. In the countryside, agriculture had often been supplemented by part-time nonagricultural work as a source of income, especially by weaving and spinning. Part-time weavers and spinners were either tied to a feudal lord or they sold their produce independently. In the latter case, a new kind of dependency had already become the rule before the Industrial Revolution. Increasingly, production was concentrated not so much physically as in manufacturing, but in the supply of capital. Middlemen put out their work to people, providing them with raw materials or loans in advance of delivery. In this manner owners of capital could finance the whole production process, with the exception of handlooms, which remained private property. At first, mechanization of spinning in the early textile mills caused a true boom in rural handloom weaving, especially in Great Britain. But by mid-century, weaving and other rural cottage industries became concentrated in urban centers, near the mills. In contrast to rural home work, this urban labor was part of the Industrial Revolution from its very beginning. In some trades this served to continue the skilled character of the trade. In others, particularly in textiles, it replaced the skilled part of the trade. Merchants and middlemen were eager to employ rural migrants, especially women, in such cottage industries. Although a number of skilled trades, like the guilds before, still excluded women, men were increasingly replaced by women in cottage industries. Where women predominated, sweated labor, characterized by very strenuous working conditions, prevailed. However. the burgeoning of urban home work only marked a time of transition to factory labor. Many mid-century rural migrants were employed in cottage industries, but in the second half of the century factories absorbed this kind of labor. Therefore, urban home work was only common in the regions of Western Europe that underwent industrialization early. In other countries there was a more direct transition to factory labor.

The work force in the mills represented the core of industrial labor. Its growth was the result of the rise of industrial technology; it was territorially concentrated from the outset, and its production speed determined the fate of home workers.

The British cotton mills started with fewer than ten workers on the average, but many of them employed hundreds of workers as early on as the beginning of the nineteenth century. A rather strict division of labor was the rule here. Men, smallest in numbers, handled heavier machines and supervised women and children. Boys, acting as piecers in mule spinning, were dependent on the (male) spinners for their labor conditions. They were often hired by the latter rather than by the employers. Women and girls comprised the majority of the work force and did most of the weaving. Their large numbers were related to two factors. First, women had been trained to be more submissive and could be paid less. The same applied to children. Second, both women and men regarded the factories with their strict discipline as an inferior type of employment. They preferred the cottage industries or other nonfactory work. Men had more opportunities than women to find employment outside the mill. This inequality with respect to work reinforced the more general inequality in work load.

In agriculture and the cottage industries work and household tasks had often been combined in one place. Work in factories meant a total separation of the two jobs. It contributed to the effect of the life cycle on industrial work. After they had given birth to children, most women left the factory and did not return until much later.

Factories were smaller on the continent than in Britain, and the division of labor was less clear-cut. The smaller size was due partly to formal restrictions and to the employers' hesitation to transcend the limits of family enterprise.

Whereas in the textile industry most workers were unskilled, the iron, metallurgy, engineering, shipbuilding, and printing industries employed large numbers of skilled workers; at times this numbered over fifty percent of the total labor force in those branches. Together with the (former) artisans in small workshops and the male supervisors and spinners employed in the textile mills, they formed an aristocracy of labor, which enjoyed some privileges over less skilled and unskilled workers. It was a new aristocracy, succeeding the old aristocracy of preindustrial artisanal masters and journeymen, and often recruited from its ranks. The concept of a labor aristocracy has been highly disputed, however, especially because it suggests large differences with the rest of labor.

Major sources of more or less unskilled employment were mining and railway construction. Throughout Europe miners and navvies (as workers engaged in railway construction were called in Britain) were rural migrants. Many continental workers in railway construction, and in Russia miners as well, returned to the countryside at harvest time. Railway construction was a rather safe type of employment, at least during the railway boom of the industrializing countries. Winter could be a slow time, but because of the lack of freedom, factory work was not a popular alternative even then.

For these reasons, industrial labor in the first half of the century was dominated by two kinds of people, each employed in different types of jobs. Artisanal masters and journeymen became the new labor aristocracy in workshops and factories or were employed as home workers. Rural migrants did less skilled work in the factories, mining, railway construction, or cottage industries. Of course there was upward and downward mobility within factories and by way of cottage industries. There was a decline in cottage industries somewhat later in the century, and from that point on rural migrants went to the factories. The category of rural migrants did not consist only of natives. Many of the navvies in Britain were Irish immigrants, while French industries also employed relatively large numbers of workers from neighboring countries. Due to differences in the timing and speed of industrialization and the main types of industry, the size of the industrial labor force varied considerably across time and among the European nations. Urbanization turned the building trades into one of the larger categories. Increasingly, it was rivaled in employee numbers by miners and workers in the iron and steel industry in countries that had such industries, or by textile workers. However, probably no industrial branch equaled the size of domestic services, mainly employing women and girls, or of agriculture. Only in Britain did industry as a whole surpass the agricultural work force before 1870.

WORKING CONDITIONS

Custom, guild rules, and statute law, some of them ancient, had traditionally regulated the working conditions of artisans and journeymen. In Britain, the Elizabethan Statute of Artificers, dating from 1563, had set the custom of "statute work against statute wage." Most of its content was officially repealed at the beginning of the nineteenth century. On the continent, the French Revolution had abolished similar customs as being incompatible with the principle of individual freedom. Many of these customs had already vanished at an earlier date. Slowly, the market replaced custom as the regulator of labor conditions in general and wages in particular. The existence of the market was not a very favorable situation for the skilled trades. They were threatened by technical innovation and by a concomitant inrush of unskilled labor. Still, most trades were characterized by higher and more stable earnings than unskilled labor. They were often able to maintain the traditional wage differential of roughly two to one between skilled and unskilled work. The skilled could also change more easily from one employer to another. British technicians had the additional advantage of being highly valued and well paid on the continent during the Industrial Revolution. In contrast, work in the cottage industries paid less than unskilled factory work. The competition of the new machines was the usual argument to lower wages. The many competitors for work constituted the real force behind the low wages for home work.

The length of the workday also differed among the various types of labor. In artisanal work and in the cottage industries it did usually not exceed the time between sunrise and sunset, while the average length of the workday in the factories probably was between twelve and fourteen hours. In the early cotton mills fourteen hours was not uncommon: from 6 to 12 A.M. and from 2 to 10

P.M. All industrializing countries also had industries or factories where the workday exceeded fourteen hours. for example, sixteen or even eighteen hours. Even here it was often the case that extra hours were put in without opposition, because the workers themselves wanted to increase their wages by working overtime. However, it was not so much the length of the workday that made conditions worse than in rural cottage industries and in agriculture, but the difference in discipline and work load. The intensity of work, in combination with the length of the workday, created a great difference from preindustrial work. The machine determined the pace of work in the textile industry, since most workers handled more than one loom. Even where the pace of a machine was not decisive, work was much more monotonous than that outside the factories. This applied in particular to children, forced to engage in monotonous work for twelve hours a day. Worst off were the children in the British mines, who were the real victims of the Industrial Revolution. Young children started as trappers, or air-door keepers, working in darkness and solitary confinement for most of the twelve hours they stayed underground. At the age of about eight they passed to ''hurrying'': pulling and pushing the coal-laden wagons through underground passages. The new labor aristocracy was less subject to strict labor discipline. These individuals worked in workshops or in small groups in the construction industry or in factories, and performed a number of jobs. They could determine their own pace of work. The symbol of this privileged position was the toolbox, which they brought to the workshop or factory. In Britain especially these relatively privileged workers could resist attacks on their autonomy, attacks like the introduction of new technology or a new type of work organization. However, the length of the workday was just as long as it was for other industrial workers.

Most British factories, as well as larger factories on the continent, enforced discipline by means of an elaborate system of fines. This approach was motivated by what the employers perceived as a general lack of discipline among their workers. This lack of discipline stemmed, first, from the difference between rural and industrial discipline, and the fixed working hours of the latter, which were independent of sunrise, weather, or season. A second cause was the work load, the nature of discipline within the factory, and the arbitrariness of its application. Rules were neither published, nor even shown to the worker in many factories, even when they were formally a part of the labor contract.

Industrial discipline started with the mill's bell. Being a few minutes tardy could mean loss of at least an hour's wages, whereas being more than five minutes late could lead to the loss of a working day. Within the factory, there were fines for any absence from the workplace without permission, for swearing, and sometimes even for speaking, singing, or whistling. Whether a fine was levied often did not become clear until pay time, so that protest was hardly possible. Protest could even bring immediate discharge. More generally, many employers reserved the right of immediate discharge to themselves, while workers had to give one or two weeks' notice. However, the regulations were not observed as strictly as the employers deemed necessary. Rules regarding the term of notice were evaded quite frequently, especially by skilled workers whose skills were in demand and who could rather easily seek new employment. Workers also evaded factory discipline by failing to show up on Monday (after heavy drinking on Sunday or just to enjoy some more sleep). Local feasts and fairs were other reasons for absenteeism. Such behavior reinforced the employers' opinion that workers were irresponsible. Consequently, the reaction was to hold workers responsible for all machine malfunctions and work accidents. In such cases, wages were withheld or the worker discharged.

Apart from suppressive measures to cope with a presumed lack of discipline, the hiring system of subcontracting tackled the problem preventively. This system consisted of skilled workers hiring unskilled laborers on their own account. Subcontractors were paid on the basis of results, while their helpers were always paid by some time unit. Subcontracting was especially common in British industry; the more paternalistic relationship between employer and workers in the smaller continental firms provided less room for it. Subcontracting increased the autonomy of skilled workers and also allowed adults to set their children to work as their assistants within the factory. Both constituted a relict of preindustrial economy, an adaptation of industrial work to a traditional economy. Subcontracting solved the discipline problem for the employer because the unskilled worker's behavior became the skilled worker's problem. Furthermore, it enhanced the discipline of the skilled by allowing them some freedom and responsibility at work to act as small employers themselves. Indeed, the other men treated them less as fellow workers than as "boss's men."

Skilled workers who subcontracted had to pay their assistants out of their own wages. Some other costs were deducted for almost all workers, too. Most mill owners charged their workers an arbitrary fixed amount for items such as machinery rental and fuel. An obligatory contribution to medical insurance or something similar was also sometimes required on the continent. Indeed, in many firms on the continent the worker might expect some very modest financial support in case of an accident at work, even though he was blamed for it. Illness or family affairs were approached in much the same way. The larger factories on the continent continued the same feudal and guild tradition of employer responsibility by creating medical funds, which were financed by obligatory workers' contributions and fines that the workers had paid. This kind of paternalism had been eliminated very early in Great Britain.

Paternalistic or not, the unequal relationship between employer and employee left ample room for arbitrary rules relating to fines, their application, and outright abuses, especially in wage payment. One of them was payment in kind (truck system) in goods that were often either inferior or more expensive than what was available on the market. A more common form of payment in kind was cash payments but with the obligation to spend part of it in the employer's shop. The truck system was more widespread in cottage industries, in which labor was rather dispersed, than in factory employment. In railway construction, where workers were often contracted in a public house, one of the hiring conditions was that workers spend money on drinks.

Of course, there were also examples of employers with social concerns. The general inequality between employer and employees could turn social provisions into another employers' weapon, however. For instance, contributions to company-provided social security funds were only accessible as long as the contributor worked at a particular mill. Were one to be dismissed or take a leave, one's contributions were lost. This also applied to workers who lived, whether voluntarily or not, in company housing near the factory under the cottage system, which was rather common in mining. Some mill owners built houses near their factories so that they could monitor the social life of their workers and keep them out of the towns.

Small plots of land were sometimes provided with the idea of keeping the workers busy outside of working hours and providing some additional income by growing vegetables. The provision of such plots also was used as an explicit argument to keep wages low. Rather exceptional were social housing plans, which were prompted less by material self-interest. Examples were the houses built by the British cotton mill owner Robert Owen, who even played a role in the labor movement.

Inequality was sanctioned by law. Legislation aimed at *liberté, egalité, fraternité*, to use the terms of the French Revolution, was confined to the first of these concepts, leaving out or even reinforcing existing *in*equality. Legislation continued to discriminate between bourgeoisie, middle class, and working class both in Britain and on the continent. The working class was quite powerless to alter the situation, because legislation deprived workers of voting rights and at the same time banned workers' organizations.

Several laws incorporated explicit inequality in their legal treatment of employer and worker, or master and servant as British law called them. Unequal treatment, mostly enacted by liberal laws, was an expression of the idea that employers were more responsible than their workers. Any infliction caused by employers was perceived as a mistake rather than malice and as a lesser danger to public order than misconduct by workers.

The British Master and Servant Act made the servant liable to punishment under criminal law for breach of contract, while the employer was liable only under civil law. A strike was considered a breach of contract, allowing criminal law to be applied. In France and the countries (such as Belgium) adopting French law after the Napoleonic conquests, civil law stated that in case of a quarrel between master and servant, the master had to be believed on his word. An 1803 French law reintroduced the *livret* in order to cope with industrial unrest. The *livret*, which dated back to the mid-eighteenth century, was a little notebook that the worker had to pass on to his employer. The latter entered the worker's financial obligations in it and did not return it until the worker had fulfilled his obligations. This represented a powerful means to tie workers to their jobs, since employers sometimes supplied new workers with a cash advance of (drinking) money. The *livret* was introduced in several countries after the dissemination of French law in Europe.

Unequal treatment also extended to government taxation. Almost all taxes were indirect. There were taxes on consumption goods, particularly food. The result was that workers paid a far higher percentage of their income in taxes than did those who were better off. Direct taxes on personal income were rather limited; yet precisely these direct taxes were linked to voting rights. In the first half of the nineteenth century the working class as well as the middle class and even the bourgeoisie had no voting rights. In theory, this could have led to some common, or at least simultaneous, action on the part of middle-class and working-class militants. However, it was already quite clear that their situations led them in different, even opposings directions.

CLERICAL WORKERS

Clerical workers constituted a distinct category. They (and their work) differed from manual workers in various ways, in skills, working conditions, and work process. The prime difference in skills between manual and clerical workers was the ability to read and write, a requirement for most clerical work. This set clerical workers apart from manual workers in the early nineteenth century, but the rising literacy rate reduced the gap as the century progressed. After that, many clerical workers, and lower office clerks in particular, no longer had specific skills. Office clerks were by far the largest group of clerical workers and the typical representatives of that category. Compared to manual workers they formed a small minority in industry. They predominated in services like banking, insurance companies, and trade agencies. In addition to office clerks, the category of clerical workers also included foremen and technicians. In contrast to office workers, however, these individuals were in close contact with the production process and occupied functions of lower and middle management. Foremen and technicians were skilled, like skilled manual workers, and they were sometimes recruited from those ranks.

Office clerks, foremen, and technicians also differed from manual workers in a second respect, their working environment. Manual workers were involved in the production process, without much hierarchy among them. Most of them remained manual workers during the course of their working life, and only some escaped by starting their own business or becoming foremen. In contrast, clerical workers were part of a bureaucracy with a continuous hierarchical line from top to bottom. This allowed promotion from one level of authority to another. Lower clerical workers were supposed to have this ambition. Though a manual worker could be successful and still remain a manual worker, for a clerical worker to remain at the same post was considered a failure.

The third difference relates to the work process. Bureaucracy implied highly formalized rules for the work process and the clerical workers' work behavior.

In contrast to manual workers, for whom mutual contact and moving around might represent an integral part of the production process, any movement on the work floor was construed as hindering the other clerks' work. Moreover, it could be interpreted as a deviation from the continuous line of authority. Thus, bureaucracy imposed a certain code of behavior, while this was much less the case for manual work. The efforts to impose such a code on manual workers were met by considerable conflict. The differences in work requirements and working conditions had a great impact on individual and social behavior, despite the fact that most clerical workers were just as wage dependent as manual workers.

Related to the clerical workers' literacy was an attitude of superiority over manual workers. This was most strongly developed in some countries on the continent, like Germany, where clerical workers adopted the corporate spirit of civil servants in the state bureaucracies. They shared responsibility and privilege, which were a source of pride and prejudice. The erosion of literacy as a distinct advantage did not affect this attitude. Knowledge of the right procedures came to function as a base of privilege. Yet, the *esprit de corps* applied more to contacts with outsiders (like manual workers) than to contacts with other clerical workers. The lack of career prospects for manual workers turned fellow workers into a group of peers and a significant reference group. The working atmosphere could remain rather informal, since all shared the same working niche. In contrast, for clerical workers those at a higher level within the bureaucracy, rather than fellow workers at the same level, functioned as the reference group, serving as a model for attitudes and behavior. Close supervision by the employer or higher clerical workers reinforced the indentification with those higher up. Clerical workers stressed their loyalty to the form and to the employer personally, proud of their white collar or clean blouse as symbols of decency and representativeness. These conditions did not facilitate overt signs of discontent and protest.

Loyalty was not a one-sided affair. Employers cherished the trustworthiness and responsibility of clerical workers. After all, the latter might be future applicants for higher functions within the firm. The special ties were expressed in better working conditions than those of manual workers. Instead of weekly wages, clerical workers enjoyed a monthly salary. In contrast to manual workers, who reached the top of their scale when they were still under twenty-five, clerical workers received yearly increments for a number of years, tying them even more to the enterprise. Old-age benefits and medical benefits had the same effect, but employer loyalty was most explicit in job security. In lean times manual workers were dismissed rather easily, while clerical workers were not. The employers' prerogative to fire at will related to them as well, but it was applied reluctantly.

The differences were also reflected more generally in social behavior. A clerical worker's social life was ruled by a much stricter code of internalized rules about how to behave, related to the aspirations cherished at work. As a consequence, family life and social contacts differed greatly from those of manual workers. Most of the norms were derived from middle-class behavior.

In contrast to the manual workers, who seemingly found solace in their common fate, the clerical workers' place in society and their identity was a greater problem to them. Manual workers ridiculed them for their servility and for their desperate efforts to dress and behave above their station in life. On the other hand, white-collar work also was seen as an improvement compared to manual work, a bright perspective for the children of manual workers. In their own view, they belonged to the middle class. But the propertied middle class considered them inferior, though regarding them as a separate category, distinct from manual workers. They were often ranked as lower middle class, because they lacked the financial base of the upper middle class, while they were sufficiently different in social behavior and social status from manual workers to be regarded as a separate subclass. The distinction between clerical and manual workers was reflected in most languages: worker-employee, *travailleur-employé*, *Arbeiter-Angestellte*, although there were slight variations in meaning.

Shop assistants represented a category of workers that shared lower middle-class attitudes and behavior. This was due less to a similarity in working conditions than to the almost permanent and close contact with middle-class shopkeepers and clients. They lacked the possibility of a career within the enterprise, and their working conditions were comparable to those of domestic servants. Like domestic servants, many shop assistants lived with the shopkeeper, were subject to strict control night and day, and were paid very low wages (motivated by the provision of free meals and lodging). Indeed, for these very reasons both types of work were considered suitable stations for lower middle- and working-class girls.

The values of clerical workers were shared by, or had even been generated by, state bureaucracies. Before the Industrial Revolution a number of countries on the continent had already been characterized by relatively large bureaucracies. Their employees had long cherished a tradition of responsibility and loyalty and abhorred the working class's lack of these virtues. State employees were still more privileged than clerical workers in the private sector, since they enjoyed job security almost for life. Even where the preindustrial state bureaucracy was small, as in Great Britain, clerical working conditions shaped attitudes and behavior in the same way as it did among clerical workers.

2

Early Forms of Workers' Action

Traditional journeymen clubs in Britain had disappeared early. Unions of skilled workers developed autonomously and faced little state opposition. Unions on the continent were more often a continuation of journeymen associations or at least reminiscent of the guilds. Due to the different pace of industrialization and to state repression they developed later and slower after 1848, except in France. In the 1860s their emergence was facilitated by economic prosperity, legalization, and international contacts. The main union instruments to stabilize labor conditions were job placement and, later, tariff lists.

EARLY WORKERS' ORGANIZATIONS IN GREAT BRITAIN AND FRANCE

Workers could react to their working conditions in various ways. Many adapted to the situation. Others evaded industrial discipline by changing jobs or even by emigrating to the New World. Still others became involved in individual protest actions, ranging from humble requests to the employer to desperate outbursts of violence. More important than individual activities were collective efforts. Such efforts differed widely between skilled workers on the one hand and home workers and less skilled workers on the other, and also between manual and clerical workers. Craft workers and other skilled workers tried to continue or revive traditional workmen's organizations in order to regulate trade practices. When such actions failed, strikes were sometimes organized. Petitioning the government represented a political move for reforms. The creation of such coalitions for organized trade or political action was outlawed in most countries, however. Under liberal rule they were deemed to be a danger to individual freedom, and under absolutism a danger to traditional authority. Under this suppression some of the attempts turned into uprisings or local revolt. In certain instances workers also became involved in riots without any previous efforts involving less conflictuous action. In contrast to skilled workers, home workers and less skilled workers lacked the means to organize. Self-imposed regulations and organized collective action were beyond their reach. Uprising and revolt were the only type of collective protest to which they had recourse.

Because of the skills required, many skilled workers had the advantage of a limited entry into the trades. Moreover, they were often descendants of families that had lived in the same town for some time and therefore had a stake in the trade as well as in urban social life. Several trades were passed on from father to son, reinforcing the urge to keep out intruders and favoring early organization. The fact that a majority of the skilled workers were literate made it easier for them to organize on a more permanent basis.

Clerical workers were mostly literate, too. Nevertheless, collective action, let alone organization, was out of reach to them because of their specific working and living conditions.

The fate of traditional workmen's organizations differed in Great Britain and France. As part of the guild order, journeymen clubs (*compagnonnages* in France) had been the traditional associations of artisanal workers. Their main aims had been social contact, assistance in meeting trade requirements, and financial help in case of illness or death. They also tried to enforce traditional guild rules and to control job placement as a means to stabilize wages. Rituals and symbols played an important role in such activities. In Great Britain most of these traditional associations had already been outlawed in the eighteenth century. Their members were liable for conspiracy in restraint of trade. The 1789 revolution put an end to the French guilds, but throughout most of the continent, France included, *compagnonnages* continued their colorful existence, at least for some time. Many of them were, at least formally, linked to the Catholic Church in Catholic countries. Priests participated in their activities, and festivities were held on the feast days of patron saints.

At the end of the eighteenth century new associations sprang up among journeymen and other skilled workers in Britain and France. They were concerned less with trade regulation and directing social life than with family security in case of illness or death. Some of these friendly societies or *sociétés de secours mutuel* were organized alongside existing *compagnonnages*; others arose in trades without previous associations. Rituals and symbols were absent or remained in the background. The main festivity was the so-called "box meeting," during which the money box was opened in the public house where it was kept. In Britain, the friendly societies were given legal status in 1793, and in the following years total membership increased to almost a million. Some of the societies were either the cover or the core of a more informal association that tried to regulate labor conditions in the trade concerned. They could also function as the backbone of temporary coalitions and support strikes.

The time of the French Revolution was one of general unrest in Britain, too.

It made the governments in both countries responsive to employers' complaints about such temporary coalitions and combinations. State action ensued, prohibiting the coalitions and *compagnonnages*. Friendly societies and mutual aid associations were not affected by these measures. In addition to the maintenance of public order, a more fundamental motive for the ban on coalitions was that they were regarded as a revival of the old corporate society, thus interfering with free enterprise and individual freedom. Accordingly, the ban also applied to employers' coalitions. The outcome of state intervention was completely different in the two countries. In France, the ban represented the beginning of a long period of suppression of workers' organizations and collective action. In Britain suppression was much weaker, and the ban was lifted earlier, allowing the rise of unions. In neither of these two countries was the ban applied to employers. They were perceived to be less of a threat to public order and did not organize openly.

The 1791 Le Chapelier Law prohibited coalitions aimed at changes in labor conditions in France. The law was enacted after the Parisian master carpenters signed a petition that asked for measures against an imminent workers' coalition. The law became the foundation for over half a century of police action against trade unions in France and other countries, like Belgium, that based their legal system on French law. The Le Chapelier Law prohibited employers or workers in any craft from organizing with the intention of refusing employment or withholding labor or offering labor only at a predetermined wage level. In 1810 the Le Chapelier Law was incorporated into the Penal Code. Articles 414–416 of the code punished employers' coalitions that were attempting to reduce wages in an unfair and unjust way. The penalty was imprisonment of six days to one month. Evidently, workers' coalitions were always deemed to be unfair and unjust, as the restriction did not apply to them. Workers could be imprisoned for up to three months, the group leaders even up to five years. The British Combination Acts of 1799–1800 made any combination that attempted to change labor conditions unlawful. Proof of conspiracy in restraint of trade was no longer required. The law was prompted by a coalition of London millwrights during a period of general unrest. In contrast to French law, the Combination Acts were hardly ever applied because the British government hesitated to interfere in mutual accusations of forming coalitions. The French law contributed to the further decline of the (by now illegal) *compagnonnages*, and to the rise of mutual aid societies, The latter continued their involvement in actions to impose regulations on trades. However, they operated in secret, often remaining a public secret.

The Combination Acts in Britain were repealed when the wave of unrest that took place at the end of the Napoleonic wars was over. As early as the 1820s there were several attempts to unite friendly societies and a newer kind of unions (engaging more overtly in the regulation of trade) into national trade associations. The first truly national craft organization was a union of spinners, founded in 1829. It was a short-lived effort, leading to the first association involving different trades: the National Association of United Trades for the Protection of Labour. Like the spinners union, it was organized by John Doherty in 1830. Although it boasted some 100,000 members, particularly spinners, construction workers, and engineers, it soon collapsed. The second effort to organize unions using an all-industry base was by Robert Owen. A self-made cotton-mill owner, Owen was the prototype of the socially conscious entrepreneur. He started the first housing project at his mill in Lanark, and in 1833 he organized the Grand National Consolidated Trades Union. It united trade unions, cooperative societies, and friendly societies and claimed a membership of 800,000. However, its only effective strength was among London craftsmen, like tailors and shoemakers. All that remained after a few years were the organization's elaborate social rituals. Nevertheless, the wave of union activity aroused official irritation, which came to the surface when a group of rural workers was sentenced to seven years of banishment to Australia because they had participated in such rituals by swearing a secret oath. The treatment of these Tolpuddle Martyrs roused the indignation of all unions. Protests were slow to disappear.

Unions on the continent had to face more repression. The new Belgian nation enforced a ban on unions very strictly. Approximately 1,600 workers were arrested between 1830 and 1860, and 946 were sent to jail. In France, union life could continue somewhat more publicly. After the 1830 revolution new associations sprang up, publicly stating that their purpose was to monitor labor conditions, in addition to providing social security programs. The new form of organization was especially popular in the heavily plagued crafts of tailoring and shoemaking. In contrast to Britain, this recasting of workers' organizations did not include any effort to unite local trade associations.

Another type of organization consisted of production cooperatives. Several unions in Britain experimented with cooperative stores or even cooperative production. Most famous became the Rochdale Pioneers, a group of twenty-eight weavers who started such a store in 1844. It paid dividends according to the amount of purchases made and spent part of its profits on common educational facilities. More than their British counterparts, French cooperatives were thought of as forerunners of a new society in line with the stronger sense of corporate ties and a more repressive government reaction.

EARLY INDUSTRIAL ACTION AND PROTEST

Workmen's organizations had various means at their disposal to influence labor conditions. Initially, their main instrument was job placement, or even a workers' veto regarding new admissions. Because population growth was greater and the labor supply was expanding more rapidly Britain found this instrument more important than France. Job placement often implied that potential new workers had to be members of the workers' trade organization (closed shop), a means of preventing illegal newcomers from entering the trade. Women in particular were targeted to be excluded, because they were considered a source of undercutting wage rates. In time, this concern was replaced by a list of wage tariffs. Entry restrictions became less effective, since they were easily evaded by cottage industries or by an increasing division of labor. Another reason for the change to wage tariffs was the erosion of the traditional rules regarding wages. In order to obtain their tariff list, workers might initially try to contact employers. If an employer would not comply, workers and their organizations would sometimes call a strike. These strikes were confined to one or a few workshops and lasted just a couple of hours, even when the employer did not succumb. Less often, a strike grew into a more general local trade movement, for instance to assist workers in a low-paying workshop. Such strikes were, incidentally, supported by masters who wanted to combat underpayment taking place in other workshops. A strike could be combined with a boycott, calling upon citizens not to do business with a noncomplying firm. One of the methods that tariff evasion was prevented was to make the tariff a formal document, sometimes very detailed, with rates for every specific operation or product.

By using individual discharge, employers had a mighty weapon against any form of workmen's action. When a conflict escalated and a strike had already closed a workshop or even a part of the local trade, a lockout would sometimes take place. In such instances, the workshop and sometimes even the entire local trade was closed. The purpose of the lockout, a rather rare phenomenon, was to pressure nonstrikers to exercise influence on the workers' coalition.

Due to the high value placed upon free enterprise, the government's policy of noninterference in industrial conflict, and the nationwide market, strikes and lockouts were the only weapons used in Britain. On the continent workers and employers not only followed this direct approach, consisting of industrial action, to fight each other, they also had recourse to a more indirect approach: political action for intervention by local and state authorities. Workers might petition or appeal to local government to interfere or impose a local tariff. Though such action was forbidden explicitly by the Le Chapelier Law, it was a rather common phenomenon in France and Belgium. It reminded the local officials of the responsibility they had under the guild system to guarantee the prosperity of local trade. Such an appeal to local government was a hazardous affair however, since it disclosed the existence of a forbidden coalition that could lead to its suppression. Indeed, local authorities were more an employers' weapon, because the latter could always call upon the government to take action against a workers' combination. Since local officials were not likely to interfere until there was a threat of conflict, local government intervention was predominantly related to strike activity.

Concentrations of strike activity, affecting a number of towns simultaneously, made their appearance in the early nineteenth century. Great Britain was hit by such a wave of strikes in 1818, when the worst postwar conditions were over, and in 1824 following the repeal of the Combination Acts. In the early 1830s the industrializing countries witnessed similar types of strike waves. The antecedent condition was a prosperous economy, buttressed in Britain by Doherty's and Owen's attempts to unite local unions and by the political campaign for parliamentary reform. Strike activity in France culminated in 1833. Various types of organizations were involved, including traditional *compagnonnages* and associations, founded only shortly before. The government responded by arresting a number of strike leaders and by adopting a stricter reformulation of the anti-coalition law in 1834. This time the ban was mainly for repressive reasons and less a matter of principle.

Not all strikes ran their course quietly without incident. Some broad local strikes were a source of, or a stage in, local unrest. Sometimes, when the police arrested the strike leaders or otherwise took strong action, strikes would escalate into an uprising. The most infamous examples were the uprisings of the *canuts*, the Lyon silk workers, in 1831 and 1834. In 1831, the mayor and the prefect of the *département* approved a still illegal tariff list, put together by the *canuts'* organization. Employers asked the national government for assistance and succeeded in having the tariff list declared legally void. The workers subsequently went on strike and occupied the city for more than a week. This action went without lasting success, however, and 20,000 soldiers restored public order.

The general strike wave two years later did not escape the attention of the trade either. A strike was called to obtain a new tariff, but this time the local officials applied the law from the beginning and arrested several strike leaders. The strike was the last event leading to the tightening of anti-coalition legislation in 1834. The passing of this law led to renewed civil strife in the city. Unlike the uprising of 1831, Lyon became a battlefield this time, with over 200 casualties on both sides. In short, both Lyon uprisings were the last stage in a sequence of events including political action, strikes, and local government intervention.

Two other forms of more violent protest were rather common in this period: food riots and sabotage in the form of damage to machines. The first represented a common historical phenomenon, while the second was typical of this period of technological change. In contrast to strikes, they represented alternative forms of protest, particularly for workers who were unable to organize (for example, home workers, including women). Because their loyalties were divided, however (that is, both to industrial work and the household), women were not very active in such actions, or in protest in general. Since organized skilled workers participated as well, the distinction between the different forms of protest was not always clear. Food riots, sabotage, and strikes could be interwoven into one protest movement. In France food riots were part of the French Revolution, while in Great Britain they were frequent during and immediately following the Napoleonic wars. Their main effect was to reinforce the impression of the upper and middle class that workers were a dangerous class of people, to be confronted by means of harsh measures and a strong police force.

Food riots gave way to sabotage during the period of industrialization. More than food riots, damage to machinery was characterized by a specific target and a specific group of actors, mostly workers from one trade or industry. Rural workers and workers from cottage industries were well represented in Britain.

They feared competition from the new machinery and the erosion of their traditional skills. In some trades, employers even requested state protection, in the form of a tax on power looms for instance. However, the government responded to such appeals only in Germany. Sabotage became known as "Luddism," named after Ned Ludd, the leader of rural workers' actions in Great Britain who soon became a living legend, acquiring the nickname "King Ludd." The first Luddist actions came in Britain after 1810, and thousands of power looms were destroyed in Manchester in the 1820s. A decade later, Luddism declined in Britain but reached a height on the continent where actions were more dispersed and more urban in character. They also lacked the romantic myths and the night raids of the British brand of rural Luddism. In 1829 coal potters destroyed the first railway line on the continent in the Belgian mine of Grand Hornu, while local actions took place in France in 1830 and 1831. During the revolutionary days of 1830, Parisian printers, gathering under the common slogan *A bas les mécaniques* (down with machines), destroyed mechanical presses. In 1831, thousands of people were involved in sabotage in St. Etienne and other towns. Elsewhere, in Germany, Solingen (1826) and Krefeld (1828) were affected.

Sabotage also constituted part of a large uprising of Silesian linen weavers in Peterswalden in 1844, at the time of a food shortage in several parts of Europe. After the arrest of a worker singing a local protest song, hundreds of home workers destroyed the mill and the home of a large employer, who was particularly infamous for the harsh labor conditions to which he subjected his workers. The uprising evolved into a local revolt, in which the army killed ten weavers. The uprising in Germany, like the uprising of the *canuts* in Lyon for France, became a symbol of the poor conditions in which workers, and in particular those in cottage industries, had to live. Strikes and sabotage took place in the Czech textile industry in 1844 to prevent the introduction of new machines. The revolutions of 1848 also included some Luddist action.

POLITICAL ACTION

Whether in the demands put forward or the individuals involved or addressed, rioting often extended the limits of the workers' own trade. Sometimes, specific political demands were voiced, such as government measures to prevent the rise of food prices or the introduction of new technology. Demands were also made for general policy changes or changes in the political system.

The parliamentary system in Great Britain allowed for questions to be raised and solved one at a time, as long as they did not imply thwarting the introduction of new technology. Liberal entrepreneurs organized campaigns to obtain the changes they desired. Parliamentary legislation was the vehicle for this change. Workers and trade unions assisted in some of these campaigns. After the liberals had succeeded in getting their reforms, skilled workers and unions continued to use the same methods, although parliamentary reform was secondary to trade regulation reform. Depending on the nature of the issue, either liberal manufacturers or conservative land owners were potentially available as supporters of workers' political demands. Between 1815 and 1818 there were numerous demonstrations against the Combination Acts, franchise limitations, and most of all the Corn Laws (which raised bread prices). During this period, actions could still result in, or had the character of, food riots or local uprisings. A major incident relating to the reform campaign was the 1819 Peterloo Massacre. Eleven people were killed when a large meeting in Manchester favoring parliamentary reform and opposing the Corn Laws was violently disrupted.

After a certain amount of worker support for the campaign to reform parliament in the early 1830s, the paths of industrial employers and workers parted again. They subscribed to opposite positions in a newly formed campaign, the factory movement, which aimed to regulate labor conditions in the factories, and the introduction of a Ten Hours Act. The campaign received support from middle-class reformers and even from the landed proprietary. The outcome applied to women and children only. The 1833 Factory Act and the laws of 1842 and 1847 made it illegal for children to work at night, banned underground mine work for children and women, and reduced their workday to ten hours.

The largest movement of all, and the first to consist mainly of workers, was Chartism. It aimed at general suffrage, but had some vague economic demands incorporated into it. The Chartism campaign started a Charter consisting of six demands relating to suffrage rights (such as secret ballot, payment of members of Parliament, and universal suffrage). The movement increased in strength and members, and in 1839 2 million people signed a petition. Its rejection led to a series of protest strikes and local uprisings but also to a split between moral force Chartists and physical force Chartists. The split and the rejection of a second petition, signed by 3 million people, squelched the movement, only to have it revive for a short time in 1848. The failure of Chartism did not undermine the workers' faith, firmly established by now, in campaigning for separate issues within the limits of parliamentary government.

On the continent absolutism prevented raising or settling questions separately. Issues remained unsettled until a series of unsolved questions was brought to the fore in a revolutionary movement. Although liberal freedom had been established in France by the 1789 revolution land owners struck back in Parliament. In 1830, artisanal workers and the middle class, without combining efforts, were each fighting for a more liberal monarchy. Artisanal workers, along with carpenters and masons, formed the majority of the Parisian revolutionaries in that year. The revolution brought hardly any change in their situation. Suffrage restrictions continued, and trade organizations remained illegal. In response, workers increasingly developed their own ideals of a new political order, based on the trade associations. These ideals were prominent in many of the cooperatives founded after 1830. French philosophy provided some ideological starting points and developed in line with cooperative activities, for instance in Claude Henri de Saint Simon's utopian socialism. In the 1830s Charles Fourier elaborated the theme in his *phalanstères*, production and consumption cooperatives. Thus, partly in reaction to the politicization of workers' organizations by the state, skilled workers politicized their associations into a substitute for state power. Their demand was not to be taken to Parliament or the government, of course, but expressed as a combination of demands in the Revolution of 1848.

Like Chartism in Britain, the Revolution of 1848 on the continent was the first movement in which workers more or less stood alone. Artisanal and other workers in France joined ranks after the king had already left the country. They occupied Paris, voicing middle-class demands of political representation and freedom. Two labor representatives were invited to take part in the provisional government: the engineer Albert and the popular publicist Louis Blanc, a protagonist of self-supporting cooperatives. One of the first decrees, in February 1848, abolished the Le Chapelier Law and proclaimed the completely new right to work. The latter was a revolutionary consequence of the idea that the nation should consist of producers' cooperatives. *Ateliers nationaux* were created for the unemployed.

The revolutionary government also established the *Commission du Luxembourg*, a kind of pseudo-ministry of social affairs under Blanc. It took measures against subcontracting and reduced the workday to ten hours in Paris and eleven hours in the rest of France. The commission became a bustling center of action of new local trade associations, workers' newspapers, political debate, and mass demonstrations, all concentrated in the capital. The new trade corporations stressed the need to set labor tariffs as a basis for a new production system. They engaged in collective bargaining and arrived at tariff agreements with the, by now, very indulgent employers. The trade associations' representatives at the commission were even given official status, and the commission itself became a serious rival of the provisional government. But after a few months of dual power the new parliament, elected through general male suffrage, put an end to this disorganization. The decision to abolish the *Ateliers nationaux* and to enroll the unemployed workers led to a massacre. Over 100,000 Parisians, predominantly workers, fought the French army, resulting in 1,500 casualties and more than 3,500 people deported to Algeria. The Le Chapelier Law was restored, the ten-hour workday changed to twelve hours, and the franchise limited again. The tariff conventions were soon dead and buried. Obviously, the measures served to reinforce workers' rejection of French parliamentary politics.

Street fighting was a more permanent feature of the national revolutions in Berlin and Vienna. Workers experimented with initiatives like those in France but were unable to carry them through. The revolutions in these countries strengthened primarily the idea of a common identity and common interests among industrial workers. Parliamentary rule had not yet been introduced; efforts to do so in 1848 failed.

Labor's revolution frightened the bourgeoisie. In some countries, notably Germany, liberals accepted existing feudal or autocratic limits to liberal freedom in order to keep labor in check. Otherwise, it was reasoned, the uprooted and dangerous labor class might be able to uproot the rest of society as well. For some years this fear overshadowed the social consciousness that had made its appearance among the liberals on the continent, and which, like in Britain, originated in concerns regarding child labor. There had been official investigations or private surveys of workers' health, housing, and labor conditions in the 1840s. In France, such a private initiative resulted in a law, passed in 1841, that prohibited night work for children and factory work for children under eight years of age, but remained ineffective, due to many loopholes. In Belgium, an official investigation of workers' living conditions was conducted in 1843, without any legislative followup. Yet, the beginning of a social consciousness was visible in the change of meaning that became associated with the term "social," from "all of society," to "regarding the poor and the working class," a sign of awareness that social life was polarized into Two Nations instead of one. The medical profession acted as the pacemaker in this process, since doctors were the only members of the bourgeoisie and middle class who had any insight into the living conditions of the poor. In 1830s and 1840s they especially feared the spread of cholera in, and even more outside, the overcrowded urban working-class neighborhoods.

NEW MODEL UNIONISM AND ITS INFLUENCE ON THE CONTINENT

At the 1851 Great Exhibition in the Crystal Palace, Great Britain demonstrated that it deserved its place as the world's foremost industrial and imperial power. The optimism that the exhibition radiated would last for some time. Compared to the first half of the century, the 1850s and 1860s were a period of relative material advancement throughout Europe. The increasing size of factories in the metal industry, related to the spread of railways, led to a change in the nature of skilled labor. The number of cottage industries declined and workers were increasingly concentrated in mills and workshops. The new aristocracy of skilled labor emerged, which was as eager as the more traditional groups of artisanal workers to develop its own unions. But they could neither stop the flow of newcomers into industry nor technological developments. Job placement became hard to impose, and unions shifted their attention to bargaining on comprehensive lists of piece rates.

A new generation of unions arose in Great Britain, the new model unions, which stressed the value of bargaining. More explicitly than previous organizations, they considered strikes to be a relic of the past, to be used only as an ultimate weapon. Other characteristic features were a strong internal organization and the emergence of elected and paid administrators. The Amalgamated Society of Engineers was the first new model union. It came into being in 1851 and was formed out of a fusion of local unions. It combined the functions of a union and a friendly society. With 12,000 members (still a minority of all engineers), it soon became the largest British union. Piece-rate payment was a primary concern of new model unions, because such payment was seen to lead to a reduction of wages and an increase in work load and working hours. Generally, however, the opposition to piece work failed.

The attempts of British unions to regulate labor conditions by means of collective bargaining did not prevent the occurrence of several great strikes and lockouts. In reaction to the rise of the new model unions, employers also started to organize, either to become active in bargaining, or to fight the unions. One of their weapons was the Document used earlier against Owen's union. It was a declaration, to be signed by workers, that they would refrain from any union activity or from supporting a union. Less than a year after the foundation of their union, engineers became involved in a major lockout. Although they had to make concessions with respect to overtime and piece-rate payment, they were able to keep the union intact, in spite of the document.

In 1859, London construction workers were locked out in a conflict over working hours. The building dispute led to the creation of the London Trades Council, an imitation of local trades councils that coordinated union action in industrial cities like Sheffield and Glasgow. The formation of these councils encouraged a development toward some kind of national organization. A national Trades Union Congress (TUC) was convened in 1868, and after some time a formal organization was set up. The TUC coordinated union activities but left the autonomy of the participating unions unaffected. British employers' organizations did not keep pace, as most employers still preferred informal bargaining.

British new model unionism and the 1848 revolution both influenced developments on the continent, although unionism remained small and scattered, even in France. New associations sprang up there, which explicitly tried to enforce tariffs. They had lost their traditional ties with the Catholic Church and increasingly adopted a new form of socialist thought, called Proudhonism. Pierre-Joseph Proudhon continued the French tradition of labor as the basis of all social activity. He supported voluntary cooperatives, but like the new model unions his anarchism expressed a dislike of political action. Another influential movement was Blanquism, named after Louis-Auguste Blanqui. He advocated (and practiced) revolt by a small and tightly knit group of revolutionaries, in order to mobilize the proletariat.

In other countries, the 1848 revolution stimulated the creation of workers' organizations like mutual aid societies, cooperatives, educational societies (*Bildungsvereine* in Germany), and a few trade unions. Frequently, as was the case in Scandinavia, the organizations were influenced by traditional guilds and journeymen organizations (*Gesellenvereine* in Germany). Only in exceptional cases, for instance in Denmark, were they a direct continuation of traditional organizations as they had been to some extent in France. Guilds and journeymen's organizations had already disappeared in most countries at an earlier date, and the link correspondingly more indirect. Most of the organizations had a liberal outlook, and some of them even enjoyed a mixed membership of workers, liberal middle class, and bourgeoisie. Exerting pressure on the government was one of their main functions. The educational societies were not only engaged in workers' education. They also sometimes took an active stand in the liberal reforms going on during this period, like the introduction of obligatory primary education. However, unions in particular remained a frequent victim of state or communal measures. In Germany book printers' and cigar makers' unions appeared in 1848 but were banned again in 1849.

The British example encouraged not only the rise of unionism on the continent, but also its legalization. At the high tide of liberal rule, in 1862, Great Britain organized another international exhibition. This time it developed into a meeting ground for British union leaders and union leaders and revolutionaries from the continent. It helped to popularize the British example of collective bargaining. Continental governments thought the time fit to legalize unions in order to encourage a similar development toward peaceful labor relations. Saxony, the most industrialized state of Germany, was the first to lift the ban on coalitions in 1861. The rest of Germany followed suit in the course of the decade. France legalized temporary combinations and strikes in 1864, but more permanent organizations that attempted to influence labor relations remained illegal. Belgium lifted the ban on organizations in 1866. The Austrian Empire recognized the right to establish organizations, at least in principle, in 1867, and Spain did so in 1868. There were a few exceptions, however. A liberal victory (or unification in Italy) in some countries caused a delayed introduction of French law, including anti-coalition legislation, rather than its disappearance.

THE FIRST HIGH TIDE OF UNIONISM

The new measures fostered a wave of unionism just as the repeal of the Combination Acts had done in 1824. Unionism was favored by prosperous economic conditions and stimulated by more regular international contacts, which resulted in the First International. The same conditions contributed to a high frequency of labor protest in the form of strikes and revolts, culminating in the Paris Commune in 1871.

In Germany, Saxony became a springboard for new national organizations. The first to appear, founded by Friedrich Lasalle, was a combination of a political movement and producer cooperatives, the *Allgemeiner Deutscher Arbeiterverein*. Its main priority was universal and equal suffrage. In line with liberal thought elsewhere, Lasalle had formulated an iron law of wages. According to this law, wages were determined by economic conditions only. Trade unions made no sense and would only harm the workers' position, it was argued. Nevertheless, the *Verein* supported some strikes, in order not to lose its members. After Lasalle's death, the Lasallians changed course and founded unions themselves. The Lasalle movement was greatly outnumbered by a federation of liberal unions, connected with the liberal party. They were called *Hirsch-Duncker* unions after their leaders, the liberal industrialist Max Hirsch and a sympathetic editor named Franz Duncker. Though they adhered to the idea of harmony between capital and labor, they occasionally supported strikes. A third German movement consisted of a combination of a political organization and trade unions organized by August Bebel, a worker. The *Sozialdemokratische Arbeiterpartei* was at its core, which had universal and equal voting rights as its primary goal. After a spontaneous strike wave in 1864–1865, the various German workers' organizations limited their activities to petitions asking for repeal of the coalition ban in force in all German states. British unionism was used as an example.

In France, strike frequency increased after 1864, and mutual aid societies, which pursued union goals more openly, were established. They were called *Chambres syndicales* and were named after already existing local employers' clubs. By this time, printers had local and sometimes national organizations in a number of countries. A nationwide union was founded in Switzerland in 1858; Holland followed in 1866 and Belgium in 1867. Printers' unions aimed at local or even national tariffs. Construction workers, cigar makers, and hatters were also relatively well organized. Although the legalization of unions on the continent did not imply their recognition by employers, the printers were especially successful at enforcing local tariffs and the official exclusion of women. Bargaining took place with leading local employers rather than formal employers' organizations. The few employers' organizations that existed on the continent were mainly trade associations. They focused on the external conditions of their trade and often explicitly opposed free trade. Only on rare occasions were they concerned with employer-worker contacts or labor conditions.

An organizational base for the increasing international contacts between union leaders and revolutionaries took shape in 1864. St. Martin's Hall in London was the site of the founding of the International Workers Association. The association, the First International, was no more than a consultative congress. The agenda had been set at the 1862 London Exhibition, where French workers met British workers and Karl Marx in exile. A small delegation from Germany was present, too, including Lasalle. Karl Marx had already called for international workers' unity in his Communist Manifesto (1848): "Workers of all nations, unite!" British unionists were reluctant to participate in the association. They preferred their ties with British overseas territories and the United States, since the continent was perceived as the source of ideological conflict. The governments on the continent feared that 1848 would be repeated. Only Switzerland, and later also Belgium, allowed the International to meet in their countries. The annual meetings were dominated by the discord between Marx, demanding political action, and Proudhonist anarchism opposing it. At the 1869 Basel congress, Marxism became the official doctrine. Member organizations of the International were quite active in founding unions and initiating strikes throughout the continent during these years.

Although the International was hardly involved in coordinating union activities, it facilitated international contacts. Combined with favorable economic conditions, this contributed to the spread of unionism. Traveling anarchist leaders, among them Mikhail Bakunin, contributed in important ways to the rise of new associations and protest movements, for instance in Spain and Italy. Of the existing unions, those of the construction workers and cigar makers adhered more often to the national sections of the International than the larger and better established printers' organizations.

Unions developed quite slowly among miners. The isolation of the miners' work and mining communities impeded organization and facilitated strong employer authority, expressed in company housing and in successful resistance to any form of unionism. Miners had led the way in the area of security provisions, occasioned by the dangers involved in mine work. In Germany, their social security funds were even supported officially and could be imposed by communal regulation. Miners' unions, however, were still absent or very weak. When employers wanted to contact their workers to discuss labor conditions, they would set up arbitration boards, which had the advantage of functioning without unions (and even preventing their rise). However, the first lasting board was established not in the mining industry, but in the British hosiery industry, where Mundella founded the Nottingham Hosiery Board in 1860. The initiative was subsequently imitated, especially in British and continental mining.

Nevertheless, mining areas were not immune from the combination of growing international worker militancy and favorable economic conditions. In 1869 strikes and revolts affected mining centers and industrial towns in France, Germany, Italy, and the Czech and Austrian parts of the Austrian Empire. The suppression of these actions caused much bloodshed, particularly in France. A miners' strike near Saint-Etienne ended in a fight between strikers and police. Thirteen people were killed in what became known as the *massacre de La Ricamarie*. Among the issues contested was a recently formed miners' association demand to control company insurance funds, paid in part by workers but without any worker participation in the administration. In Waldenburg (Germany) the issue was the recognition of a *Hirsch-Dunker* miners' union. Miners came out on the losing end of this action, and union membership dwindled. Heavy fighting in Belgium between the police and rioting Charleroi miners, who were on strike against wage reductions, caused six casualties in 1868. Workers in other industries were also involved in strikes. A conflict in the Aubin metal industry in France resulted in another bloodbath, in which fourteen people were killed.

The climax of this period of worker militancy came in 1871. The defeat of the French army in the short war against Germany caused a political crisis in Paris. While the city was still surrounded by German troops, a *Garde national*, consisting of unemployed artisanal workers, kept order. The new republican government was fearful of challenging this rival power and decided to settle in nearby Versailles. It provoked Paris with measures like the official dissolution of the *Garde national* and an attempt to remove arms from the city. The *Garde* then proclaimed the Commune, the beginning of a new social republic. It took a number of unprecedented social measures, like handing over workshops from which the employers had fled to new cooperatives, wage tariffs, and a maximum wage. The city was governed by a number of councils. In contrast to the period of dual power in 1848, Paris was now an exclusively revolutionary center. The French army recaptured it in May, after a bloody series of fights, conquering one street and barricade at a time. More than 20,000 *communards* were killed. The attempt to establish a social republic had lasted from March until May, but it lived on in workers' memories for a long time, due partly to Marx's description and praise of this first attempt to create a social revolution. Its crushing temporarily ended Parisian unionism and even some local trades whose workers had been killed. Though these events represented less of a rupture elsewhere in France, other national sections of the International suffered considerably. Governments became more severe in their attitudes toward unions, and some forced the sections to discontinue their activities. Most unions could continue, but they were very cautious for some time. Some lost all courage. The collapse of the Commune and internal discord dealt a fatal blow to the International itself. At the 1872 meeting in The Hague the anarchist Mikhail Bakunin was expelled. This move implied a factional split. Because of the hard times now at hand the secretariat was moved to New York, where it disintegrated more or less silently.

This period of union activity, strikes, and uprisings provided high hopes and great expectations for some time. It also demonstrated poignantly the weakness of unionism on the continent and the failure of its political activities. In France it further alienated workers from parliamentary politics. Elsewhere workers did not lose faith in parliamentary procedures, but census restrictions and plural voting kept them from positions of influence.

This situation contrasted with the one in Great Britain, where unions were now well established. They were able to influence Parliament through successful campaigning, though they preferred to abstain from political activities. Two events at the end of the 1860s could have endangered the position of the British unions, but the unions withstood both challenges. A first event was the Sheffield Outrages, in which members of cutlery unions violently attacked blacklegs who refused to become union members and undermined union control of craft rules. The incident prompted a royal commission to investigate union activities, without much effect. A second incident involved a civil lawsuit (*Hornby vs. Close* in 1867) in which the Boilermakers' Society demanded that its secretary return £ 24 to the union funds. The Supreme Court judged that the law in question did not apply to unions. The unions subsequently started a new campaign for official recognition. The result was the 1871 Trade Union Act. A group of London Trades Council leaders, referred to as the Junta, was actively engaged in lobbying in this and other campaigns, such as those against franchise restrictions and the century-old Master and Servant Law. Voting rights were extended to most skilled workers, and in 1875 the Master and Servant Law was replaced by the Employers and Workmen Act. It was more than a change in wording. Under the new law, workmen and employers were treated alike, and contract breaking was no longer subjected to criminal law.

Campaigning was not the only political activity of British workers. Though rather reluctantly, they also sought representation in Parliament. Suffrage extension especially favored the miners' unions. Though rather weak as organizations, they organized large numbers of voters at the local level and had a tradition of lobbying for labor protection in the mines. The first two workers' representatives were miners: "Lib-labs" (liberal-labor), representing labor within the Liberal party. In light of the successful campaigns of the 1860s and the recognized status of the unions, the liberals seemed perfect senior partners indeed. The Junta was replaced by a parliamentary committee under the leadership of Member of Parliament Alexander MacDonald.

The British unions had been officially recognized, had campaigned successfully against inequality in legislation and for some social laws, and had secured a firm national organization. Neither this union performance, nor the social legislation record, was rivaled on the continent. On the contrary, many a union founded under the First International's guiding light succumbed, mainly due to internal strife and to a sudden change in economic conditions during the mid-1870s.

3

The Era of Organization

From the 1870s on, Marxism became a powerful force on the continent. As a movement, it incorporated a combination of political and economic objectives, focused on organizing the less skilled in the craft workers' protest tradition. Marxism gave rise to a distinct model of union development, unlike the types of unionism that existed at the time in Great Britain and France. Employers' organizations developed as a reaction, with less variation.

THE RISE OF MARXIST ORGANIZATIONS

After liberalism peaked in the 1860s, and after the period of rapid economic growth in the early 1870s, 1874 marked the start of a reaction. Prices dropped and unemployment increased, signaling the first lasting industrial depression. Nevertheless, industrial growth continued. Germany and other industrial new-comers could either maintain their pace of industrial growth or else embark upon a course of industrialization. From 1896 on, a new industrial boom spread across Europe. Despite some minor interruptions, it lasted until World War I. The rise of the steel industry and the electro-technical industry, in factories much larger than the textile mills so characteristic of early industrialization, was the most conspicuous sign of this Second Industrial Revolution. It was anchored most strongly in the German Ruhr area, which mushroomed into Europe's largest industrial region. Throughout Europe, population growth and urbanization led to the industrial proletariat being concentrated in expanding industrial towns and cities.

Labor relations and politics in this period were affected and completely transformed by the rise of Marxism as an international movement. The existing guild and anarchist ideologies combined some ideas about what had been lost and

about the ideal order of future society. In essence, the aim was to restore preindustrial society in the form of craft cooperatives. Toward the end of the 1860s
such ideas had been complemented by a strategy of attacking the capitalist social
order. Although the First International had a mobilizing effect, the dissemination
of the ideas remained limited and socialist organizations succumbed along with
the First International during the recession. In the course of the 1880s this all
changed as Marxism became a dominant ideology in the labor movement.

Marx provided a more forceful ideal of an egalitarian social order by placing
industrial laborers instead of craft workers at the core of his theory. Industrialization was no longer seen as an aberration but as a transitional stage in societal
development. All aspects of social life were explained by referring to technological development and the production relations created during each phase.
Liberal social life could be attributed to capitalism, which would eventually give
way to socialism.

After 1848, when Marx published the Communist Manifesto, followed by
extensive studies in later years, the influence of Marxism increased slowly. Its
spread across Europe was related to the alliance it formed with political and
industrial movements. Politics was at the heart of the movement in answer to
unfavorable economic conditions and to the high level of state involvement in
various industrializing countries. Economic conditions as well as state involvement encouraged political rather than strictly industrial action. It was possible
for a political movement to be viable in the 1880s, while the emergence of a
strong industrial movement (in the form of unions) had to wait until economic
conditions improved in the 1890s.

The strategy leading toward a socialist industrial future was rather open in
Marxist socialism. Capitalism was to be displaced, if not by revolution, then by
the existing political channels, in other words, a parliamentary majority. This
strategy included the struggle for universal suffrage. In the meantime, the labor
movement would have to wrest concessions from the ruling class in order to improve the workers' living and labor conditions. In contrast to conservatives and
Catholics, who were not very interested, Marxists contributed a great deal to the
general knowledge about those conditions. They were eager to disseminate information about social life and to reveal the relationship between abuses in one domain and poor conditions in another. Several movement leaders engaged in social
research and described and analyzed social problems in lengthy discourses.

Political parties adhering to Marxist socialism arose in the 1870s and 1880s.
In order to attract workers who might reject belonging to an organization bearing
the label "socialist," they adopted names like Workers' party, Labor party, or
Social Democratic party. The political arm, which took the form of a political
party, was intended to be just one part of the labor movement. The second part,
considered less important, was formed by the unions. They were to be organized
nationally, as well as internationally, like the political parties. Their task was
the daily struggle with employers for bread-and-butter improvements and the
recruitment of a following for the party among the less committed workers. In

some cases, the party itself organized a union federation to coordinate socialist unions. The German *Sozialdemokratische Arbeiterpartei* of 1869 founded a *Generalkommission* for socialist unions in 1890. The Belgian Workers' party of 1885 followed suit in 1898. However, newly created unions were not the only way that socialism entered the field of labor relations. Numerous existing craft unions turned to socialism and joined the socialist movement. Socialist parties were already in existence in Scandinavia when a joint Danish-Norwegian-Swedish workers' congress in 1897 provided the impulse for an autonomous (but party-linked) national union organization in each of these countries. Even in countries without such formal links, party and union organizations were sometimes created by the same individuals, as happened in France. Socialist labor movements, consisting of both a political and a union wing, developed throughout Europe. The Second International was established in 1889 to coordinate and stimulate the socialist movement. In contrast to its predecessor, it did become an influential body. It discussed matters of direct relevance to the national party and union organizations and to some degree directed their course of action.

In addition to the spread of socialism, economic conditions and new technologies also contributed to the rise of a labor movement transcending craft boundaries. The rise of large enterprises, in combination with production rationalization and standardization, affected the position of established crafts. Subdivision of work operations facilitated managerial control and even allowed the replacement of skilled workers by less skilled newcomers. Toward the end of the century came waves of strikes that focused on workplace autonomy of skilled workers and the admission of semiskilled workers. In 1897 the British engineers, the strongest British union, lost a major conflict that centered around these issues. They resisted the introduction of new work methods but were defeated by a national lockout. The struggle between employers and craft workers was probably fiercest in French artisanal production. Around the turn of the century, the control of the work process was the main issue in a series of strikes that affected various trades throughout the country. The rise of many national unions in skilled trades on the continent was intimately linked with this issue. Skilled workers looked for support among the less skilled newcomers to the trade or craft, though such a step could imply a partial loss in their own privileged position. On the other hand, the result was an extension of the unions' sphere of influence over all workers in the trade. In most countries and industries the battle was lost. Tariffs became a last union refuge and consequently the major issue in employer-union contacts. The Amsterdam diamond workers proved to be an exception to the rule. Their union, by far the largest and best organized in the country, withstood two general lockouts, which were intended to end its monopoly and its veto on new admissions. Because British national unions had already obtained a firmly established position, the engineers fought their struggle alone, without the assistance of the less skilled.

On the continent, the combination of political and economic motives to organize not only the skilled but also the less skilled workers was often at the root of large nationwide labor movements. National governments responded to their rise. The empires of central and eastern Europe (Germany, Austria, and Russia) attempted to crush this challenge to authoritarian or absolutist rule. Germany suppressed socialism by means of a special law (*Sozialistengesetz* in 1878), which affected the socialist unions more than it did the party. Although unions continued their activities and their growth, they had to exercise caution and forgo national coordination. Accordingly, the party could act as the leading force in German socialism. After the repeal of the anti-socialist laws in 1890 and the creation of the *Generalkommission*, the Socialist party became quite large and developed into a model for other countries. Characteristic were its large membership (mainly of skilled workers), its organizational strength, and its party discipline. Indeed, the movement was organized as a strong bureaucracy, in the tradition of German state bureaucracy. In this way it could fight the state with its own weapons. Its strength made it a major influence within the international socialist movement. The parliamentary nations did not oppose the existence of a socialist movement, even though some socialist actions led to clashes with the police. France even removed its last restrictions on the trade unions when, in 1884, it repealed the 1791 Le Chapelier Law. It had become clear that the German suppression of socialist unions had been a failure. Moreover, the French Parliament probably did not want to impose a strict ban. The purpose of a new law, replacing the Le Chapelier Law, was to stimulate the unions to organize and to act in a way that was comparable to the British situation: negotiations instead of conflict. But almost a century of persecution did not pass without consequences.

MARXIST VERSUS ANARCHIST SOCIALISM

Marxist socialism challenged all the more traditional labor ideologies, including liberalism and, most of all, anarchism. Anarchism shared the political primacy of Marxism, but it was much stricter in its rejection of capitalism and parliamentary government. It stressed the role of spontaneous individual or collective action as a means to remove capitalism, thereby establishing an ungoverned society of free individuals and collective small-scale economic activity. Elements of anarchism had been prominent in workers' cooperatives, particularly in France. Indeed, it preceded Marxism as a labor movement ideology. In the Marxist view, anarchism was a thing of the past, obsolete in its emphasis on spontaneous action and its "petty-bourgeois" ideal of small-scale cooperatives. It prevented workers from becoming conscious of their interests, that is, of taking part in development in order to establish a society of coordinated industrial activity. To anarchists, the Marxist ideas of organizational discipline and coordinated economic activity substituted new organizational and economic coercion for the existing suppression by employers and the state. Parliamentary activity could only serve to strengthen the state. It kept workers from spontaneous direct action and from developing individual freedom and social equality.

There was a very lively debate between Marxist and anarchist socialism around the turn of the century, which almost represented a clash between organization (by workers) and inspiration (by intellectuals). The differences of opinion frequently amounted to scolding ("traitors of the working class") and on occasion even open fights. Both sides obstructed each other's strike actions and demonstrations and even called strikes against each other. In an unending flow of booklets and leaflets, anarchists accused Marxism of extinguishing the fire of struggle through its disciplined organization. In defense, Marxists pointed to the concessions employers had been forced to make when confronted with Marxist-inspired strikes. They also pointed to their large strike funds and their prestigious buildings, libraries, and other recreational and cultural facilities—in short, to the symbols of their movement's power. Anarchists considered these institutions, and the increasing number of full-time party and union officials, as mere expressions of the growing gap between the Marxist leaders and the mass of the workers. The symbols were perceived to be symbols of "embourgeoisement," paid by the workers' contributions. In contrast to the high contributions and high strike pay of the Marxists, anarchists served a free meal daily during a strike (later called the *soupe communiste*), paid for by voluntary contributions.

While Marxists contributed to the knowledge of social conditions, it seemed that anarchists were almost too conscious of social abuses to spend any time studying them. Neither were they interested in expanding their efforts to include nonworkers. Consequently, they spent more energy than the Marxists in their mutual fight. The debate between the two factions dominated the first years of the Second International. Marxism won the political tug of war after it had already gradually taken over most of the national labor movements. Anarchists were excluded in 1896, but this time the International did not collapse.

However, the symbols of Marxist socialist power also symbolized its stake in society as it existed. In contrast to anarchism, it had something to lose. This led to cautious and responsible behavior, with the goal of not provoking police or army attacks on its organization. Divisions within the movement also arose, some questioning the movement's revolutionary zeal, others the sense of such zeal. If socialist practice was to be reformist instead of revolutionary, wasn't a shift in ideology necessary, too? Two events that intensified socialist debate regarding this issue were an 1899 publication by the German Marxist Eduard Bernstein and the acceptance of a minister's post by a French socialist, Alexandre Millerand. The International condemned both Bernstein's "revisionism" and Millerand's "ministerialism."

Marxism and anarchism differed not only with respect to their ideologies, but also in their appeal and recruitment of workers. The divergence was due mainly to three factors: the relation with existing forms of worker protest, political conditions and prospects, and the nature of enterprise and employers' reactions.

First, anarchism tended to appeal to workers from all countries who were unable to organize, such as rural workers and industrial workers in the countryside. Their spontaneous and preindustrial action resulted rather easily in local uprisings and revolts. The anarchist emphasis on spontaneity and its total rejection of any kind of authority fit that type of protest. Indeed, from the south of Italy to the north of Sweden, rural industries and rural workers were anarchist strongholds. In contrast, the Marxist creed of organization was more suited to the pattern of protest practiced by skilled workers. This allowed skilled workers in the urban craft industries and metallurgy to assume a leading role in the Marxist movement and to retain the distinction they made between industrial and political action. Unskilled workers in industry were subject to contrasting influences. Marxist organizations attempted to draw them into their movement. Rural migrants to urban areas, however, would sometimes remain oriented toward a tradition of preindustrial protest, valued by anarchism.

The second factor, politics, led to national variations in Marxist and anarchist appeal. Probably most important were the prospects of a workers' majority in parliament. In countries where suffrage extension was slow or gradual, such prospects were brighter than nations where parliamentary politics was not developed at all or where workers were unable to influence parliament. Like Britain, Scandinavia and the Low Countries introduced gradual suffrage reforms. Parliamentary politics was less developed in the German and Austrian empires, but workers could cherish their hopes of a future majority. In the countries on the continent where gradual reform took place and in Germany and Austria, Marxists soon dominated workers' political activities. In other countries like France, however, the anarchist rejection of parliamentary politics had a wider appeal or even became a dominant force. In France, universal male suffrage had been introduced, abolished, and reintroduced. Moreover, workers did not obtain more than a small and scattered minority, and Parisian workers had fallen victim to parliamentary violence in 1848 and 1871. A new bloodbath, the *massacre de Fourmies* continued that tradition of violent clashes: On May Day 1891 nine people were killed when armed forces shot at a demonstration of workers on strike. In some southern European countries and in Russia, parliamentary rule probably was too far off to be of importance.

Third, the nature of industry and employers' reactions influenced the labor movement. Although Marxism started a movement of craft workers in urban trades, it increasingly attracted skilled workers in large and heavy industry, to whom the anarchist ideal of artisanal cooperatives was no longer seen as a viable alternative. The size of enterprises itself probably also facilitated organization. Large-scale industry molded a proletariat that was subject to rather uniform labor and living conditions. Consequently, expectations of individual social mobility within or outside the factory were reduced. The notion of the existence of one large working class also became more prominent, especially in Germany with its rapidly developing large enterprises. On the other hand, anarchism took hold among artisanal workers in small workshops. The very small scale of production impeded organization in a number of ways. First, it nurtured the hope of social mobility, of establishing oneself as an independent small employer. Second, it implied direct employer supervision over the work force, which also discouraged organization. Third, labor and living conditions varied among the workers employed in different workshops. A single movement could hardly appeal to all of them. France provided a good example. Aside from the long tradition of suppression in that country, the opposition of artisanal *patrons* to workers' organizations, or (more accurately) against any encroachment upon their authority in family-owned enterprise, fostered anarchism. The powerful ideal of becoming independent *patrons* also kept artisanal workers from organizing as dependent workers. Marxism in France was more developed in large-scale industry. But just as is the case concerning the first and second explanations of Marxist and anarchist growth, there were many exceptions to the rule. Exceptional cases could be due to foreign influence, the availability of organizational or oratory talents, and other specific conditions.

THREE MODELS OF UNION DEVELOPMENT

The underlying differences between Marxism and anarchism were at the root of two different types of union development. As a consequence, two types of labor relations arose. Since most countries still lacked a tradition of unionism outside the skilled crafts, both types represented a continuation of existing traditions to only a limited degree.

The Marxist pattern consisted of unions coordinated by a national federation, closely linked to the Marxist political party. The federation not only coordinated union work, but also established new unions and pressed for the admittance of the less skilled into craft and occupational unions. The ideal was industrial unionism rather than craft unionism. The former would allow the mobilization of less skilled workers for both political and industrial action. But the principle was hard to translate into effective practice, and craft unions continued to prevail. Where craft union opposition to the admission of the less skilled was too strong, separate unions consisting of factory workers or general workers were set up without affecting the ideal of industrial unionism. Less organized trades, as well as members of newly created unions, were attracted by the federations' common strike fund, financed by the stronger member unions.

The existence of both political and industrial activities did not imply that the two were combined in any single action. On the contrary, a fine distinction was made. The unions confined themselves to industrial action (against employers), leaving politics and parliamentary action to the political branch of the movement. Of course, they would support the party's political claims with a political strike if specifically requested or ordered to do so by the party. Industrial and political actions were not the only weapons of the Marxist labor movement. The party and the union federation also created, or encouraged the creation, of an extensive network of services by member unions, including social security benefits, educational and recreational facilities, cooperative stores, and related services. Most of these services had already been part of earlier craft unionism, but their scale and scope were vastly expanded. The main union function, however, was to represent its membership in contacts with employers. Preferably, workers were to leave any contacts with their employers to the more independent union officials. This process would stimulate uniformity in labor conditions and would prevent employer pressure on workers. The wide range of union activities required membership discipline, and it fostered bureaucratization. In combination with the party's parliamentary work, reformism was also reinforced within both the party and the unions. Moreover, many union leaders knew—and cared—little about Marxism. They left the task of intellectual debate and political affairs to the party leadership. Their own concern with organization made them oppose all kinds of anarchist action, as well as outbursts of individual protest and desperation. This weakened anarchism and contributed to the rise of collective structures in labor relations.

Germany provided the foremost example of this kind of development, and what happened here influenced a number of other countries. The Marxist type of unionism might thus be dubbed the German model. The major factors were growing numbers of skilled workers, favorable prospects of parliamentary politics, and large-scale industrial enterprise. The German model of unionism created a specific type of labor culture, which would have a great impact on political and social life in the twentieth century. Prominent features of this culture were unity, representation, and restraint. The labor movement claimed to represent the objective interests of its membership. Since the rest of the working class shared those interests, the movement claimed to represent the class as a whole. Unity of the entire working class required an end to spontaneous and unorganized action. Instead, continuous organizational efforts and disciplined restraint were seen as a means to improve the position of the working class. The powerful combination of organization and discipline by an entire class posed a possible threat to large portions of the middle class, as well as to the lower middle class. The middle class was caught between large industry and the organized working class.

The anarchist type of union development did not link unions to a party and indeed rejected parliamentary politics. Unions were to be political movements in their own right but were to operate outside the domain of parliamentary politics. They were to mobilize workers for political purposes, that is, political protest in the form of strikes. This type of political mobilization also encouraged industrial unionism. But development of power was slower than in Marxist unionism because the unions did not create a standing organization. In accordance with the aim of mobilizing—rather than organizing—workers, they were primarily active during strikes. Anarchist unions lacked the means to shape a more lasting solidarity between skilled and unskilled workers, or between different trades and industries. The process of creating such a sense of solidarity had to be constantly initiated and reinitiated. Moreover, the results of anarchist action, which amounted to political action, were often meagre. The importance of spontaneous action reduced the need for a formal leadership or any kind of representation. This approach to social change also opposed the rise of collective structures in labor relations.

Since this type of unionism was especially pronounced in France, it might be called the French model. The aim of the French union movement was protest rather than organization. Unionism was locally dispersed and became a unity only during larger protest eruptions. Nationwide unity functioned more as forceful idea than as a current practice. The establishment of a socialist confederation took place later than in Britain and Germany. More than the TUC and the *Generalkommission*, it remained plagued by ideological discord between anarchists and Marxists, since it lacked the organizational instruments to cope with internal strife. The road to one national confederation also was one of disagreement between conflicting trends, and of local rather than national strength.

After union legalization in 1884, French unions made use of newly created local labor exchanges, *Bourses de travail*, to coordinate union work (more or less the way the British trades councils did). The predominance of local activities hardly affected the very slow trend toward industrial unions, which lacked a central organization and engaged in fighting new technology more than in political mobilization. Nevertheless, the general strike was a major issue at national workers' congresses of the *bourses* and the unions. The typographer Jean Alleman and the *allemanistes* stressed the central importance of the general strike as a revolutionary weapon, which was counter to the ideas espoused by the Marxist *guesdistes,* led by the journalist Jules Guesde, and also counter to the more reformist *possibilistes*. The *allemanistes* also organized a national federation of *bourses*. The *bourses* and the nationwide unions were confederated into the *Confédération générale du travail* (CGT) in 1901. Like its member organizations, it was loosely organized and lacked formal ties to the socialist parties. This served to prevent the Marxist-anarchist strife from intensifying. Although Marxism enjoyed increasing popularity in France, several factors made anarchism the dominating ideology. These included the long tradition of anarchism, a lack of confidence in parliamentary rule, the scatteredness and small size of industrial enterprise, and the value attached to individual social mobility. French anarchism developed into syndicalism, which stressed the crucial role of unions (*syndicats*) in the general strike, deemed the starting point of the revolution, and also in the postrevolutionary society of producer cooperatives. Local strikes should provide training for, and ultimately should result in, the general strike.

Like the *Generalkommission*, the CGT claimed to act on behalf of the working class as a whole, but the claim was effectuated only at the time of a general strike. The pattern of dispersed protest and mobilization for unified action only occasionally shook the authority of the family enterprise *patron* and the position of the middle class and bourgeoisie.

Both the German and the French model contrasted with the by now well-established British model of union development, which did not include a need to organize or mobilize workers for political purposes. Consequently, the British unions did not claim to represent the working class as a whole. They were basically craft unions, which attempted to steer clear of politics, and only occasionally campaigned against specific legislative restraints placed upon their activities. The craft unions engaged in bargaining with employers and also valued the more traditional ways of managing labor conditions through job placement and the closed shop. Both activities prevented industrial unionism. Indeed, British unionism put little effort into educating or integrating the working class as a whole or even to pursuing a common policy. The working class shared only a popular culture of hedonism rather than a culture of restraint or protest.

Toward the end of the 1880s the already established British unions were challenged by an autonomous movement of the less skilled. A number of strikes in London led to a unionization wave among unskilled workers. This "new unionism" not only organized specific industrial branches, but also general workers. It was more militant than craft unionism and embraced political action. Both the employers and the existing craft unions tried to curb the new unions. The craft unions feared the erosion of their privileges, a predominance of political action, and the spread of socialism. The general workers were allowed to occupy a modest place within the TUC, but were not able to move the congress to become involved in politics. Although there were also some separate women's organizations in the other models, they were more typical in Britain. This model lacked a central authority that could argue for the admission of women to the craft unions.

Up to this point, only national variations between Britain, France, and Germany have been taken into consideration. Developments in each of the three countries also led to the rise of unions and forms of worker protest that fit somewhat better into one of the other models. Indeed, the domination of one national model in each of these countries was the outcome of a process reflecting many regional and industrial differences. The British model was most uniform, especially after new unionism secured its modest place within the TUC. The German model also applied both generally and nationwide in Germany, with only minor variations. A few craft workers' union initially adhered to British model craft unionism and political neutrality. There were also spurts of spontaneous French model actions, particularly among miners. French unionism was least uniform. The absence of strong organizations allowed internal strife to continue within and between unions, and there were wide regional and industrial variations in forms of action and organization.

Miners occupied a special place in France, too. They contributed most to the practice of spontaneous action, often without reference to anarchism. Strikes would spread from one shift and from one pit to another until they became local or regional and achieved national significance. Indeed, some of the larger strikes in this period were miners' actions. In areas like the Ruhr, miners were only occasionally involved in large outbursts of protest, while spontaneous actions were more endemic in the Saint-Etienne region of France. Newly formed unions tried desperately to control the actions in order to gain acceptance by miners and to become recognized by employers. They were almost as concerned about stopping spontaneous strikes as about organizing strikes themselves. Their weak base and their fear of new outbursts, which were likely to endanger their organization, made them a reformist force within Marxist or anarchist federations.

In spite of the differences within each nation, the three models may be treated as distinct national forms of union development. Each form also applied to one or more other European countries. The British model served as an example for some of the early craft unions on the continent. The rise of Marxist organizations, however, swept this type of unionism from the continent. The only country outside Britain that remained loyal to this model was Ireland, where craft unions had originally been linked to their stronger British counterparts. The model was thus increasingly confined to the British Isles. Starting as a great example for the rest of Europe, it later became the exception, though still influential because of its relative power. The French model had served as an example for many anarchist unions founded at the time of the First International. It, too, gave way to Marxist organizations. The only country outside France where this model found a foothold was Spain, partly due to direct French influence. Spanish anarchism was concentrated regionally. Catalonia's textile industry, the scene of many anarchist actions in later years, was a prime example. Anarchism was challenged or even pushed into the background by Marxist organizations in other industrial regions of Spain. However, anarchism greatly influenced the development of Spanish unionism.

Its organization and the growing importance of parliamentary politics made the German model almost the continental standard. The model was borrowed in Scandinavia, the Low Countries, Switzerland, and the Austrian and Czech parts of the Austrian Empire. None of these countries had much artisanal or craft union tradition, except for a few crafts like the printing industry. Basically, the union movement could make a fresh start. Unionism was linked to a political party, which had favorable future prospects if equal voting rights could be introduced. German influence contributed to the spread of the model. Most of the countries involved bordered on Germany and spoke a Teutonic language. Of course, the spread of the model was not uniform, and there were as many variations as there were countries involved. In some cases, the typographers continued British model craft unionism. They were well organized and rather reluctant to join socialist federations. But they slowly overcame their objections and became major centers of reformism within such national organizations. Most countries involved also had their share of anarchism, challenging the Marxist organizations either occasionally or more regularly. Anarchism was mostly a rural affair, practiced by rural workers, workers in rural industries, and miners. Its hold was probably the strongest among the miners of (French-speaking) Wallony. Though some countries witnessed bitter conflicts between Marxists and anarchists, the Marxist movement gradually incorporated this rural or miners' anarchism. A Marxist federation was not established until 1906 in Holland, but it soon became more influential than the existing anarchist organization.

Marxism also became a growing movement among workers in the industries of southern and eastern Europe. Three characteristics of these countries, however, hampered its growth into a national model of unionism. First, industry was still small and confined to a few and scattered industrial towns in most of these countries. As in France and Spain, this discouraged or even impeded the foundation of a strong national union organization. Second, rural workers by far outnumbered industrial workers. Protest movements were often more in line with anarchism and established national traditions of anarchist protest. Third, heavy suppression, often by feudal or almost absolutist state authority, hindered organization or parliamentary pressure. On the contrary, suppression and anarchist protest reinforced each other and radicalized those Marxist organizations that were founded. Unable to build up provisions like those in the German model, the organizations had less to lose, while they simultaneously had less to win by a more reformist stand. Thus, one might say that the predominance of agriculture and political conditions (like autocracy or feudal rule) favored the rise of French-model unionism, while the spread of industry added to the force of the German model. Indeed, Marxist organizations gained force, but their radical struggle against employers and the state set the labor movements in these countries apart from those in the German model. This applied to eastern Europe (the Russian Empire including Finland and Poland) and to southern Europe, including the Balkan Peninsula, Italy, and Portugal. Italy, the most industrialized country in this region, also had the largest Marxist movement. To some extent, unionism in northern Italy even resembled the German model. However, unionism here was part of a national movement that shared the three characteristics typical of southern and eastern Europe.

MINOR TRENDS

In addition to Marxist and anarchist unions there were other minor varieties of unionism. The largest of these were Catholic organizations, which developed at the end of the nineteenth century. The rise of Catholic workers' organizations passed through three stages. In all of them priests, rather than workers, dominated organizational work. The first stage was paternalism. In the 1860s and 1870s Catholic workers had been drawn into organizations and clubs organized by priests and led by employers. The organizations were comprised of a mixed membership of workers, members of the middle class, and the bourgeoisie. Most of these clubs provided educational and recreational facilities in addition to religious activities. Labor conditions were hardly ever a topic of conversation or debate. Corporatism, the second stage, became a leading principle in the 1880s. Workers became a distinct category and labor conditions a recognized topic of discussion in mixed employer-worker organizations. The organizations' primary aim was to demonstrate the harmony of interests and to foster corporatist cooperation, more or less in the guild tradition. Although there were already some Catholic organizations for workers exclusively, the rise of such organizations did not gain momentum until 1891. In that year, Pope Leo XIII condemned liberalism as well as socialism in his encyclical *Rerum Novarum*, and called on employers and workers to cooperate. In the third stage, priests stepped up their efforts and founded distinct workers' organizations. Almost everywhere, these were intended as a reaction to, or even represented a split from, socialist organizations. Motives for such a split were related either to religion, like Sunday meetings or socialist anti-religious propaganda, or to the nature of Catholic social life. The latter still implied the existence of paternalistic contacts between employers and workers outside the workplace. Such contacts provided Catholic workers with different loyalties from those of socialists.

Though the new organizations were set up explicitly as unions, labor conditions were only a minor theme. Main topics of debate were Catholic unions' relations with the older paternalist and corporatist clubs, the basis of organization (industry or diocese), and interconfessionalism (that is, working with Protestants in one organization). Most attempts to set up interconfessional organizations failed, sometimes due to clerical intervention. Catholic unions valued cooperation and compromise rather than conflict in contacts with employers. The sense of Catholic community made them very cautious in calling for or supporting strikes. This provided Socialists with a motive to condemn them as traitors but did not prevent incidental coordinated action. Catholic unions were strongest in the Low Countries, especially in the Catholic south of Holland and in Flanders, where they outnumbered socialist organizations. In Europe's Catholic South their appeal was confined to rural workers: The Church had lost its hold in industrial towns. Despite small numbers, Catholic unionism contributed to the ideological pluralism of continental unionism in most countries. It set the two continental models even more apart from British model. It also made Scandinavia, lacking Catholic organizations, a distinct category within the German model. Protestant unionism was far less important. The organizations that arose in Holland, Germany, and Switzerland were also reactions to socialism. Jews had separate organizations and also dominated some craft unions, due to their concentration in specific urban trades.

Liberal unionism had preceded socialism. Its following consisted of craft workers attracted by British new model unionism and the liberal reforms of the 1860s. Like the Catholic unions, it propagated class cooperation, but without the paternalistic connotation that this assumed with the Catholics. Liberal unionism succumbed under the influence of socialism in all of Europe, however. Only in Belgium and Germany (the *Hirsch-Duncker* unions) was it able to survive until the First World War.

The fate of liberal unions was shared by a small and religious-socialist form of craft unionism, the so-called Knights of Labor. Originating in the United States, the Knights took the form of a secret society and engaged in seemingly mysterious rituals. In Europe they only impacted small and dispersed groups of craft workers.

Unionism developed with great difficulty among clerical workers. The small office clerk and commercial travelers' unions that originally paved the way remained at the margins of the union movement. Working conditions and strong employer resistance discouraged organization. Moreover, the industrial unions that arose in some countries not only often refused to admit clerical workers, but also denied unions which exclusively organized clerical workers a right to exist. Indeed, there was some discussion in the socialist union federations, particularly in Germany, of whether clerical workers were wage-dependent workers who needed to be organized, or a *Neue Mittelstand*. In the end, the problem was solved by allowing separate clerical unions to join the federation. Still, many clerical organizations preferred to remain independent rather than join a socialist federation of manual workers.

By 1914, 10 to 20 percent of all industrial workers were organized, and in Great Britain and Germany more than 25 percent were. The large majority of these workers were members of socialist or related unions, with the TUC and the *Generalkommission*, each boasting 2.5 million members, being the largest. Craft workers formed the most important category of members. Despite a rise in their organization level, women still played a very minor role in the union movement.

Unionism was becoming a conspicuous part of social life. Previously, union meetings had been held in public houses, in the guild tradition. Socialists wanted to rid themselves of this public house image and increasingly concentrated their activities in one building. Such a *Maison du peuple* or *Volkshaus* became the seat of local unions and sometimes of the party. They sometimes also housed mutual aid societies, a library, and other educational and recreational facilities and became small worker strongholds in a hostile environment. Cooperatives, mostly bakeries, small publishing agencies, and socialist union and party papers were part of the movement as well. Stores and papers had resounding names like Progress, Ahead, Harmony or Aurora, *Avanti, Vorwärts*, or *Vooruit*. On certain occasions their colorful banners filled the streets. Catholic unions had their own services and festive meetings, though on a smaller scale.

THE RISE OF EMPLOYERS' ASSOCIATIONS

Employers founded a number of debating clubs and local syndical chambers even before the 1890s. Their main concern tended to be the economic condition of the trade or the local community. Labor conditions were seen as the individual employer's responsibility. British competition was a major source of debate and concern on the continent. Clubs and chambers had petitioned for trade tariffs in the 1860s, the peak of international free trade. In the 1870s, when economic conditions deteriorated, they turned into true political pressure groups. In addition to influence through personal contacts, a series of requests for trade tariffs were sent to governments and parliaments. The reluctance to discuss labor conditions was almost a matter of principle. Typically, in their search for local tariffs, workers in the printing industry encouraged the creation of employers' associations to facilitate bargaining. Employers were reluctant, however, to participate.

After this early phase of trade associations, a second phase of development started in the 1890s. A large number of employers' organizations emerged, often coexisting with the older trade associations. Their emergence represented a re-action to the rise of trade unions. Some combined the function of trade asso-ciations and employers' organizations, while others acted exclusively as employer organizations, coordinating employer activities vis-à-vis the unions and the craft workers' opposition to technological change. Whether or not they combined the two activities often depended on the specific characteristics of the trade. Com-bining both functions was rather common in the construction trades but not in the metallurgy or steel industry, because different economic conditions char-acterized various branches of metallurgy. The opposition of craft workers to rationalization and mechanization was a particularly strong inducement to set up employers' organizations. Employers in craft industries opposed union attempts to interfere in working conditions (such as wages and working hours), but they resisted union efforts to influence technological change and workplace organi-zation even more fiercely. The rise of industrial employers' associations in a number of countries was related to this struggle.

Many of the new employers' organizations were created after a large strike movement. From their outset, they adopted a more offensive stance, calling or threatening lockouts when confronted by new union demands. British engineer-ing employers organized in 1896, initiating an enormous lockout a year later. Diamond-cutting employers in Holland called two major lockouts within a few years after their organization started. Indeed, the new organizations often man-aged a common strike fund, which allowed members who were not strong enough individually to survive a lockout or to cope with selective union strikes, so-called whipsaw actions. On occasion, the strike fund was the only element in such an employers' alliance. In general, the associations were orga-nized more loosely than the unions to which they were a reaction. Employers were willing to hand over responsibilities to their organizations only reluctantly under strong pressure from increasing union power.

During the first years of the twentieth century, social legislation became a third motive for employers to organize. (Trade conditions in the 1860s and union growth in the 1890s constituted the other two). Since the third and second motives were often intertwined, it is hardly possible to speak of a distinct third phase of development. Though employers' associations would often start as political pres-sure groups, they soon found themselves dealing with unions. Political action resembled that of the earlier trade associations, but the main participants were no longer such trade associations, but employers' organizations concerned with labor conditions. The employers' federation in French metallurgy started by opposing social legislation introduced by the socialist minister Millerand (notably relating to the introduction of joint management-union committees).

When a strike or lockout was followed by a settlement reaffirming the hold of the employers' organization over its members, more peaceful relations might develop. The way in which such relations developed was related to the prevailing model of unionism. The rise of industrial employers' organizations as such was not determined by the model of unionism. Rather than the type of unionism, the concentration of union growth and activities around the turn of the century, and the beginning of social legislation during the same period, were decisive factors.

In contrast, the pace at which central employers' federations were founded did vary according to the model of unionism. The early rise of central employers' federations or confederations reflected the trend toward rather strong central union federations in the German model. The central union federations functioned more as a facilitator than as a direct target of the central employers' federations. The number of direct contacts was very limited. Denmark formed an exception, followed by the other two Scandinavian countries, where employers' federations were a driving force behind the centralization of employer-union contacts. The existence of German-model unionism, combined with the absence of Catholic or other rival organizations, facilitated such central level contacts. Most of the smaller countries characterized by German-model unionism preceded Germany in the formation of central employers' federations (for example, Belgium in 1895 and Denmark in 1896). The *Vereinigung der deutschen Arbeitgeberverbände* (League of German Employers' Federations or VDA) was not formed until 1913. The German employers were years ahead of their British and French colleagues, however, who failed to develop such federations before the First World War. The union movement was less developed at the central level in both these countries when compared to German-model unionism, so that there was less of a need to react. Differences in the nature of enterprise and employers themselves may have also influenced the unequal pace of development. The predominance of family enterprise in France may have retarded it. Although large entrepreneurs tended to organize very late, they were probably important in helping transcend the industrial level of organization and stimulating the foundation of central federations. The availability of organizational talent and the nationwide prestige of industrial tycoons and magnates may have facilitated their role in national federations. They were well represented in the German federation and constituted the Belgian organization's backbone. Employers' associations developed in southern and eastern Europe, but their importance did not transcend regional boundaries. The Italian confederation was a good example: Like the union organization, its base was located in northern Italy's industrial area.

Most employer associations refrained from drawing up explicit ideological documents or even more practical policy platforms. They had in common worries about the growth of trade unions and the initiation or expansion of social legislation. They maintained contacts with conservative and Catholic, rather than liberal, parties, but there were no formal links to political parties. Indeed, large employers preferred their informal contacts, allowing access to government and parliament without causing discord within the organizations. Free enterprise was cherished within national boundaries, not internationally, as pleas for trade tariffs and state involvement, colonial or not, in foreign trade bear evidence.

Catholic unionism was in no way matched by Catholic employers' organizations. The mixed paternalistic and corporatist clubs often aimed explicitly at organizing workers rather than employers, to whom they were of only secondary, if any, importance. To the Catholic Church, employers were of less concern than the growing socialist appeal among workers. The few Catholic and Protestant organizations that emerged (Holland had both) remained in the shadow of non-religious organizations, even more than did unions. Although Catholic employers might prefer Catholic unions for their workers (at least compared to socialist organizations), they themselves had no need for any Catholic organization.

In addition to common action, whether linked to an organization or to a more informal arrangement, large enterprise on the continent had at its disposal a specific weapon against autonomous workers' movements. The large German firms that arose during this period offered their workers a range of social services, including housing, health care, and vocational training. The provisions were expressions of strong paternalistic authority and concern, intended to reinforce the power of the industrialists over their local communities and to tie the workers to the company. In order to arrest the growth of the Marxist labor movement, firms reserved at least part of these services for members of company-originated and company-dependent union organizations. Most steel companies on the continent, not just those in Germany, had such yellow unions (named perhaps for the color of its press). Initially, they often outnumbered socialist unions. Yellow unions, and employers themselves, also fought socialist organizations more directly by recruiting blacklegs from the outside, by preventing picketing, and by dismissing militant socialists. Of course, ''yellow union'' also rapidly became a popular term of abuse, used by anarchists against Marxists and by both against Catholic unions, due to the latter's restrained policies.

In sum, by the turn of the century both workers and employers had their industrial—and in many countries also national—organizations. National models of unionism were not to any great extent matched by national models of employers' organizations. The contacts between both sides, as well as the system of labor relations that would emerge, would be largely determined by these organizational characteristics.

4

The Impact of the Organizations

Three models of labor relations and political action developed in relation to the three types of unionism. The labor movement's political activities influenced the concentration of social legislation at the turn of the century.

THE EIGHT HOUR DAY AND THE TREND TOWARD COLLECTIVE CONTRACTS

A universal demand by the socialist unions in their contacts with employers and the state was the implementation of an eight-hour workday. The idea was borrowed from the United States, where it had been an issue during a nationwide strike on 1 May 1886 that had ended in bloodshed. From then on, May 1 became a day of socialist actions and demonstrations throughout Europe, especially devoted to the eight-hour workday. In 1889, an international workers' congress in Paris, representing the beginning of the Second International, put forth the eight-hour day as a major aim. The demand was propagated as the "3 × 8" formula, that is, eight hours each of work; the combination of recreation, education, and family life; and sleep. A shorter workday had been a traditional demand in most industries. A major argument was that working for ten hours or more blunted workers because it did not leave any time for family life, recreation, or education. The argument became more powerful when the workday of women and children became regulated. A secondary argument was that working less would lead to a fairer distribution of work when unemployment existed. Socialist unions and parties considered both arguments equally important, and advanced both, although priority shifted according to the economic conditions of the moment. Both arguments incorporated the idea that shorter working time would increase wages. The excesses of competition, that is, workdays in excess of ten to twelve hours, would disappear, and the burden of competition no longer would be shifted completely to the workers. A condition was attached to these changes: Legislation would have to enforce the eight-hour day throughout all of Europe. The eight-hour issue provided the international socialist movement with a powerful slogan, relevant to all workers, irrespective of their skills, age, nationality, or sex. It transformed the first of May (May Day) into a symbol of socialist strength and determination.

Employers reacted fiercely. First of all, an eight-hour workday entailed a drastic reduction compared to the standard at the time, which had been decreasing gradually to ten or eleven hours in the 1880s. This reduction was due more to slackening economic conditions and the regulation of women's working time than to union action. Second, such a demand implied state interference on the continent. Socialists exerted considerable pressure for legislation, if not for eight hours then for nine or ten, and if not for everyone then at least for specific groups as a start (such as miners). The employers' determination was revealed in the sanctions they imposed against workers for celebrating May Day. Dismissals resulting from such celebrations were a frequent source of labor conflict. Important examples were a miners' strike in Bilbao in 1900 and a strike in the Berlin breweries in 1894. The latter conflict even included a local beer boycott, which lasted several months, obviously requiring a disciplined union organization.

Work time was not the only topic in employer-union contacts. Socialist protest also contributed to the decline of abuses like the truck system, arbitrary fines, and dismissal without notice. However, it is not surprising that wages were the most frequent bone of contention. Especially the better organized craft unions or craft-based industrial unions tried to engage in local or regional collective bargaining in order to set uniform wage tariffs. Tariffs had a long tradition as a more general craft workers' demand. They also served a novel goal: to defend craft workers against the effects of new technologies and new work processes, especially where resistance against these innovations had failed. The typographers had set, and still set, the example. Locally concentrated craft industries like diamond cutting, cigar making, and hat making followed, as well as the building trades, characterized by their local agreements with joiners, carpenters, and bricklayers. In the last decade of the century the German printers set the tone by means of a nationwide formal contract, the *Reichstarif*. The *Generalkommission* expelled them initially for this collaboration with employers, but in 1899 such formal contracts (*Tarifverträge*) were accepted as normal practice. Soon the typographers were used as an example. Collective contracts, though still rather exceptional, became a major aim of German type unions from then on. They spread to various industries in the countries involved.

Decisive for the development of collective agreements was the aim of German-model unions to obtain uniform tariffs (taking after craft unionism) and to put an end to employer arbitrariness in the area of wages and working time. The unions' organizational structure and expansive strike funds allowed them to surpass the workshop or factory level. They were also able to guarantee their members' adherence to the contract. This changed the nature of strikes. In order to enforce a better new contract, frequent and spontaneous direct action in a specific workshop was replaced by a well-organized and well-prepared strike in local industry at the time a contract expired. In practice, the transition was very gradual.

Employers were reluctant to engage in formal bargaining. However, the rise of their own organizations, created to fight the unions and to coordinate actions by means of anti-strike funds, encouraged bargaining. Increasingly, employers' associations were able and willing to impose bargaining results upon unwilling members and to ban undercutting. Employers in small-scale craft workshops, unable to influence the local labor market, gradually came to value uniformity in wage tariffs and working hours. Large industries, including the textile industry (with its many less-skilled women), the large steel industry, and mining were less affected by the new trends. Large employers, either alone or in local coalitions, could set wages at the local labor market and did not allow any outside force to impose uniformity. The process of industrial rationalization at the end of the century made them even more opposed to fixed labor conditions.

The collective agreements on the continent regulated wages, working hours, and other conditions. They covered piece rates as well as time rates. Some of them also provided for mediation to settle conflicts or individual complaints. The typographers' contracts were the most elaborate. They consisted of several pages filled with specific piece rates for the various types of letters, commas, and blank spaces, and tariffs for time workers. Industries like tailoring followed this example of using detailed piece rates. Agreements in the construction industry were less detailed, however, since most construction workers were paid by the hour. Agreements or contracts served to reinforce existing differences in wages, relating to age and sex (if women were not excluded totally from the trade). National agreements prescribed higher tariffs in cities than in rural areas, reflecting labor market differences.

The early collective contracts each lasted a number of years, some up to ten years, and included provisions for a fixed yearly wage increase. This was advantageous for the workers during periods of slack and low prices, but not when prices were on the rise, as the German typographers experienced. The organizations on both sides, or the coalition of employers in case there was no formal organization, were held responsible for upholding the contract against dissenting members (that is, against undercutting and overcharging) during its term. When problems occurred, one was required to make efforts to bring dissenters in line again, or expel them. In exceptional cases the contract included a closed shop, which could lead to exclusion from the trade. On occasion, employers and unions promised explicitly to refrain from strikes and lockouts during the term of the contract. Such a clause amounted to a mutual obligation to maintain labor peace (*Friedenspflicht*) for one or more years. Implicit in this type of collective bargaining was the unions' noninterference in matters of new technology and changes in work organization, apart from complaint procedures. Indeed, one of the unions' arguments to promote collective contracts among employers was that the agreements left this employer prerogative with respect to technology and work organization intact. In Scandinavia, the long-lasting Danish guild tradition, the socialist unions' monopoly position, and the rapid rise of central employers' organizations contributed to nationwide mutual recognition and understanding, as well as to a more explicit formulation of this employers' prerogative. The first central-level agreement in Europe, the 1899 Danish September Agreement (*Septemberforlig*) stipulated a mutual recognition of the right to effect work stoppages and the employers' right to direct and supervise work. Under the pressure of the employers' federation the central organizations assumed responsibility for monitoring contracts that their affiliated organizations had agreed to. They set up a procedure that needed to be followed in case of a breach of contract. The Danish basic agreement, not a contract itself, was followed by less obliging central agreements in Norway (1902) and Sweden (1906).

The rise of collective contracts changed the extent and reduced the frequency of industrial conflict in the countries involved. It certainly did not pacify labor relations. Instead, it made employers and unions even more determined because contracts might influence labor conditions for a number of years. Indeed, most of the early contracts were the outcome of a large strike movement. The Danish basic agreement was an example. It put an end to a large strike and a lockout, which had started among the Jutland joiners and lasted four months. The conflict aroused international union solidarity, reflecting national variations in financial strength. French unions donated 1,900 francs, the TUC more than fifty, and the Germans more than a hundred times that amount. The Swedish agreement of 1906 came after a protracted engineering conflict, resolved by means of a collective agreement.

Industrial bargaining and well-organized strikes became distinct features of labor relations in countries characterized by German-model unionism. Indeed, they developed into main features of the German labor relations model. Centralization and bargaining were related and reinforced each other in this model. This model thus consisted of several elements: centralization of the organizations involved, industrial bargaining (mostly regional but also nationwide in the smaller countries), and industry-wide organized strikes and lockouts. Another feature was that union representation within the enterprise or in the workshop was relatively weak. The Scandinavian unions in particular had their enterprise representatives, but they allowed them little autonomy. The activities of the representatives were confined to executing agreements and handling complaints. Yet, there were many variations within the model, ranging from the national Danish September Agreement, to Switzerland, where the unions were unable to enforce formal bargaining. Moreover, the model did not develop overnight. Its distinctive features developed gradually into a consistent model of labor relations. Even then, large industry was hardly affected. It continued to embrace exclusive employer competence in labor conditions. The attitude of large entrepreneurs had a wider impact in Germany, with its concentration of heavy and large industry, than in the smaller countries characterized by the German model of labor relations.

Anarchists and dissenting Marxists strongly rejected collective contracts as being in league with the enemy. How could capitalism ever be replaced if the unions prevented their members from striking, thereby crushing their fighting spirit? The anarchist inability and refusal to persuade workers to move toward labor peace, as well as fierce employer resistance, prevented the spread of collective bargaining in France. Printing was the only industry practicing it, later followed by regional bargaining in mining, with its reformist union organizations. In most industries the loosely structured unions continued the *action directe* tradition, that is, plant and shop-floor militancy. It did not use any form of official union representation within factories. The contentious opposition of both sides did not allow for such formal devices. Consequently, France developed a distinct model of labor relations, characterized by rather weak organizations without contacts at the industry level. Union activities remained highly decentralized and shop-floor based, but without formal union representation at that level. The French model also had some impact in Wallony, where it challenged the German model.

Great Britain remained loyal to its own tradition of craft rules enforced by a closed shop. However, the craft unions and employers also had developed a system of industrial bargaining (that is, craft bargaining for each industry separately). Such industrial agreements consisted mainly of general rules and procedures. Specific labor conditions were the subject of large numbers of local and workshop regulations. The 1897 lockout in engineering affirmed this tradition of decentralized bargaining within the framework of industry-wide guidelines. The employers won the lockout and in 1898 imposed formal Provisions for Avoiding Disputes, directed against the autonomy of district union committees. The provisions did not contain substantive labor conditions, as would have been the case in the German model. The relative decentralization of British organizations did not allow a shift to substantive agreements at the industry level. The provisions actually reinforced decentralization to plant and workshop. Instead of the unions themselves, their shop stewards had to deal with the introduction of new technologies and work processes. Though their position was not formalized, the shop stewards rose to considerable power in a number of industries, and they were determined to defend their interests in bargaining. In addition to their role in industrial strikes and lockouts, the shop stewards instigated shop-floor or plant actions. Therefore, the emergent British model of labor relations shared the predominance of bargaining with the German model, but it differed in the subject matter and the level of negotiations. Plant and workshop bargaining ruled by industrial dispute procedures prevailed, rather than the industrial and substantive agreements that characterized the German model. The British pattern was similar to the French model with respect to its shop-floor and plant level of militancy and its degree of decentralization, but it differed in the nature of employer-union contacts, stressing bargaining instead of the mere expression of protest.

The fierce opposition between unions and employers in eastern and southern Europe was not conducive to substantive or procedural bargaining. Only the typography industry and a few skilled trades developed collective contracts. Labor relations in other industries resembled either German large industry, with centralized unions trying in vain to enforce bargaining, or France, where direct action was advocated. Labor relations tended to be a mixture of these two models, as was the nature of unionism, rather than conforming to a single model. In this way, three different models of labor relations emerged throughout Europe, closely related to the models of union development and reinforcing the main features of unionism. The nature of employers' organizations, which were determined by the existent unionism models, was less decisive. Still, it was also a force in shaping the different models of labor relations.

At the close of the century (a highly contentious period) the differences between the continental models became overshadowed by similar conflicts in mining. Some of the conflicts surpassed all previous labor conflicts in the countries involved. Relevant issues were the repression of the truck system and forced company housing, the reduction of the workday to eight hours, the recognition of newly created unions, and wage fluctuations due to the gliding scale. The latter implied a link between wages and coal prices. It originated in Britain, reflecting the British dislike for fixing wage tariffs independent of economic conditions. On the continent, the gliding scale could take the form of a compromise between union demands for fixed wages and employers' wishes for a free hand. However, it was usually imposed by the employers, and on occasions a decision to lower wages was not even known to the workers until payday. Mine accidents and the dismissal of militant workers were a frequent last cause of strikes, most of which started spontaneously.

In 1886 such a strike spread through Wallony and almost became a regional uprising, despite socialist appeals to resume work. The army, committed to end the strike, killed a number of demonstrators. The Ruhr area was confronted with a similar situation in 1889, but the action there continued until the emperor himself received a miners' delegation and called upon the employers to compromise. The Saint-Etienne region of France was the scene of a major strike in 1890, in which the socialist party leader, Jean Jaurès, was able to mediate. In the same year, Basque miners went on strike when four socialist militants were fired. There was another wave of miners' strikes around the turn of the century in the Czech mines and in Saint-Etienne. The miners' federation in France was eventually able to prevent an extension of the strike. The potential embarrassment of the socialist minister Millerand produced a motive to prevent a nationwide strike movement. The union's reformist stand and its hold on the miners allowed the (rather exceptional) rise of collective bargaining in French mining. In 1905 efforts failed to coordinate actions in Britain, France, and Belgium against the export of coal to Germany, where a major mine strike was taking place. The

German strike and the increased export of Belgian coal even encouraged the Belgian miners to initiate a major strike themselves, in which higher wages were the main goal.

Especially in France and southern Europe, and occasionally where the German model of labor relations applied, miners' strikes and other local actions were the beginning of local or regional uprisings. They were common during the depressed economic conditions of the 1880s and early 1890s. The commitment of troops to restore order contributed to the transition from strike to uprising. Some of the major miners' strikes, particularly in Belgium and France, belonged to that category. Italy witnessed a series of uprisings in 1894 and 1898, probably brought on by rising prices. The most dramatic events in 1898 were the *Fatti di Maggio*, the May events in Milan. Police violence at a demonstration was the motive for a local general strike and heavy fighting between police forces and strikers, resulting in over a hundred casualties. In Spain, local general strikes were endemic in the first years of the twentieth century. They started in one trade or industrial branch and were spread by anarchist groups, representing a form of political rather than industrial action.

POLITICAL ACTION

The beginning of the century can be characterized as the high tide of the nationwide general strike. In countries with a German model of unionism and labor relations, Marxist organizations were by now better able to control such action. Main issues in these countries were universal and singular voting rights, which had an even higher priority for Marxists than the eight-hour workday. The general strikes (*Massenstreiks*) for suffrage rights or for other aims strained party-union relations because they interfered with collective bargaining.

Anarchists attached more value to the general strike. The French syndicalists regarded it as the culmination of union action, bypassing parliamentary politics. Revolutionary Marxists shared that view. Anarchist organizations were hardly able, however, to organize nationwide strike movements. As a consequence, any French general strike was doomed to failure. Chances of success were better, and the probability of any general strike at all greater, where German-model organizational talent was combined with French-model pressure for action.

Indeed, general strikes were most pronounced in Belgium. The Belgian socialists organized three such strikes for universal and equal suffrage: in 1893, 1902, and 1913. The first two were called only reluctantly and hastily after Wallonian miners, traditionally under the influence of French anarchism, had already tried to expand local strikes. Both actions (in 1893 and 1902) resulted in rioting and bloodshed during fights with police forces. Nevertheless, the 1893 action was one of the few examples in the nineteenth century of a nationwide strike with at least some effort to coordinate and control activities. The second strike lasted ten days and involved almost half of the industrial work force.

Two other general strikes, in Holland (1903) and in Italy (1904), also combined reluctant German model organizations with anarchist French-type pressure for action. The Railway Strikes in Holland started with the refusal of railway workers to break a strike in the port of Amsterdam. This led the government to propose legal measures against strikes in public services. Reacting to this move, anarchists called a general strike. Marxists opposed it, but their disciplined organizations became the backbone of the action, and they were later condemned by anarchists as strikebreakers when they discontinued their participation. The discord resulted in the foundation of the Dutch Marxist union federation. The beginning of the Italian general strike was a spontaneous protest strike in Milan against the shooting of demonstrators in the rural south. The Socialist party, or more accurately its anarchist faction, turned the strike into a nationwide movement, lasting several days without fighting or rioting. For a short time this success managed to mitigate the quarrels between Italian Marxists and anarchists.

The only nationwide strike in a country characterized by German-type unionism and lacking any substantial anarchist pressure was a three-day Swedish strike in 1902. Like the Belgian strikes, it aimed at expanding suffrage rights, but in contrast to Belgium the Socialist party was able to control the action.

The general strike became an even more hotly debated topic among socialists after two other attempts, in Russia in 1905 and in France in 1906. In addition to their national significance, these strikes were extremely important in shaping union-party relations more definitely in other countries as well. The Russian strikes in 1905 were part of the 1905 revolution, which started with the shooting of peaceful demonstrators on "bloody Sunday." Strike committees in Petersburg organized a local "soviet of workers' deputies," led by Leon Trotsky. The soviet organized two general strikes to expand the revolution. Both started as local actions of divergent groups (railway workers and printers demanding tariffs). Liberal industrialists even supported the strikes by continuing to pay wages. After the second strike and the soviet proclamation of the eight-hour workday, the soviet members were arrested. In the Polish and Finnish parts of the empire, general strikes were more nationalist in nature.

Although France became the real locus of the general strike (*grève générale*), the CGT encountered many difficulties and much opposition in coordinating local actions and preventing internal discord. Indeed, the first general strike (in 1906) can hardly be considered a general strike at all. The cause of the strike was the CGT decision not to allow its member unions to organize May Day strikes. The confederation wanted to organize a nationwide movement itself, if only to bridge the distance between anarchists and Marxists. Some unions decided to start with actions in April, which allowed the police to arrest the CGT chairman (the shoe worker Victor Griffuelhes) and to send troops to Paris. In this insurrectionary atmosphere the May Day strike was a failure, but many industrial or local strikes continued.

The general strikes of the early twentieth century, including a number of local and regional strikes, influenced the German attitude toward political strikes and German party-union relations. The chairman of the *Generalkommission*, the metal worker Carl Legien, had never been very enthusiastic about such actions. In his view, shared by most German socialists, decades of organizational work would be endangered in case of a crushed general strike, a fate no general strike could ever escape. This German view also prevailed in the *Massenstreikdebatte* within the International. Under the influence of the defeats suffered up to that point, the 1904 congress declared the general strike to be a strategy of last resort only. The 1905 Russian revolution intensified international discussion about the issue but did not change the decision. The German unions wanted more. In their opinion, political mass strikes and May Day actions hampered them too much in their union activities. They demanded more autonomy from the party and veto power regarding political strikes. At the 1906 party congress in Mannheim, they could enforce those rights. Intimate links were maintained, but the party and the union federation became more equal partners, as was the case in Scandinavia. In Italy, party-union relations were settled in a similar manner. Thus, the general strike led the German-model organizations to distinguish more clearly between political action, pursued by the party, and industrial action, coordinated by the union federation. The two might be combined, but only if both sides agreed.

The French union movement also codified its attitude toward the general strike and the Socialist party. As early as 1892 a French workers' congress had adopted the idea of a general strike as the only means to overthrow capitalism. That this view prevailed so early was due in part to the powerful speeches by the lawyer Aristide Briand, who as a minister was later to crush a French attempt at a general strike in 1909. Neither Millerand's ministerialism, nor the fusion of the socialist parties under the International's pressure in 1905 induced the syndicalists to change their opinion in favor of parliamentary activities. The failure of the 1906 general strike only added to the grievances. Later in that year, the CGT, at its congress in Amiens, adopted the Charter of Amiens. It confirmed the confederation's total abstinence from parliamentary politics and reaffirmed the importance of the general strike, considered to be nonpolitical, as the ultimate and most important revolutionary weapon. The charter banned parliamentary politics from CGT meetings, though this did not prevent local contacts between the party and unions or party activities by CGT officials.

The resolutions drawn up in Mannheim and Amiens left two patterns of party-union relations on the European continent: intimate informal or formal bonds in German-model unionism and complete separation in the French model. As an odd coincidence, the British unions also changed their attitude toward political activities in 1906, a change that bore little relation to the debate about the general strike on the continent. Two incidents made the TUC decide in favor of establishing a political party of its own. First was the Taff-Vale case, in which a railway company was awarded damages from a union because of a strike. In 1906, during the course of the campaign to have the relevant law changed, the unions established the Labour party. Second was the Osborne case, in which a union member successfully proceeded against the political levy of the unions

for the new party. This led the unions to start a new campaign for changes in
the law. This campaign firmly established the Labour Party and put an end to
liberal-labor cooperation. Thus, after they had organized only reluctantly in the
political domain, the British unions became the only ones in Europe to establish
and dominate their own party. The party was socialist in outlook, but far less
committed than the socialists in the rest of Europe.

By then, the three models of unionism had not only given rise to three different
models of labor relations, but also to three divergent patterns of political activities
and union-party relations. The German and British models had incorporated into
them a clear distinction between political activity directed at the government and
industrial action aimed at influencing employers. The relation between the two
forms of action differed. In the British model, the party was an instrument to
be used by the unions. It served to guarantee government nonintervention in
labor relations, clearing the way for union activities without any legal restrictions
or regulations. In the German model, the unions and the party each had their
own arenas. The party was to gain a majority and assume state power through
the lengthy process of parliamentary activities. In the meantime it would enforce
legislation (for example, relating to the eight-hour workday). The unions would
wrest concessions from employers through industrial action. The state was not
involved directly in the latter arena, which allowed it to act as an intermediary.

The French model operated differently. The *Charte d'Amiens* rejected political
campaigning and substituted the general strike. Refraining from involvement in
parliamentary politics (related to the distance from the Socialist party), the CGT
became a direct party in politics, using both industrial and political action. Strikes
were not merely a weapon in the industrial struggle, but also, even predominantly,
a political weapon. Parliament was bypassed, and the result was to be an immediate usurpation of power. In the meantime, strikes were to be used as a tool
for fighting and wresting concessions from the government, representing a substitute for parliamentary pressure by the party. Because of its role as a target in
any action, the state was too much involved to act as an intermediary. This
partisanship of the French state in labor relations contrasted with the trend toward
neutrality in the German model and nonintervention in the British model. In the
French model any state action was envisioned as either a hostile act or a victory
wrought by the labor movement pending the final blow.

LABOR LEGISLATION

The definition or codification of political activities, not coincidentally, took
place in a period of increasing labor legislation. Though social legislation, apart
from the eight-hour workday, was not a primary concern of socialists, the latter
were affected by it and were also engaged in pressure or protest. The wave of
labor legislation in this period was very wide in scope and characterized the true
beginning of state social policy. It was preceded by two concentrations of more
limited scope in the nineteenth century, partly overlapping in time. First was

the protection of children and women during the 1860s and 1870s and second was Otto von Bismarck's introduction of social security in Germany during the 1880s.

The first wave of labor legislation, involving the protection of children and women, consisted of a ban on child labor (with age limits ranging from nine to twelve), a prohibition of underground mine work for older children and women, and reductions in the number of hours they worked. Legislation was instituted in the liberal period of the 1860s, but it was continued by conservatives and Catholics, who rose to power during the crisis. To the liberals it was a precondition for freedom in adult life, while conservatives and Catholics stressed the value of family life. Indeed, middle-class and upper-class concerns were the force behind this kind of labor protection. The labor movement was still too small and dispersed to exercise pressure, and it was hardly interested in this reduction of household income. Moreover, legislation was no help to craft workers like printers, who were determined to exclude women from their trade.

Protection of women evolved into an issue of conflict between socialists and feminists. The latter, including middle-class activists in particular, opposed any legal protection of women because it was a deviation from the principle of equality and would only lead to a further deterioration in the position of women. It would reduce female opportunities to obtain economic independence and reinforce the social isolation of women by condemning them to be housewives. Feminist priorities were full equality in the eyes of the law, equal pay for equal work, and admission of women to trades traditionally reserved for men. Women in the socialist movement adhered to the principle of equality, but argued that middle-class feminists made no allowance for the existing double burden of many working-class women. Legal protection and a division of labor between men outside the home and women at home would reduce that burden and improve the living standards of the working class as a whole. In practice, the socialist support for protection dominated their more fundamental adherence to the principle of equality. The Catholic labor movement was less ambiguous in its support for the role of women as housewives.

In some countries, the first wave also included the legal prohibition of abuses like the truck system and the *livret*. Generally, however, governments subscribed to the sacred principle of not interfering in the labor conditions of adult male workers.

This principle was cast aside in the second major labor legislation: Bismarckian social security. This time socialism played a prominent role, not so much by exercising pressure, but by its mere existence. The system was introduced a few years after the *Sozialistengesetz* and represented another device in the battle against socialism. Illness was covered first, in 1883, followed by work accidents, invalidism, and old age. In accordance with its function, the system was confined to industrial workers. All conditions were financed by workers' and employers' contributions, except for work accidents. That risk was considered inherent to economic enterprise, so that coverage was to be financed solely by employers—

a complete transfer of responsibility because it had been a workers' risk until that time. The system of contributions was basically a concession to employers, who opposed a tax-based system because it provided the state with too much power. The socialists shared this objection, but they stuck to their opposition. Moreover, they had other priorities, like union legalization. Bismarck's social programs were influenced by existing municipal provisions, the social welfare scheme of miners, and by pleas from outside the labor movement for more state concern with social conditions. In the early 1870s a small movement of *Kathedersozialisten* (Chair-socialists) arose, lecturing about the *Arbeiterfrage* and pressing for more state activity. In this respect it was comparable to Great Britain's Fabian Society, although the latter had less academic interest and style, and was more akin to the labor movement and socialism. A few Catholic aristocrats shared their social concern. A major effect of the Bismarckian social programs was that they made industrial workers a distinctive category and facilitated the socialist claim to speak on behalf of the class as a whole. It also contributed to the rise of separate clerical workers' organizations, eager to demonstrate that they were a distinct category from manual workers.

Although the German example was followed only by Austria and Denmark, it influenced the third wave in the first decade of the new century. Several countries sent representatives to report on the Bismarckian system. Another influential factor was the concentration of strikes and uprisings at the end of the 1880s, which resulted in official investigations of working and living conditions. At the same time, left-wing (or social) liberals drew attention to recent social legislation or social practice in some of the Australian states and New Zealand. By doing so, they made social legislation an accepted topic of parliamentary discussion. Liberalism was in decline, however, due to the rise of socialism and internal discord regarding social and other affairs. This provided another group with a crucial position in social legislation: progressive intellectuals within the Catholic and conservative parties. Catholics organized special meetings or even entire Social Weeks devoted to the social question. The socialist pressure for change and its surveys of living and working conditions lent force to the arguments.

The distance in political priorities and style between Catholics and conservatives, on the one hand, and socialists, on the other hand, was still great. This made it difficult for the socialists to influence legislation without outside support. Moreover, socialists were interested mainly in legislation concerning working hours and labor contracts. Nevertheless, the German model was characterized by pressure from the socialist parties and with respect to specific measures also by unions for particular regulations and for amendments in Parliament. The French syndicalists were less interested in piecemeal reform, but they had no choice but to address the state when attempting to persuade unwilling employers. Occasionally, they joined a political campaign, but it was more common for them to mobilize protest against legislative proposals. British unions were not very interested, and even tended to reject social legislation, since it might weaken their position. In short, socialist activities with respect to social legislation differed according to the existing models of labor relations and political action. Pressure prevailed in the German model, protest in the French, and an attitude of "wait and see" in the British one. These patterns were not uniform, however. Some bills provoked fierce protests in countries characterized by the German model, while in France there was pressure for specific measures (for example, regarding working hours). Social legislation was less developed in eastern Europe. It remained an expression of the benevolence and paternalistic concern of feudal and absolutist rulers or it was due to a (short-lived) liberal rise to power, for instance in some Balkan countries. Socialists played only a minor role.

Labor legislation during this period represented part of a wider range of social legislation, covering living conditions more generally. Urbanization had caused housing problems that were solved by the rise of slums and by jerry building. Housing standards subsequently became another state concern, following the educational reforms during the 1860s and 1870s. Laws regulating labor conditions became the core of this concentration of social legislation, however.

The most important laws at the turn of the century were those relating to work accidents. They were the first piece of social legislation covering male workers in several countries. A main issue was whether employers should be obliged to insure this risk and whether the insurance company should be a state agency. Employers feared too much state involvement and in some cases even created new organizations to fight social legislation. The labor movement was content with state control of the insurance funds, though it preferred a more active role for the friendly societies or related union agencies.

Legislation regarding work accidents was followed by laws relating to sickness insurance, old age pensions, and unemployment insurance. Initially, social insurance remained a voluntary affair, but soon new laws included the obligations to insure one or more risks as in Great Britain in 1908 and 1911. The trickiest issue and least subject to legislation was unemployment insurance. Unemployment was considered to be less the result of circumstances beyond one's control than illness. The distinction between unemployment and being on strike was also less clear than the other risks. Sometimes countries with a tradition of municipal social assistance subsidized union assistance. Two examples were the Danish system, where the state subsidized social insurance contributions, and the Ghent system of 1898, where the benefits paid were subsidized. Other Belgian, French, and Dutch towns imitated the Ghent system, but unions preferred the uniformity of the Danish system. France lagged behind: Social security was a controversial issue, not only within the CGT, but also for those within the large middle class, who often had limited personal savings.

Social legislation in the early twentieth century also covered the individual labor contract. Removal of specific abuses had already taken place during the liberal 1860s and after industrial action. This time the regulation of the labor contract was more detailed. The truck system and payment in public houses were forbidden. The employers' right to fine workers was limited by instituting a procedure to this end and by limiting the part of one's wages that could be withheld. Fines were to be used for sickness or other insurance funds. A minimum term of notice, to be observed by the employer, was set at one or two weeks. A maximum term of notice was set for workers. It was often dependent on the number of years the worker had been employed. Legal obligations applied not only to the contents of labor contracts, but also to their publicity. Henceforth, the employer was obliged to hand a copy to the worker, instead of simply allowing the worker just a few minutes to sign the contract. In some cases regulation of the term of notice did not answer the question of whether a strike was to be regarded as a breach of contract. If so, workers terminated their contract by going on strike. Intense socialist pressure contributed to the creation of a legal distinction between a strike and a breach of contract. Socialist resistance to strike legislation was even stronger, except where it was part of laws pertaining to collective bargaining. A bill calling for a referendum when strikes took place was withdrawn in France under the pressure of the CGT, which objected to this parliamentarism within the factory. The act constituted a serious challenge to the *action directe* tradition.

Working time was hardly ever subject to regulation. After the short-lived French restrictions of 1848, Switzerland became the first country to impose a more lasting limit of eleven hours in 1877. The eight-hour workday practiced, or even made mandatory, in Australia and New Zealand was more important as a model. Still, Switzerland remained an exception. Regulation remained confined to specific categories of workers (for example, miners) in the rest of Europe. In some countries local government was involved more actively in setting a maximum limit on the number of working hours in a day and a minimum limit on wage tariffs. Local governments would occasionally require contractors to observe mandatory labor conditions for their workers. Socialists serving on city councils encouraged this kind of local control of labor conditions, which applied mainly to the construction industry.

Shop assistants also came to enjoy some protection, more because females predominated in this kind of work than because of union action. Some countries passed a shops closing act in order to regulate the number of hours that shopkeepers and their assistants could work.

Collective bargaining and conflict mediation were the last subjects addressed by social legislation. The spread of collective contracts increasingly created the need for their legal status. Some countries provided this status under civil law. It applied to the members of the unions and employers' associations that were involved in bargaining. Other devices used to reduce conflicts were arbitration and conciliation councils of paritary composition, that is, with equal employer and union representation. Again, Australia (with its wage boards) served as a model, as did the collective agreements in typography, which already provided for conciliation institutions and procedures. Pioneering work in conflict settlement took place in Denmark, which adopted rules after a major labor dispute, in a pattern resembling the 1899 September Agreement. This time the dispute took place in typography. In line with the development of collective bargaining, a distinction was made between conflicts of interest (concerning conditions of new labor contracts) and legal disputes (regarding the interpretation or the alleged violation of a contract still in force). Legislation passed in 1910 sanctioned this distinction officially and accordingly introduced different institutions and procedures to settle conflicts. The distinction was applied in other countries characterized by German-model labor relations as well, although legal consequences associated with this distinction remained confined to Scandinavia.

Pioneering work in institutions at the nation level occurred in France. A consultative body was set up in 1891, first as a state institution, later as a tripartite body. But the slow pace of social legislation and CGT objections weakened its role. In line with its tradition of law codification, France also became the first nation to create a separate Ministry of Labor and to codify social legislation into one *Code du Travail et de la Prévoyance sociale* in 1910.

Indeed, social legislation had undergone quite an evolution. In several countries the first step had been taken in the 1860s. Legislation had removed barriers to formal equality, like the *livret* or the difference in treatment of master and servant. The legalization of unionism was a second phase, allowing workers, as the weaker party, to defend their interests collectively. The third step was the state's recognition that it had a more direct responsibility to enforce factual (rather than legal) equality and to protect the weaker party by regulating the contents of labor contracts. State concern for more factual equality was also apparent in the change from state repression of worker protest to state efforts to conciliate in employer-union contacts. Labor disputes, and not the working class itself, became a matter of state concern. However, the transition was slow and far from universal. Furthermore, it would be put to the test in the years immediately preceding the First World War.

THE UPSURGE OF SYNDICALISM

After the spread of labor relations patterned after the German model throughout large parts of Europe and the setback of syndicalism, there was a last rise in syndicalism beginning in 1908. It consisted of a politicization of unionism and major union action directed at national governments. The French and British model, the latter influenced by the former, were the most prominent scene of syndicalist action. Syndicalism had already been part of French-model labor relations, but it became more intense both in France and in Spain. It was also on the rise in Great Britain and Ireland, where strong national organizations that might have deterred its growth were absent. Within British-model labor relations syndicalism even gave rise to a new ideology of guild socialism, a combination of ideas from syndicalism and Marxism. In guild socialism, syndicalist worker, or more accurately, union control of industry was to be embedded in the framework of a coordinating state. The idea gained support particularly among miners, but its appeal did not reach beyond the British Isles, and even here it failed to attract a large following. Labor relations of the German type were also affected by the rise of syndicalism, but without lasting effects. The existing organizations were less willing to challenge national governments and did their utmost to keep their members under control. Only in Norway was a more revolutionary union wing, under Marten Tranmael, able to rise to importance within the union movement.

Four developments contributed to the growing popularity of syndicalism. First, though economic expansion continued, conditions and prices were unstable. Rising prices even caused a temporary drop in real wages. Of course, this did not add to the popularity of collective bargaining. Second, experience showed that socialist pressure could enforce legislation or changes in bills. Unions rather than the party had rallied support or opposition on specific topics of social legislation, such as working hours in mining. This implied that the separation between industrial and political action was not complete, while in France it was totally absent. Third, imperalist expansion caused growing international tension. The danger of war and pacifism dominated the meetings of the Second International. More directly, the expectation of a war undermined organizational discipline and restraint and favored immediate solutions by means of direct action. It also made governments eager to compromise in large strikes, especially by miners, that might affect national power. Despite the fact that the government was not involved directly, miners were well aware that it would be eventually. Indeed, governments responded quickly to the larger strikes by issuing mediation proposals.

Even more important was the fourth development, the rise of unionism among workers in public utilities like municipal transport and more particularly, in railway transport. What applied to miners applied even more to railway workers, because the railways were under state control (if not in state hands), making any strike a political action. Most parliamentary states did not oppose public sector unionism, though France prohibited the affiliation of public sector unions with the CGT for a long time. Governments were not willing to bargain with public sector unions, however, since that would imply a transfer of state power. This problem was solved more easily for municipal workers because many town councils were at least willing to hear the unions' viewpoint before making decisions about labor conditions.

Railways and, at the local scale, tramways, not only facilitated a rapid extension of any strike, but also allowed transport workers to disrupt a large part of national economic activity. Indeed, railway workers had been at the heart of the general strikes that took place in Holland (1903) and Russia (1905). It made them aware that "their mighty arm in a strife might stop the wheels of social life." In turn, governments tried to impose regulations with respect to strikes in the public sector and related branches, such as postal services, gasworks, and electricity. Nevertheless, the great railway strikes probably were the most conspicuous feature of these years. These strikes were romanticized and celebrated as a lasting symbol of labor's fighting power from their very beginning.

The railway strikes around 1910 were either part of, or attempts at, general strikes. French actions influenced such strikes outside France. The French railway strike of 1909, the largest attempt at a general strike thus far, was crushed by minister Briand, who had argued vociferously in favor of the general strike at an earlier time. He arrested the strike committee, placed the *cheminots* under martial law, and fired 3,000 strikers. This made the CGT, under its new leader, the matchmaker Leon Jouhaux, more cautious in its activities. French syndicalism crossed the English Channel and especially influenced transport workers. London dock workers lost a large action for a closed shop, while railway workers won a strike in 1911 because the government gave in after only two days. Railwaymen, dock workers, and miners even formed a Triple Alliance of mutual support to be used in the case of a major dispute. Like international state alliances, however, it was short-lived. Spain was a late participant in nationwide general strikes. But the foundation alongside the Marxist federation of an anarcho-syndicalist union federation in 1911, concentrated in Catalonia, added to their popularity. Both organizations already called a general railway strike in the same year. The minister of transport tried to initially follow Briand's example, but he was less familiar with the subject and finally gave in. France was thus the only country left without union success in a railway or a general strike. The failure contributed to the force of the ideal.

The issues at stake in the major railway and miners' strikes were the same as in less syndicalist labor disputes. Working hours, union recognition, and pacifism were main issues in addition to wages. Voting rights remained in the background, though the Belgian general strike in 1913 was by far the largest single action in this period. Craft workers' autonomy was no longer a matter of dispute. Craft workers had lost their struggle, and new technology was introduced at a pace determined by employers rather than the unions. Only in Britain were shop stewards able to influence such decisions.

Working hours were a source of conflict especially in craft industries. Some unions were able to enforce a gradual introduction of the eight hours. The English Saturday represented a new issue in such industries: a free Saturday afternoon after a working week of forty-four hours. This was something that was already practiced in some British trades. The argument used was more time off to compensate an increasing work load. The second argument, work allocation, hardly played a role. Working time was a major issue in mining, too. There were major strikes in Germany and actions for a nine-hour shift in the Basque region. The 1912 German miners' strike for the eight-hour workday was the first such action that was well organized in advance. Despite 2 million marks of strike pay it did not produce any positive results. British miners even went on strike to protest legislation regarding the eight-hour day, in spite of union pressure for the law. Wages were the central issue in the British miners' strikes of 1910 (lasting six months) and 1912.

Union recognition was at stake mainly in industries employing large numbers of less skilled workers, like the textile industry, and public utilities (for example, transport). A general workers' union that was attempting to organize dock workers and others in Dublin had to face a major lockout in the winter of 1913–1914. The employers' reaction was all the more fierce because of the union's syndicalism. In France, postal service workers' permission to affiliate with the CGT was at the heart of two strikes in 1909.

More than the other issues, opposition to war was a real syndicalist theme and the cause of major strikes. The French were the most active anti-militarists. Syndicalism and its complete rejection of the capitalist state facilitated this attitude. French Marxists, too, advocated pacifism. While the British were less interested, German socialists faced a predicament. They foresaw the nightmare of another period of illegality if they supported pacifism and so refrained from pacifist declarations, and the International followed their example. Pacifism was the most frequent strike issue in Spain and Italy. In 1909 actions against Spanish warfare in Morocco, intermingled with other issues, resulted in the *Semana Tragica* (Tragic Week) in Barcelona. Clashes between police forces and workers involved in a local uprising killed eighty people. A similar *Settimana Rossa* (Red Week) in Milan and other Italian towns in 1914 ended less violently. By 1911 Italy had already witnessed a successful general strike against warfare in Libya. These actions, however, represented mere incidents on a continent preparing for war.

5

The First World War and Its Aftermath

Three years of increasing state regulation of labor relations were followed by three years of strikes and revolutionary ferment. Outside Russia, capitalism survived both, though not without concessions.

THE FIRST WORLD WAR

The First World War put a sudden end to a period of intense socialist anti-war activities, including demonstrations, strikes, and appeals by the International. Socialists now supported their national cause, except in Russia, where they remained suppressed, and in Italy. The transition was easiest for the German *Generalkommission*, which was convinced that an attempt to block war efforts would be ineffective anyway and that support for the war would encourage bourgeois and middle-class acceptance of socialism and of the laboring class in general. It pressed the party to discontinue civil strife, too. Indeed, during the war a *Burgfrieden* (civil truce) was in force, soon followed by similar arrangements in other countries.

Workers were suddenly plagued by two problems: a rapid increase in prices and growth of unemployment. In their efforts to compensate for rising prices, unions were bound by their pledge not to strike and sometimes by collective agreements as well. Like the unions, employers preferred to uphold the contracts. They offered a cost-of-living allowance as a temporary solution, a sign of national responsibility in accordance with the unions' restraint. New price increases soon surpassed this compensation, however.

The second problem, unemployment, forced the unions to use up most of their strike funds in the form of unemployment benefits. When they ran out of money, they requested state subsidies. Several countries agreed to measures that eased the depletion of the unions' unemployment funds, either directly or indirectly by subsidizing municipal unemployment insurance schemes (for example, the Ghent system). Another route to coping with unemployment was the establishment or the activation of paritary labor exchange offices under state supervision. Like wartime socialist participation in government and the unions' cooperative behavior, state support of the unions' unemployment funds and the labor exchanges contributed to the political integration of the unions. They almost became part of government administration in the area of unemployment insurance.

During the course of the war, the problem of unemployment was solved in a more definite manner. The weapons industry and the replacement of soldiers lost on the battlefield generated so much new employment that many skilled jobs had to be relegated to unskilled workers. The British craft unions were the most sensitive in this respect. Their major wartime focus was to combat this dilution process and to guarantee the unskilled a skilled wage in order to prevent general wage reductions. Women were the main diluters. Union requests for equal pay, however, were motivated more by the desire to protect their male membership than to do justice to women. Dilution was less of a threat to the unions on the continent. All unions in the belligerent countries also had to face another problem: the military mobilization of skilled workers (who constituted the backbone of the movement). The *Generalkommission* was the major loser; membership fell from 2.5 to 1 million. Union membership continued to grow in the neutral countries, partly because of unemployment benefits.

In 1916 and 1917 the belligerent nations substituted provisional measures with direct or indirect state supervision of strategic industries. To some of the socialists actively involved in this regulation (like Albert Thomas, who had become the French defense minister), partial state control of the economy represented training for full-fledged socialist state planning. Once socialists could establish a parliamentary majority after the war, or usurp state power otherwise, the same structures could be maintained and used to start socialist planning. Indeed, handling the state was especially attractive to French socialists, in view of fierce employer resistance toward any union initiative. Revolutionary opponents spoke of state capitalism instead, brought to bear by so-called socialists. In the view of these revolutionaries, the Socialist leaders and organizations were engaged in officially sanctioning worse forms of worker exploitation than had existed before the war. The impression that a system of state capitalism had come to existence was reinforced by the increasing power of employers' representatives. To some extent, the war economy was based on oligopolistic arrangements, legalized and transformed into elements of state regulation. Powerful circles of large industrialists, like the French *Comité des forges*, prepared and implemented economic policy. One of the effects of this regulation, and of the war effort itself, was the concentration of production in very large enterprises.

Within such enterprises, the employers' power was reinforced. The belligerent countries on the continent introduced some diluted form of military discipline for workers particularly in strategic or state-protected industries. Of course, employers were quite willing to impose stricter discipline. Measures ranged from worker mobilization for specific tasks or industries to full labor militarization characterized by a system of total military discipline.

The transition to a war economy was especially profound on the continent, and in particular in Germany. In Austria, it included a form of military control similar to that in Russia, which put an end to independent union activities. The unions in the other belligerent countries were involved in some decisions. German unions cooperated in preparing and implementing a bill on auxiliary war service, which the socialists viewed as a further step toward state socialism. The war ministry, content with the unions' cooperation, even defended the unions against prominent employers in heavy industry, who were eager to impose even more discipline on the labor force. In France, the unions' main activity was to prevent strikes and to participate in paritary committees, which supervised regional labor exchanges. The British unions were more recalcitrant in their opposition to anything that might stimulate dilution and wage reductions. However, in 1915 they reached the Treasury Agreement with the government, which provided for compulsory arbitration and a relaxation of trade practices.

The hands of the unions were tied, while labor conditions deteriorated rapidly. Wages decreased disproportionately to prices. The workday, reduced to nine or nine and a half hours immediately prior to the war, again surpassed ten hours. Safety regulations were observed less strictly, and the number of work accidents rose steeply. The unions attempted to stop this process and the return to full employer authority within the enterprise in two ways. First, they advocated national minimum standards, like a statutory minimum wage, or at least sectoral standards. National collective agreements and arbitration devices were to enforce such regulations. Though minimum standards failed to materialize, there was a slight increase in collective bargaining both in Germany and in France. A second way in which an attempt was made to salvage some union influence on labor conditions was the recognition and formalization of union representation within the enterprise. Enterprise and shop-floor representatives were introduced, or given formal status. *Vertrauensmänner* (men of confidence) in Germany and *délégués d'atelier* (shop delegates) in France were examples. There was not much tradition in this area, however, and employers distrusted them. Their tasks did not go beyond acting as individuals to whom one could complain. In contrast, British shop stewards had already interfered in managerial decisionmaking before the war. They revived and extended their activities rather spontaneously. Accordingly, British workers had more maneuvering room, and they made full use of the opportunity. While unions on the continent were asking for arbitration in order to keep employers in check, the government in Britain was attempting to impose arbitration with the aim of keeping the unions in check. British miners were less compliant. A major miners' strike was called in South Wales in 1915, immediately after all miners' strikes in South Wales had been declared illegal. Nevertheless, the prime minister made some concessions.

In the neutral countries socialist gladly hailed neutrality, and the unions were also rather cooperative in their stance. In exchange for formal promises, informal agreements or just the ruling parties' hope that the unions would refrain from strikes, they were treated with much respect. Union unemployment funds were subsidized, paritary labor exchanges set up, arbitration devices and modest forms of shop representation introduced. Regulation was less strict than in the nations at war, and unions gave up strike activity only hesitantly. In some countries strike movements against governmental emergency measures arose, condemning the widening gap between prices and wages and the uneven distribution of food supply. Norwegian unions even called a general strike in 1916 to oppose the Compulsory Arbitration Act. However, the more common practice was to refrain from striking but to call for demonstrations against increasing prices and for a better food supply.

Only small but zealous minorities of revolutionary or pacifist socialists in the belligerent countries rejected participation in the war and the unions' war support. This was an imperialist war, in their opinion, fought by national industry and the finance world to expand their foreign influence. The main victim was perceived to be the working class, which was wrongly deserted by the unions. It was argued that the unions were using their strike funds to curb the protests of the unemployed, while assisting the government in its effort to send workers to fight other workers. The rapidly growing gap between this anti-war group and the majority collaborating in the war efforts was one of the causes leading to the wartime or postwar split in the socialist movement. The anti-war socialists met twice in the neutral country of Switzerland (in Zimmerwald in 1915 and in Kienthal in 1916). The most radical participants there were the Bolsheviks, represented by Vladimir Ilyich Lenin and Leon Trotsky.

1917

In 1917 the continued absence of peace, combined with deteriorating living conditions, caused a change from initial enthusiasm to widespread deception. The consequence was insurrectionary ferment in which political demands were forwarded. Skilled workers in the metal industry were the first to express their discontent. They constituted the core of the unions that had fought for a shorter workday but were no longer able to protect labor. Working hours increased, while wage differentials with the less skilled and work freedom were reduced. Metal workers took two actions: They activated their unions, and they also started alternative movements to force improvements. These groups became the core of a more general protest movement. Its following consisted of the new arrivals in industry: young men making rapid career advances from unskilled to semi-skilled or skilled work. Although they might have had some respect for the skilled, shared their aspirations, and had a position to lose, they lacked respect for the unions. British shop stewards organized in the form of local workers' committees and called for strikes against dilution. In Berlin skilled metal workers and foremen (*Obleute*) organized groups to activate the unions.

The transition from economic to political demands was easiest in Russia. Strikes and demonstrations in Petrograd resulted in a general local strike, issuing a call for bread and peace. Strike committees were set up, as they had been in 1905. They elected a "Petrograd soviet of workers' and soldiers' deputies," which took over part of the local administration and food supply. Increasing revolutionary turmoil and the inability of the imperial government to commit troops to itself led to the February Revolution. Control passed to the provisional government, but its authority was challenged by local soviets, which had their base in factory committees. Employers hastily gave in and recognized the factory committees as official workers' representatives. Craft workers established trade unions independent of these factory committees. The Bolsheviks had only a small following in the latter, but they dominated some of the factory committees, including the Petrograd soviet. This allowed them to claim "all power to the soviets."

Among workers in the rest of Europe, and particularly in the two remaining empires, the February Revolution also encouraged peace demands. In April a strike wave paralyzed a number of German towns. Demands included the abolition of the auxiliary war service and immediate suffrage reforms. National independence for various language groups was a central issue in Austria. The rest of Europe, too, became the scene of major strikes, hesitatingly backed by the unions. This union support put an end to the wartime civil truce.

In Russia protest culminated in the end of dual power, shared by the provisional government and the soviets. Trotsky, presiding over a session of the Petrograd soviet, proclaimed the revolution on October 25. One of the first acts of the new workers' state was to proclaim the eight-hour workday.

The October Revolution encouraged strike activity throughout Europe. Local *Räte*, or *Arbeiterräte*, resembling the soviets, appeared in major industrial towns of the German and Austrian empires. Although most actions were spontaneous, the unions increasingly tried to direct their course. Only the *Generalkommission* remained somewhat detached. Other unions loosened their ties with the national government and intensified contacts with their members, even taking an active part in the *Räte* in the Austrian Empire. General claims like bread and peace now were turned into more specific demands, such as general suffrage and an end to the war economy.

The main targets in the 1917 and early 1918 strike wave were the national governments. Fearing revolutionary upheaval, they responded by means of sweeping reforms. The call for bread was met by the introduction of rationing or, more commonly, by improvements in the functioning of the rationing system. The demand to put an end to the mobilization or militarization of labor hardly required any concessions, because governments no longer dared apply sanctions to workers bending the rules. The major issues were universal and equal voting rights. Wartime mobilization of labor and socialist support for the national cause had already given rise to government promises, but the strikes served to remove the last objections. In countries where no advances had been made, provisions were made for general suffrage (or at least male suffrage) in the first postwar elections. The main socialist goal was thus finally accomplished, though it had required a war and in some countries also a wave of strikes and the threat of revolution. Employers were less involved in the actions. They viewed governmental concessions with clear suspicion.

While employers desired a quick return to normal conditions, the unions failed to develop any elaborate plans for postwar labor relations. They were too preoccupied with organizing and controlling the strike movement. The only blueprints for the future were made in Great Britain (by the government and not the unions) and in Germany (where the unions dissociated themselves from the actions). In Britain the Whitley Committee proposed the creation of paritary councils in each industry and within the larger enterprises. The councils were not to engage in negotiations about wage rates but instead establish more general forms of cooperation. Such Whitley councils were set up in several industries. The opinion prevailed, however, that they limited the unions' freedom too much, and they were soon discontinued. The enterprise councils never came into existence, due to employer resistance. The proposals materialized only in the public sector, which lacked collective bargaining devices.

The *Generalkommission* was still rather fanatically searching for employer recognition, in order to regulate the postwar economy without state intervention. In 1917 it contacted employers about the possibility of a kind of paritary council that would supervise the economy and continue union-employer cooperation, at least during the process of demobilization. The employers in large industry opposed this prolongation of outside interference in the economy, whether by the state or by the unions. Yet, the prospect of a socialist majority or even a revolution at the end of 1918 made the *Generalkommission* the lesser of two evils, especially because it did not press for the nationalization of industry. In November the industrialist Hugo Stinnes and Carl Legien, chairman of the *Generalkommission*, as well as some other industrialists and Catholic and liberal union leaders, signed the Stinnes-Legien Agreement. It contained provisions for demobilization, recognition of the unions as legitimate labor representatives, and a ban on employers' support for yellow unions. The workday was to be limited to eight hours. The agreement also laid down the creation of workers' committees in large firms. They would function to monitor the upholding of collective agreements and other regulations. Though no more than a tactical move for the industrialists, the agreement was even extended to a complete *Zentralarbeitsgemeinschaft*, or ZAG (central labor community). The agreement also called national and industrial paritary councils into existence, intended to supervise demobilization and tackle economic and social problems. This constituted an extension, on a wide scale, of the prewar efforts exerted by the German unions to enforce collective bargaining.

THE AFTERMATH

After the February and October revolutions in Russia, the wave of strikes received a third and even more powerful stimulant toward the end of 1918, when uprisings and mutinies put an end to both the German Empire and to the war. The new German republic and some of the new nations created from the dissolving Austrian Empire became the scene of widespread revolutionary ferment. These developments frightened the bourgeoisie and middle class in the rest of Europe more than the Russian events. Their fear was justified: No country remained unaffected by strikes and turmoil.

In Germany employers complied hastily with the ZAG but could not prevent the rise of *Betriebsräte* (factory committees) in the shadow of the local *Arbeiterräte*. The committees demanded nationalization or socialization of large enterprise, but only occasionally took over total factory control themselves. Local and regional *Rätepublike* were proclaimed in Bremen and Bavaria. In Berlin a revolutionary general strike and uprising failed, and two leaders of the revolutionary movement, Rosa Luxemburg and Karl Liebknecht, were killed by volunteer corps, who were committed to restoring order. After elections in December failed to provide a socialist majority in the government, revolutionary zeal decreased. In contrast to the situation in Russia, German revolutionaries faced a very determined government and union leadership (apart from the army), while they lacked a determined leadership themselves. Although there were some major strikes in 1919, they aimed at changes in labor conditions rather than political changes. An important demand was the implementation of the eight-hour workday, enacted right after the Stinnes-Legien Agreement had been signed. The continuation of the *Räte* was at stake, too, since they were not mentioned in the first draft of the new constitution.

The revolutionary movement lived on in some other areas of central and eastern Europe. Hungary became another revolutionary republic during the summer of 1919, reforming social and economic life along Soviet lines. But these and other attempts to establish such ''Red'' republics were crushed by ''White'' (rural) opposition or by outside forces. The adversaries were the same as in the Russian civil war, which broke out in 1919. Outside the former empires, strikes for changes in labor conditions (mostly the eight-hour workday and wage increases) alternated with strikes demanding workers' control or the nationalization of industry. Sometimes such political demands were added only during the course of action. Demobilization was a minor political issue, confined to France and Britain, partly intended to prevent further intervention in the Russian civil war.

More than during the war, established socialist organizations tried to aggregate demands and direct them toward specific points, turning strikes into actions that would incorporate socialist goals. The organizations were handicapped in this search for leadership by the still expanding gap between the more reformist leadership and radical activists. The latter, well represented among the new work force in the metal industry, challenged the unions and found a response among the workers returning from the front. In several countries, the gap, partially visible even before the war and extended during the war, became a true split. It gave rise to a competition in strike activities. Governments and employers contributed to the increasing number of strikes by rapidly giving in on a series of issues. Never before had the bourgeoisie and the middle class been so frightened by the expectation of an early socialist victory. Socialist disappointment was widespread when elections all around Europe failed to provide the socialists with the majority they had depended on. The electoral failure encouraged the more revolutionary groups, and sometimes the union leadership itself, to demand in strikes what they could not accomplish through parliamentary activity. Catholic unions during this time of upheaval either remained aloof or hesitantly followed the socialist example.

The most common demand, put forth or supported by all unions, was that of the eight-hour workday, a highly salient issue both in strikes and in pressure on various parliaments and governments. In several countries, the socialists made an attempt to enforce the eight hours in industrial branches by supporting strikes. They forged the strike movement into a large, combined action for legislation by these same methods. While the sectoral actions pushed the eight hours as an improvement in labor conditions, the socialist federations added the second argument, that of a better allocation of work, particularly in view of the ongoing process of demobilization. The eight-hour workday was at stake in a series of strikes that hit various industries in Belgium at the end of 1918. The outcome was the introduction of eight hours and a new system of bargaining. The Italian union federation took the initiative to contact the new employers' federation about the eight-hour day, a relatively early example of central-level bargaining (following the Scandinavian agreements around 1900 and the German ZAG). The employers' federation cooperated and recommended that its member organizations introduce the eight hours. The metal employers were the first to comply. French socialists devoted May Day 1919 to the eight hours, but socialist leaders were determined to prevent revolutionary turmoil in order to prevent any slowdown of economic recovery. This position was taken in spite of their disappointment that employers refused to introduce the eight hours as compensation for wartime union cooperation.

Wage demands were often secondary to more sweeping demands. Nevertheless, calls for wage increases were a frequent cause of strikes, and a frequent outcome as well, since employers tried to silence other demands by granting such increases. Wage cuts could also be at stake: A number of strikes were called to prevent or stop wage cuts resulting from demobilization and the termination of the war economy. A general railway strike in Britain, in which the government gave in, and a strike of French miners, combatted by the official mobilization of the workers involved, were examples. In some cases, unions tried to funnel wage demands into the demand for a minimum wage, either for specific industrial branches or for the nation as a whole. This demand had already been raised during the wartime food shortages. Again it did not meet a positive response. In actuality most unions confined themselves to demands for improvements in labor conditions, which, along with various specific political grievances, were the issues in a national Swiss strike that took place in November 1918. The action was well organized but discontinued after a few days

due to government pressure and because certain groups of workers had resumed work.

In most countries, sweeping demands like nationalization and workers' control were generally expressed by revolutionaries and more radical union members. Nationalization had been a traditional socialist aim, and it remained an
important topic in socialist discussion, but German-type unions expended few
resources on the issue. They preferred to develop their bargaining relationship
with employers. German unions had recently enforced the joint employer-
union supervision of the economy embodied in the ZAG and had refrained
from expressing further demands. Only small minorities in the countries characterized by German-model labor relations called for action, and they only occasionally could make nationalization a more general union demand. In France
and among British miners (the latter under the influence of syndicalist-inspired
guild socialism), nationalization obtained a wider appeal. The CGT demanded
the nationalization of transport, large credit institutions, and coal mines without calling for action, however. Some of its member unions were divided on
the question, in particular the railway union. In 1920, after a change in leadership, this railway union called for a general strike demanding the nationalization of the railways. The CGT gave in under pressure, but it was confronted
with fierce governmental reactions, including the arrest of strike leaders. The
strike, which lasted for a month, became a national trial of strength between
the government and the unions. The government won and dismissed 15,000
railway workers.

In the eyes of many socialists, nationalization was connected with the issue
of worker control, since the former would provide opportunities for the latter.
Worker control was also a demand in itself. It often implied a search for more
democratic supervision of managerial power rather than a total overthrow of the
system. In most countries demands were soon toned down to more modest ones,
like the right to have union representation within a company.

Union recognition and nationalization were the issues in a rather peculiar form
of labor strife in Italy: factory occupations. In 1919 *commissioni interne* were
set up in Turin metal industry factories to handle grievances. But revolutionary
engineering workers, led by Antonio Gramsci, demanded workers' supervisory
powers in factory committees without union tutelage. Workers perceived opportunities for change in 1920. The union feared a general lockout with respect
to issues like wages and overtime. Since it was hardly equipped after the many
other strikes that took place in 1919 and 1920, it ordered its members not to
leave the factories. The metalworkers occupied hundreds of factories and workshops in Milan, Turin, and other towns, and continued production under workers'
control for a month. The union federation took over and demanded increased
supervisory powers for workers. The resulting agreement between the federation,
government, and employers, however, contained only vague recommendations
about workers' control.

The French general strike and the Italian factory occupations represented the last outbursts of the European strike wave. The movement came to an end in the summer of 1920.

THE OUTCOME

The accomplishments of the revolutionary and insurrectionary times varied according to the extent of socialist power. The Soviets set the tone, immediately followed by the short-lived *Räterepublike*, or soviet republics, of central and eastern Europe. In Russia, most changes were incorporated into a labor code (*Kodeks o Trude*) that took effect in 1918. Socialists throughout the rest of Europe were unwilling or unable to wage a revolution, and elections proved deceptive. In spite of general (male) suffrage, they could not turn out a socialist majority. Nevertheless, the very threat of revolution made employers and governments agree to a number of important reforms. Numerous social laws were passed, not only on labor conditions, but also in the areas of housing and social security. Usually, the first law to be passed dealt with the length of the workday. The eight-hour workday was introduced first in new republics with socialists in the government, that is in the former Russian, Austrian, and German empires. Employers in other countries would occasionally raise objections, but the fear of even more strikes made them comply. Legislation had been passed throughout Europe by 1920. Like universal and equal (male) voting rights, this socialist demand had become a reality after thirty years of action, after a war and its revolutionary aftermath had given the final push. Minor changes in work time included the scattered introduction of an English Saturday and vacations. Whereas a few craft industries had allowed workers to take several days off before the war, this became a more general, though far from universal, phenomenon after the war. The Soviets even introduced four weeks of vacation but soon reduced this period to two weeks.

It was rare for any country, apart from the short-lived *Räterepublike* and the soviet republics, to follow the Soviet example of instituting a minimum wage. Nevertheless, wartime food shortages, rationing, and wage supplements had affected the relation between wages and labor output, and reinforced that between wages and basic needs. Subsequently some countries, like Austria and Belgium, experimented with a new type of gliding scale. It related wages to retail prices, instead of the prices of industrial produce, as was the case in the gliding scale formerly used in mining. Social legislation introduced a number of other changes in labor conditions. Indeed, within two years a large number of laws gave a new boost to social policy. Some of them had already been prepared earlier but had been postponed either before or during the war. In addition to large housing projects, labor legislation provided for the expansion of labor inspection, better restrictions on heavy and dangerous work, and some extension of social security. In particular, unemployment insurance had proved defective in the first years of the war and was improved. The 1918 Russian Labor Code even introduced the right to suitable work, as a corollary to the obligation to work.

By 1920 Russia was the only country where a revolutionary transformation of society was still underway. The country became the socialist, or more accurately Communist, laboratory of the world at this time. Initially, the Communists were unable to constrain the spread of autonomous worker control, and they officially sanctioned it, if only because it further undermined capitalism. The rising union movement was a junior partner in worker control and played a role alongside the factory committees. The railways were the exception, where the union dominated (in line with the best syndicalist principles). In 1918 a large part of private enterprise was nationalized to facilitate central control and planning. Consequently, the tasks of factory committees and unions were limited. The need to mobilize the country for the war effort during the civil war facilitated central control. Many decisions taken under this War Communism were in essence tactical measures, though hailed as strategic steps toward full communism. Gradually, worker control was curtailed and one-man management imposed. In Lenin's view unions (*profsoyuzy*) might still be concerned with labor conditions at first, but increasingly the workers' state would be able to guarantee workers' rights. Unions were to shift their attention to worker exhortation and labor discipline. They were to act as what would later be called transmission belts (*privodnye remny*) in the service of the Communist party, providing the party with a large and active following for its actions. This scenario was opposed from two sides. Trotsky wanted to extend and continue labor conscription, which was imposed upon miners, railway workers, and others under War Communism. All workers were to be mobilized as soldiers of labor, under military discipline. This would guarantee labor discipline. Others wanted the unions and even the factory committees to retain more autonomy from the party and perform functions beyond those of exhortation and disciplining.

Gradually, Lenin's ideas on unions as Communist party transmission belts were carried out. They implied a fourth model of unionism. This Soviet model imitated the dependent and subordinate position of trade unions that had characterized party-union relations in Germany until 1906, but the pattern was carried to its very extreme. A concomitant Soviet model of labor relations was also developed in the Soviet Union. Formally, collective bargaining between unions and management was a part of these relations. In practice, the Communist party made the important decisions on labor conditions and controlled both unions and management. Strikes and other forms of labor protest were prohibited and severely punished, since they challenged party rule and interfered with economic development.

The economic structure of the rest of Europe was left intact. The issue of nationalization was solved by committees called into existence to investigate the problem. In Great Britain, the Sankey Committee argued in favor of nationalizing the coal mines, and a German committee also advised in that direction, but in both countries the government refused to follow the advice. Other governments rejected nationalization from the outset or allowed committees to postpone their investigations until the end of the revolutionary aftermath. Consequently, private enterprise was not challenged by state control or by workers' control.

In most instances, the issue of workers' control was solved by instituting a form of union representation. Sometimes this constituted a continuation of wartime provisions for union presence in factories. In Scandinavia, enterprise councils came into existence during the war and became legalized. Shop stewards continued their work in Britain, while *commissioni interne* started in Italy. The German *Betriebsräte*, originating in 1918, were legalized only after heavy pressure was exerted by the existing councils and their responsibilities were then curtailed. Social affairs such as evaluating the performance of collective contracts and the administration of social enterprise funds became their main tasks. All workers were eligible and entitled to vote, but manual workers and office workers would have separate councils. Council members enjoyed some, but not complete, protection against arbitrary dismissal. The councils were independent from the unions, and the latter could only act as an adviser, as was the case for the employers' organizations. This autonomy was almost as much a victory for the radicals, who despised union tutelage, as it was for the employers. In larger companies, one or two members could act as delegates to the company board, thereby enjoying full voting rights but without extra pay. In general, both sides were devoid of enthusiasm about this kind of representation at the top. Austrian socialists were less cautious. Outside union officials could be elected into the Austrian enterprise councils and the protection against dismissal was more extensive.

The lack of sweeping reforms in the structure of economic control did not imply a complete return to prewar conditions. An important change concerned the status of the unions and consequently of union-employer contacts. Governments provided the unions with a new kind of official recognition. As members of newly created consultative councils, they were treated as market representatives, as were the employers. Unions were no longer perceived as merely disturbers of the market and the employers as the market representatives. From now on there existed two market parties. The employers, unwilling to go that far, were ready to recognize the unions as labor representatives but not as a market party. They nevertheless complied with the paritary institutions of deliberation and consultation that were established on the continent. They could find solace in the fact that state recognition and paritary consultation focused on social rather than economic decisions.

Paritary consultations with the government, and direct central-level contacts in Germany, covered subjects like labor exchanges, arbitration, and general economic and social problems. Paritary labor exchanges had already been created in some countries before the war or at the beginning of the war in order to fight unemployment. A smooth course of demobilization became their main concern after the war. In Germany, where paritary labor exchanges replaced former employers' exchanges, demobilization was one of the ZAG's major goals. The

unions wanted to be involved in coordinating policies, and the employers preferred union assistance over state regulations. But employers considered the
entire structure as temporary, to be removed as soon as possible.

Another common task for paritary committees was arbitration. It usually took
place at a regional level and for each industry separately. Both the Whitley
councils in Britain and the industrial committees created in Germany had an
inflated arbitration function, including initiatives for more general cooperation
and the solving of common problems. In general, the unions were more interested
in collective bargaining, and they sometimes requested state support in their
efforts to get employers to sit down at the bargaining table. State encouragement
could consist of informal government pressure or legal provisions to provide
collective agreements with more status. Belgium was the only country that created
a new structure for collective bargaining. It followed the example of the Whitley
councils and set up paritary committees. In contrast to the British example,
however, these committees were regarded as negotiation bodies. After government intervention had broken fierce employers' resistance, the first committees
were established in the steel industry, mining, and engineering. The first issue
on the agenda was the eight-hour workday, and once it had been introduced,
the committees shifted their focus to wages. The French government, too, promoted collective bargaining in the face of employer resistance. A law on collective agreements issued in 1919 recognized them as binding contracts. The
government itself set the example by demanding collective bargaining procedures
in firms supplying government agencies, which represented an extension of a
wartime measure requiring arbitration bodies in such firms.

In addition to all these changes in labor conditions and the position of unions,
the war and the revolutionary turmoil had two other effects, one on the international coordination of social legislation and one on unionism itself. The International Labour Office (ILO) was created to coordinate legislation. The
American unions had taken the initiative to devote part of the peace talks to
labor issues, since they blamed backward social conditions at least in part for
the outbreak of war and the Russian Revolution. An international commission
was formed at the peace conference. The first ILO meeting was held in Washington in October 1919. It passed six conventions. The first provided for the
eight-hour workday and the forty-eight-hour work week. The other conventions
concerned labor exchanges, maternity leave, night work for women and children,
and child employment in general. The popularity of measures protecting women
was related to the renewed emphasis on family life and the exodus of women
from industry once the war was over. Since the fear of a spread of Communist
revolutions was one of the motives for the foundation of the ILO, the Russians
were barred from the organization. The latter, however, were hardly motivated
to participate in an organization dominated by capitalist governments. In later
years, the ILO engaged in advising governments on matters of social legislation,
on collecting and exchanging information relating to social matters, and on
organizing regular international meetings to discuss and pass conventions on

social legislation. The French socialist Albert Thomas was the first director of
the ILO, which was located in Geneva.

The years 1918–1920 brought radical change to the unions, too. An enormous
growth in membership had started in 1917 and continued until 1920. Membership
rates were doubled compared to those of 1914. Unskilled workers, women, and
even clerical workers were well represented among the new members. Women
at least doubled their share of total membership to 20 or 30 percent.

On the continent, clerical workers had occasionally participated in the revolutionary turmoil at the end of the war. In a number of countries this activity
stimulated the rise of new organizations and of coordinating federations of clerical
workers. The growth of the existing *cadre* organizations of technical staff in
France gave rise to a lively discussion about their place in the CGT: Were they
corevolutionaries or *bourgeois* intruders? By this time, the growing unionism of
clerical workers, both within and outside the major federations, had become
characterized by some of the distinctive features of unionism models: reformist
umbrella organizations in the German model, highly politicized and dispersed
movements in France, and a number of small craft-like organizations in Britain.

As was the case before the war, socialist unions enjoyed the largest following.
In the small nations of Luxembourg and Iceland they had by now also set up
national federations, more or less in the tradition of the German model. The
cautious stance of Catholic unions during this period of upheaval had varying
effects upon membership numbers. Membership rose in Germany and Holland,
but numerical equality became transformed into a large socialist majority in
Belgium. Postwar events provided the motivation to establish Catholic union
federations in France, Spain, and Poland. The French organization (very small
like that in Spain) was called *Confédération française des travailleurs chrétiens*
(CFTC). Their Polish counterpart was for some time the largest organization in
the country, but slowly gave way to the socialist federation. Apart from France
and the less industrialized countries of southern and eastern Europe, at least one-
third of all manual workers were organized by 1920, and this figure was as high
as three-fourths in Germany (that is, 8 million workers).

The most important effect of the war and the postwar events on the unions
was perhaps the split between reformist and parliamentary socialists on the one
hand, and Communists on the other. Though almost complete, the split would
become definite only in the following years. In addition to membership growth,
the split represented another reason to replace the *Generalkommission* with an
independent union federation. In 1919 a trade union conference at Nürnberg led
to the foundation of the *Algemeiner deutscher Gewerkschaftsbund*, or ADGB
(General German Trade Union Federation). Carl Legien remained in charge.
Although it was a socialist organization, it was not affiliated with any political
party. This approach was chosen in order to remain attractive to members of
other political parties, especially the Communists. The 1906 Mannheim Reso-
lution, which had regulated party-union relations since the general strike debate,
was revoked to establish this neutrality.

Although they were affected less by the turbulence, employers' organizations became somewhat more centralized. Wartime regulations had already strengthened their sectoral organizations. In Britain employers founded the British Employers Confederation (BEC), while in France government pressure was decisive in the foundation of a nationwide confederation, the *Confédération générale de la production française* (CGPF). It combined economic and social functions, but remained very weak as an organization. The central federations were directly involved in bargaining only on rare occasions, but they were important instruments in the consultation process with the government and in providing industrial bargaining with some coordination. Indeed, the introduction of formal arbitration and negotiation structures and procedures clearly transformed the industrial (sectoral) organizations into bargaining parties, sometimes in spite of employers' resistance.

In conclusion, apart from the rise of a Soviet model of labor relations, the impact of the war and the revolutionary aftermath on labor relations generated more uniformity. Wartime economic policy and the strike movement had brought about a certain degree of centralization (from the industrial level upwards to that of the central federations), as well as some decentralization (from the industrial level downwards to the enterprise, plant, and shop-floor levels).

The effects of the trends differed in the three models. In the German model, the position of union representatives in companies was too weak to make it a lasting force in labor relations. Company activism could, however, force unwilling employers to engage in industrial bargaining, if only to reduce pressures within the enterprise. This extended the tradition of industrial bargaining. In Britain, the stop stewards were able to retain their relative autonomy. This reinforced the system of multilevel bargaining, at both the industry level and within the enterprise. In France, and to some extent also in the Belgian paritary committees, the government was a decisive force in pressuring the employers to sit at the bargaining table. The consequence was a partial transition of French-model labor relations toward more collective bargaining. In combination with the socialist role in the war economy, this strengthened the union idea which posited the state as a force to be used against the employers (as was the case with the local tariffs in the nineteenth century).

6

The 1920s

The 1920s started with an employers' counteroffensive, evoked by a sudden change in economic conditions. Bargaining had taken hold, however, as a pervasive phenomenon. Its spread, as well as the interruption of bargaining by major labor conflicts, were the main features of labor relations during this decade.

THE EMPLOYERS' COUNTEROFFENSIVE AND THE RISE OF SCIENTIFIC MANAGEMENT

Until 1920, American and British capital flows had concealed the level of general impoverishment caused by the war. These flows were reduced in 1920. National differences in war losses and war reparations disturbed the nineteenth-century system of stable currencies dominated by the British pound. By the fall of 1920, economic conditions had deteriorated. Unemployment increased, and there was a steep rise in inflation.

The sudden change in economic conditions put an end to the union offensive. Employers could now exert pressure on the work force to accept a longer workday again, as well as cuts in pay. The major reason offered was intensified international competition. Lockouts, rather rare in 1919 and the spring of 1920, again became a more common phenomenon. Strike frequency declined, though it remained at a high level. The threat to recent achievements like the eight-hour day, the suddenness of the employers' reaction, and the still militant mood of many workers motivated the unions to strike back rather than compromise. Union militancy assumed a defensive nature now, resisting deterioration in labor conditions rather than demanding new improvements.

Employers' response took various forms where the issue of working time was concerned. First, in the few countries where a law had not yet been passed, employers attempted to delay or prevent the introduction of legislation invoking the eight-hour workday. The arguments were the same as those applied to previous social legislation. The law would affect national production and reduce the competitive power of national industry. It would also limit the freedom of workers to work in the manner they desired. The latter argument was illustrated by occasional workers' opposition to the eight-hour workday or by collective agreements embracing more than eight hours (for instance in the case of the English Saturday). Concealed in these arguments was the more general fear of state regulation of labor conditions. A second way to evade the eight hours was to request the government not to sign the Washington Convention. Indeed, the ratification of that convention was upheld in most countries under employers' pressure. By 1922 the only industrial country that had signed was Czechoslovakia. Some governments even decided to wait explicitly until others had ratified it. In the course of the decade international contacts would standardize the interpretation of such terms as work breaks (and lead to new conventions), but the ILO was slow to clear the way for the larger industrial countries to sign the convention. A third method that was employed to return to a longer working day was to ask for new exemptions or a complete removal of the law. The argument put forth was that it did not take changed economic conditions into account and that it gave rise to unemployment. Employers professed that the extra hours of free time had not been used for educational purposes or to improve the workers' home comfort. Instead, they had been wasted in activities like cycling and visiting theaters. In most countries the granting of exemptions provided a solution to employer grievances. Lockouts also helped employers evade the law. German industrialists combined such lockouts with the official request to retract the law. They repeatedly made their contribution to the war reparations dependent upon this withdrawal. The issue became hotly political, a source of conflict between socialists and nonsocialists in government.

In addition to their urging more working hours, employers also attempted to reduce wages. Because the early 1920s were a time of escalating inflation, the easiest way to accomplish this was to delay the adaptation of wages to inflationary prices. If wages were linked to a price index, as was the case in Belgium and Austria, indexing became a discussion topic at the time collective agreements were to be renewed. The unions sometimes agreed to forfeit one or more wage increases or to stabilize wages for a certain period, irrespective of the price level. More often, such concessions had to be won in protracted labor conflicts. Some strikes even exceeded those of 1919, particularly in mining, where unions were under fierce attack. Miners in Great Britain won a strike against wage reductions in October 1920. Unable to revive the prewar Triple Alliance with railway workers and dock workers, they were forced to accept lower wages in 1921. In Norway, actions against wage reductions developed into a large national strike. The strike failed, and after two weeks the government imposed arbitrage. In some countries, governments set up committees to investigate the need for and the extent of wage cuts. This presented a striking contrast with the situation in

1918 and 1919. During those years committees had only been set up to study drastic changes in economic structure, while wage increases had been agreed upon very early to save the country from revolution. Generally speaking, the committees advised or imposed about half the wage cuts the employers had proposed or had tried to impose themselves.

The employers' attack affected not only wages and the eight-hour day, but also union representation on the shop floor and workers' councils. French *délégués d'atelier*, Scandinavian workplace representatives, British shop stewards, Italian delegates, and German *Betriebsräte* all became targets of employers' reactions. Moreover, they were impaired by a lack of worker interest as unemployment rose. Performance declined, managerial pressure increased, and disappointment grew. Consequently, most of the institutions became impotent or disappeared altogether. The most powerful of all enterprise and shop-floor representatives, the shop stewards in British engineering, were defeated in 1922 during a lockout reminiscent of that of 1897. This time the engineers had to accept that management proposals relating to the replacement of skilled by less skilled workers should be communicated to the workers but that replacements could be made pending the procedure. By the early 1920s most of what the unions had attained after the war was being jeopardized again. Wages, not yet at the prewar level, were reduced, the eight-hour workday abolished, suspended, or evaded, and enterprise and workplace representation weakened.

In some southern and eastern European countries employers were favored by a general autocratic or feudal reaction against the workers' postwar offensive. The small socialist movement was suppressed or at least regarded with suspicion. Employers' reaction in countries with parliamentary rule remained within the limits of the parliamentary system, except in the German Weimar Republic and Italy. In Germany, employers attempted to fight the socialist rise to power in government. In Italy they were determined to overcome government irresolution in the face of a rather revolutionary but equally divided socialist movement. In the Weimar Republic, there was a certain amount of employer support for the *Kapp Putsch* in March 1920, a half-hearted attempt by a conservative politician to restore traditional values in politics. Prominent heavy industry leaders eagerly sought some kind of settlement. The coup failed, partly owing to a general strike called by the socialist, Catholic, and liberal unions. The unions participating in the ZAG were even able to get their strike days paid by the employers.

Italian developments had wider implications. By the time of the 1920 factory occupations, disaffected and uprooted young agricultural laborers and urban middle-class youth had spontaneously joined forces in physical attacks on local socialist leaders and union offices. Once these fascist black shirts had gained some local control by force, they were welcomed by industrialists and the middle class. This novel movement seemed to offer better guarantees against socialist actions and intrusion upon managerial prerogatives than the state could. Textile enterprises and other rural industries even contributed financially. Neither socialists nor Communists were very firm in their opposition: both considered fascism to be a last gasp of bourgeois rule. A desperate effort to unite socialist, Communist, and anarchist groups in a general strike to stop fascism failed for lack of participants. The effort only served the fascist cause because it provided new arguments to proclaim the fascists as the true defenders of public order, protecting the nation against any repetition of the revolutionary wave of 1919 and early 1920. Employers in other countries attempted to mobilize rural laborers as strikebreakers, but such movements of blacklegs remained rather marginal in labor relations and politics. The revival, mostly short-lived, of yellow unionism was more common.

The rise of scientific management, which led to a further extension of managerial control, also represented a partial reaction to the eight-hour workday and the quest for workers' control. Scientific management, also called Taylorism after its inventor, and also rationalization, aimed to rationalize management and increase productivity by reducing the scope of control that skilled workers had over their own jobs and the large amount of free time or "natural soldering" that such control supposedly implied. Management was to increase its knowledge of the tasks that skilled workers carried out. Managers could then break down skilled work into a number of tasks, prescribe rules for each task separately, assign each task to a different worker, and allot a specific amount of time for each one. In the United States, Henry Ford adapted Taylorism to mass production and mass consumption by introducing the assembly line, the extreme separation of very small tasks, each performed by different workers. Fordism retained or reestablished some aspects of traditional paternalism. It combined a high wage (to encourage mass consumption) with job security, but demanded that workers adhere to rules like decency in their behavior at work and at home.

Although Taylorism reached Europe before the war, it had been applied in only a small number of automobile plants. Renault had attempted to introduce the timing of work by the *chronomètre* in 1912, but these steps led to protest strikes. The concentration of capital during the war, and the increase in the number of industrial giants through the continual merging of firms after the war, encouraged rationalization. The reduction of working time also contributed to its rise. Indeed, rationalization became—if it was not already—the almost natural reaction of employers to movements calling for work-time reductions. Rationalization evolved into an expanding movement during the 1920s and became a popular subject of discussion at employers' meetings. It also gave rise to a more systematic study of the relations between management and the labor process in the burgeoning sciences of organizational sociology and psychology. However, the actual impact of scientific management on European industry was rather limited. The smaller size of companies and national markets when compared to the United States, the greater importance of family-based enterprise, and the stronger unionism of skilled workers were impediments to its prospering. Its main province remained the large automobile industry. To the extent that it was applied, it implied a process of "deskilling," that is, the replacement of skilled by less skilled jobs. Nevertheless, a process of "reskilling" was also involved.

Manual workers were taught to work with new machinery, and new groups of white-collar workers became involved in new technology and in managerial planning and decisionmaking. Taylorism affected office work, too. In combination with the growing popularity of the typewriter, it contributed to the feminization of lower-level office ranks, jobs lacking career prospects.

Rationalization did not arouse much opposition on the part of unions. One of the more debated parts of the entire movement was the further spread of payment by results, consisting of either piece rates or premium bonus systems, that is, a combination of piece rates plus a time allowance in case the task was completed within a certain amount of time. Piece rates and other wage incentive schemes were not only part of the rationalization drive, but also constituted an alternative to it in those instances where employers desired to speed up production but lacked the means to rationalize. The spread of the use of piece rates did not meet many objections. In some cases the new union position was a break with prewar attitudes, when craft workers had resisted such rates. The change was made possible by the transition to the eight-hour day and by the unions' self-confidence that they would be able to withstand any rate reduction. The unions also saw advantages, including less strict surveillance on the work floor and increased worker responsibility for the less skilled. The latter point demonstrates that the new developments were regarded less as an attack upon the autonomy of skilled workers than as a growth in responsibility for less skilled workers. A specific union concern was the reduction in size of the enterprise work force as a consequence of rationalization.

The only groups to condemn these developments as a further intensification of capitalist exploitation were revolutionary socialists and the Russian Communists. In their view, the capitalists would reap the fruits while the workers would carry the burdens. Yet, within a few years after the Russian Revolution, Taylorism became accepted as a means of labor discipline and industrial growth in the Soviet Union. Its introduction was justified by the absence of capitalists. According to the prevailing ideology, workers themselves would be the beneficiaries of increased production.

THE SPLIT BETWEEN SOCIALISTS AND COMMUNISTS

The blows dealt to recent union accomplishments had important effects on the union movement. They were part of a series of developments that split socialist parties and socialist unions into social democrats, who accepted parliamentary rule, and Communists, who rejected it. First, friction between the two factions had started before the war, when minorities believed that the revolution had been betrayed by reformists and consequently either challenged the socialist organizations or split off. A second divisive issue had been the wartime support of the national cause, challenged by the pacifists' meeting in Kienthal. Third, in the wave of revolutionary upheaval most party and union leaders had shied away from actual attempts to initiate a revolution. This posture alienated revolutionary minorities even further. Once Communist rule had been firmly established in Russia, the Russian Revolution became the fourth issue. Social democrats rejected the lack of democracy and liberal freedom in the Russian dictatorship of the proletariat.

The employers' offensive and the return to more normal economic and social conditions became a fifth divisive issue. The gap was transformed into a split that had international repercussions: The forging of international allegiances became a major issue among socialists. Though heated discussions took place mainly within the parties, socialist unions were affected as well. The twenty-one entry requirements, which adherents to the new Third ("Red") International, founded by the Soviets, had to meet, became a crucial issue in the international split. In order to speed up revolution outside Russia, the requirements followed the example of Russian Communism, including central control, iron discipline, the purging of reformists, and the formation of cells or factions within various social organizations. They also implied complete union subordination to the party. The intention was to transform the unions into Leninist transmission belts of the Communist parties. The twenty-one conditions were a definitive breaking point in most socialist parties. Most of them had supported the efforts to revive the Second International, and they were soon joined by parties that had tried to unite the Second and the Third International in a short-lived Second-and-a-half International. Christian (that is, mainly Catholic) unions founded their own international organization in 1920, dominated by the German Catholic federation.

British-model unions were hardly affected by the breach among socialists. Viewing unions as an extension of party politics was part of some far-off ideology on the continent. German-model unions, and the parties to which they were formally or informally linked, chose the social democratic side almost without exception. Only smaller organizations followed the Soviets. They were as yet unwilling to set up their own unions and remained active within the larger social democratic unions. Once in a while this would give rise to radical movements and to serious internal strife.

Unions in the French model and in the more agrarian countries of Europe were affected more severely. In France, the separation between the CGT and the Socialist party turned the party and the unions into scenes of fierce discussions. The minority obtained a stronghold in the railways, the construction industry, and in most large cities. In line with the rules of the Red International, Communist-dominated cells were organized (*comités syndicals révolutionnaires*, or *CSR*) within the unions where representation was the most limited, like the textile industry and mining. The union leadership tried to ban the committees. In doing so it not only had to fight opposition from Communists, but also the syndicalist tradition, which strongly opposed central control. For some time the discussion dominated all the meetings of the CGT and its member unions. At a very rebellious congress at Lille in 1921, CGT leader Jouhaux was only able to secure a small majority that would support his plan for union discipline. Shortly thereafter, the minority left the organization and set up its own union, the CGT-

U(nitaire). It called itself "unitary" because it had not desired the split. The Spanish union movement had already been split into a (reformist) Marxist union and a more revolutionary anarchist organization. Revolutionary syndicalism (or anarchism) and Communism had thus formed a combination against creeping or traditional centralization and reformism. Because the anarchists and syndicalists could not match the organizational activities of Communists, the latter were able to increase their hold of the CGT-U and the Spanish anarchist organization. Though only a minority in France, the existence of Communist unions and the continued tradition of Spanish anarchism widened the gulf between French-model unionism and the British and German models. Union involvement in politics was reinforced, and the road to collective bargaining was blocked. The traditional radicalism of the Marxist organizations and of revolutionary rival movements caused a rather easy transition to Communism in eastern and southern Europe (for example, in Finland, Yugoslavia, Bulgaria, and Greece). This development set these countries more clearly apart from the rest of Europe with respect to unionism and labor relations. The Communist movements became tied to Soviet policy, which made them an even easier target for repression.

The bloody suppression of the Kronstadt Revolt in Russia sealed the breach between indignant reformists and loyal Communists. Henceforth, the latter strictly observed policy guidelines from Moscow and changed their organizations accordingly. The socialist-Communist rift weakened the unions, already affected by rising unemployment and the employers' offensive. Within two years, most socialist unions (at their peak in 1919 or 1920) lost between one-third and one-half of their membership, although they remained above the 1914 level. Generally speaking, the high tide of socialism was over, and a conservative reaction in politics set in. Sweden proved to be the exception. Union membership did not decline, and Swedish social democrats dominated the government after 1920.

Among employers, the offensive during the early 1920s buttressed the self-confidence of the new central organizations that had been founded after the war. The federations did not undertake efforts to coordinate the employers' position in bargaining or in conflict, but they tried to influence politics. Given the pressure of changed economic and political conditions, they were increasingly certain of a sympathetic response by the national governments.

THE SPREAD OF COLLECTIVE BARGAINING

Unemployment soon began to drop throughout the continent. Currency fluctuations and the resulting price movements continued to dominate labor relations during the remainder of the 1920s. Unions monitored rising consumer prices and regularly demanded wage increases. Large employers were more concerned about the fluctuating prices of their products. More than once they pressed for wage cuts. Due to the lack of price stability the 1920s became a decade of frequent major strikes and lockouts.

Despite labor conflicts the by now regular or even institutionalized contacts between unions and employers or employers' organizations continued. Indeed, the 1920s were a period of collective bargaining rather than a period of conflict. The German model of labor relations extended it tradition of substantive agreements on a number of matters for a fixed period of time, mostly one or two years. The socialist organizations' more explicit reformist position after the socialist-Communist breach facilitated bargaining. A second and related development was the spread of industrial unions. The wave of recruitment among unskilled workers reinforced the principle that unions should leave their craft base and become industrial unions or industrial branch organizations. In Norway, the more radical union wing, which had arisen before the war, put forth this demand. Several union federations followed this example and decided that the idea of industrial (branch) unions should be put into practice, instead of being merely an ideal. They did not force craft unions to leave but promoted a transition to industrial unions by way of union mergers. They subsequently restricted the right to join the federation to industrial unions.

The spread of incentive payments and the resulting detailed wage rates also stimulated enterprise-level negotiations. However, many large firms still refused formal bargaining. They allowed only informal union, formal union, or workforce consultation. Some large factories had their own agreements, offering additional advantages to standard industry agreements. Enterprise agreements point to one of the differences in structure between unions, presiding over almost all collective bargaining, and the employers' associations, not involved in enterprise bargaining. On occasion, enterprise agreements strained the relationship between individual employers and their organization. Recalcitrant employers sometimes gave up their membership.

The spread of bargaining also applied to the British model. British craft unionism was too well established to give up traditional rights. It had been left intact or even strengthened by wartime cooperation and the lack of a revolutionary aftermath. A series of amalgamations reduced the number of unions, but only some of them opened their doors to unskilled (general) workers. As a result, the Transport and General Workers Union (TGWU) became the largest concentration of unskilled workers. Craft unions continued to adhere to their own tradition in bargaining. Most agreements consisted only of a dispute procedure, relegating the domain of labor conditions to informal local and enterprise agreements.

Various efforts to engage in bargaining were undertaken in France but proved abortive despite recent legislation. By now, the CGT was in favor of collective bargaining. However, the existence of a Communist opponent, Communist enterprise cells, the syndicalist tradition, and the lack of organizational discipline prevented the confederation from signing contracts or guaranteeing the absence of conflicts. Attempts to turn wartime contracts into collective agreements also failed because of heavy resistance by the French *patronat* against intrusion upon paternalist authority. The 1919 law on collective bargaining did not persuade French employers. In line with the idea of the French government's partisanship in labor relations, employers regarded the law as a hostile act, enforced by the revolutionary turmoil. Bargaining remained confined to industries like printing, where contracts had already been introduced before the war.

In the rest of Europe bargaining remained rare or completely absent. Unions tended to be dominated by Communists and remained small. Employers were unwilling and even repressive. These conditions also prevented the spread of bargaining in countries where social democrats held a majority in the union movement (for example, in Poland and Hungary).

The central issues of the 1920s, currency fluctuations and the resulting changes in prices, gave rise to conflicts in three periods. Working time was sometimes an issue as well. The major scene of conflicts was mining, which was plagued by the currency problems and by strong international competition.

The first period refers to the time of rising prices in 1922–1923. Wages followed prices to some extent, either by wage indexing or by successive agreements that took inflation into account. Frequently, such adaptations needed to be debated. Belgian mine owners restored the gliding scale, lost before the war. It mitigated the effects of wage indexing by partially linking wages to consumer prices and partially to coal prices.

In this same period, Germany fell victim to extreme inflation, affecting labor relations both directly and indirectly. For some time France and Belgium occupied the Ruhr area to enforce war reparations. Despite strained mutual relations, employers and unions in the mines and railways in the occupied territory agreed on passive resistance. A combined private aid program would finance this action, which almost amounted to a strike without conflict. After two Communist attempts to organize a general strike in the same year, the German government put an end to this passive resistance. The occupation also served to raise the issue of the eight-hour day again. Representatives from heavy industry and mining even wanted to invoke the assistance of the French army to impose a ten-hour workday (eight and a half hours underground), but the French refused any commitment. A new government complied to the employers' demand and revoked the law on the eight-hour day. The argument put forth related to the need to recover completely from the war and to pay war reparations. The measure added to the unions' disappointment about the employers' offensive and to the employers' determination to confine union influence to sectoral collective bargaining. The ZAG was dissolved in 1924, after five years of rather ineffective functioning.

The second concentration of conflicts affected labor relations in 1923 and 1924. Prices started to drop again, and the unions had to face wage reductions, sometimes in nominal rather than real wages. Since the unions had regained some of their previous strength, they were unwilling to accept lower wages during this period of increasing productivity and profits. Consequently, the price index was not applied to a lesser extent or, on occasion, it was abolished altogether, sometimes to be restored when prices started to rise again. Indeed, the general outcome of conflicts was that employers made sacrifices with respect to wages, lessening wage cuts or accepting wage increases, while the unions made sacrifices in the area of working hours, complying with the demand for more than eight hours of work a day. The unions could not evade all wage reductions or cuts in real wages, however. In the fall of 1923 almost a million Polish workers, including postal and railway workers, were on strike against wage cuts. The government attempted to militarize the railways and postal services and declared martial law in a number of towns. In response, the socialists called a general one-day protest strike (in Kraków the strike resulted in an uprising), but wage cuts went through. Wage reductions in Great Britain were often the consequence of the introduction of a four-day working week. Employers decided to take this step to combat the high level of unemployment.

Inflation was less of a problem during the second half of the decade. Instead, the stabilization of currencies became a new source of labor conflicts, which were concentrated in Great Britain, the first country to stabilize its currency (in 1926). This pioneering role served to safeguard the international financial interests of the London City, but it damaged the British trade position and gave rise to repeated employer demands for wage cuts. A continued high level of unemployment, widespread labor unrest, and the Great Strike of 1926 were the consequences. Other countries became rather reluctant to stabilize their currencies, for they wanted to avoid such problems. Indeed, wages continued to increase in most countries, and in the late 1920s they again surpassed the best prewar year, 1913.

Events leading to the Great Strike started with the mine employers' demand, repeatedly voiced since 1921, for wage reductions. After the stabilization of the pound in April 1926, a committee reported in favor of wage reductions, and the employers, backed by government, insisted upon such reductions. The miners refused, using the slogan "Not a penny off the pay, not a second on the day." They went on strike facing a lockout. Without much preparation, the TUC called for a general sympathy strike. In addition to the million miners, 1.5 million strikers stopped working. As was usual in mine disputes, the strike gave rise to foreign solidarity activities. Some national union federations even temporarily increased membership fees to collect money. A large sum of money offered by Soviet unions was refused, because the strikers feared that the strike would be denounced too easily if they accepted. In spite of this solidarity, the refusal by government to negotiate made the position of the TUC rather difficult. The Great Strike was called off after nine days without any government concessions. The miners felt betrayed again and continued their strike until the winter, when they admitted total defeat and accepted wage cuts. In fact, the general strike had been an attempt by the miners to import syndicalist action against the state, a characteristic of the situation just before the war. This failed strike remained the only British example of a large political strike until the 1970s. Both the TUC and His Majesty's Government defended the British tradition of labor relations with even more determination than before. The Trade Disputes and Trade Unions Act of 1927 can be considered evidence of the government's attitude. This act outlawed general sympathy strikes and simultaneously put an end to the automatic political union dues for the Labour party.

The course of the labor conflicts in mining and other sectors demonstrated the firm determination of European governments to stay out of labor conflicts. In accordance with their more conservative inclination, most governments were willing to meet employer demands, but they also remained interested in solving industrial conflicts. One means to accomplish this was to introduce arbitration, preferably on a voluntary basis. In Holland four regional state mediators were appointed in 1923 to engage in voluntary mediation. When friction occurred, governments in the German-model sometimes shifted to compulsory arbitration. This had the disadvantage of being a source of dispute in itself and of affecting the neutral position of government in German-model labor relations. Norway was an example. Compulsory arbitration, introduced during the war, was given up in 1923, only to be reintroduced in 1927 for some time. In Germany, compulsory arbitration (*Zwangsschlichtung*) was imposed in 1923, the year of the Ruhr occupation. While the unions often resorted to arbitration, employers preferred direct negotiations, because they viewed the arbitration judgments as biased in favor of the unions. The dispute was another factor leading to the end of the ZAG. The spread of bargaining also made some governments sanction collective agreements through legal means where they had not yet done so (for example, in Holland in 1927, and in Sweden in 1928).

In addition to this legislation on collective agreements and arbitration, labor legislation and unemployment insurance in particular also remained on the agenda. Since such programs could not be financed out of existing funds, state contributions to unemployment insurance became a major parliamentary issue between Catholics and conservatives on the one hand, and socialists on the other. For two of the three social democrat cabinets in Sweden it even proved to be an unsurmountable obstacle. A second issue involving unemployment insurance was the degree of uniformity and centralization in the system. This topic became an important source of friction especially in the Weimar Republic. Conservatives and employers attached great value to private initiative (in other words, to employer influence) and to the distinction between manual and clerical workers. Socialists favored uniformity and centralization. Socialist aldermen in local government were better able to pass social reforms, most of all in housing. The measures improved the social integration, as well as the living standards, of the working class. These developments allowed the working class to participate in the "roaring twenties."

FROM BARGAINING TO CORPORATISM

Industry-level and enterprise-level bargaining commonly took place between one group or organization representing each side. The existence of Communist unions (in the French model) and Communist factions within the socialist unions (in the German model) complicated negotiations. If they were active within the socialist unions, Communists called strikes before their union had decided to do so and continued to strike after the union had called it off. The former activity often created a predicament for the unions. They could either support a strike, thereby breaching a collective agreement, or lose their hold on their members. Catholic organizations (and some less important Protestant and liberal unions) stood at the other pole. In contrast to the Communists, however, they were willing to negotiate side by side with the socialists. Their relative strength was the greatest in Holland and in Belgium. Socialists in these two countries grudgingly accepted the Catholics as co-bargainers, if only because the latter were able to break socialist strikes and because the employers wanted them at the negotiating table. The Belgian paritary committees, founded in 1919, could not start functioning until disputes had been solved about the number of seats for each of the organizations. In Holland, Protestant unions were often involved as well. The various union organizations that were to sit on one side of the table only occasionally standardized their demands. Sometimes a breach occurred when the socialists were less willing to compromise than were the Catholics. Employers would sometimes attempt to reach an agreement with the Catholics only, in the hope that the socialists would be unable to strike without Catholic support. Mutual relations were affected even more when Catholics would give up a strike before the socialists were willing to do so. In general, the socialists were not only eager to hold out longer, but also able to do so since their strike funds were much larger, in spite of more frequent use. The growing importance of collective bargaining reduced conflicts between the various unions. It reinforced the reformist stand of the unions involved and also tended to contribute to some form of mutual understanding and cooperation. There was less divisiveness on the employers' side. Catholic organizations remained in the shadow of the larger neutral industrial organizations. Frequent debates took place between conservative and more liberal and bargaining-minded employers, however, within these industrial organizations.

The rise of collective bargaining during and after the war gave rise to a growing amount of literature relating to the ordering of economic and social life by means of peaceful relations between employers and unions. One solution that was embraced to cope with unwilling employers or workers was the legal extension of collective agreements to include nonmembers of the signing parties. The extension would give the contracts force of law for all employers and workers within a specific industrial branch. Proponents of legal extension were found mainly among Catholics and social democrats. Most large industrialists rejected this imposition of agreements upon unwilling employers, including themselves. In several countries their opposition sufficed to keep governments from introducing legislation.

Especially among Catholics collective bargaining was considered to be a sound base of a more all-encompassing ordering of social and economic life. This fit the tradition of class cooperation, stressed by Catholics in the nineteenth century, and represented an alternative to both the high degree of state involvement that was characteristic of the war economy and to the anarchy of the free market. It was reasoned that because too much state involvement would paralyze private initiative, employers and unions should regulate social affairs within the industrial branches. In order to accomplish this, paritary corporate councils were to be established. As corporate institutions they were to be endowed with some discretionary power in social matters. The contentious German ZAG, struggling for survival in the early 1920s, hardly served as a model, although it was an example of such union-employer cooperation. Some partisans of the corporate councils, mainly Catholics, regarded them as the basis for a new corporatist political order, encompassing all aspects of social life. The corporate councils could even be complemented by a general corporate chamber, representing various interests in addition to unions and employers, as a substitute for parliamentary representation.

These ideas offered Catholic unions an alternative to socialist ideas and strengthened self-confidence within Catholic organizations. However, occasional efforts in countries characterized by German-model labor relations to introduce corporate arrangements on a voluntary basis failed because of resistance by large employers, including Catholics, and a lack of interest among social democrats. This experience, plus the improvement in economic conditions during the second half of the 1920s reduced interest among Catholics as well.

Another reason for the growing lack of interest was that Italian fascism, in power since 1922, had annexed the notion of corporatism rather violently. Indeed, corporatism provided an easy means for Catholic dictatorship in southern Europe to pacify labor relations and to outlaw socialist organizations. This state corporatism was an instrument of state rule rather than an alternative to it. Existing Catholic unions were too small to play a role in it. The Italian version was a mixture of Catholic corporatist ideas and old syndicalist ideals about the organization of producers being the base of society. In the Italian New Order, socialist unions were suppressed and the *fasci* (local fascist groups) set up their own unions to engage in collective bargaining. Employers increasingly broke off their agreements with the socialist unions and subsequently signed new agreements with the fascists. Soon the fascist government suppressed the right to strike and the celebration of Labor Day on May 1. The national employers' federation and the leader of the fascist union organization signed the Pact of Palazzo Vidoni in October 1925, which affirmed the fascist monopoly in collective bargaining with employers or employers' organizations. The fascists agreed to discontinue the practice of enterprise representation (*commisioni interne*) without getting the wage indexing they had asked for. The socialist union federation more or less dissolved. In 1927 a charter of labor was introduced (*Carta del Lavoro*), which contained some basic labor conditions, including the eight-hour day, paid holidays, and the recognition of labor exchanges. No controls with respect to the observance of these regulations took place, however. The charter also introduced corporate commissions of employers and fascist unions as part of a more comprehensive corporatist order.

After the 1923 military coup in Spain, this country also experimented with corporatist elements like paritary industrial councils, but with less direct state control of labor conditions. The large anarchist union was outlawed; the other socialist unions were allowed to participate.

In summary, the 1920s caused a further spread of bargaining in German- and British-model labor relations, as well as a sharper distinction between political activities and industrial action. The outcome of the Great Strike consolidated the separation between the two in Britain. The French model retained its features of politicization and protest. Corporatism gained popularity in the Catholic south of Europe as a means to pacify labor relations and to silence socialist organizations. The coming crisis would only add to its appeal.

7

Europe in Crisis

During the 1930s Europe was split by the polarization between the Soviet Union, engaged in a tremendous industrialization drive, and the rest of Europe, immersed in a stifling economic crisis. Labor relations in both parts of Europe were deeply affected, while the unions were placed under great stress. Attempts to achieve national economic recovery from the crisis turned labor relations into a political problem, to be dealt with by the government. Union-employer relations were subject to a process of pacification, either forcibly under fascism and corporatism, or voluntarily.

THE RUSSIAN INDUSTRIALIZATION DRIVE

In the Soviet Union in 1921 Lenin had put an end to War Communism and introduced the New Economic Policy (NEP). Private initiative in small enterprise was encouraged again, and there was a certain amount of relaxation in labor relations. Main accomplishments in labor conditions like the eight-hour workday were incorporated into the new Labor Code of 1922, and a minimum wage came into force. In all other areas, however, labor conditions were determined through collective bargaining, implying a reduction of state control and a stronger position for management. The unions had to surrender the degree of enterprise control they had become accustomed to under War Communism and accept their subordination to the party, a distinctive characteristic of the Soviet unionism model. Dependence was not complete, however, and there was still some maneuvring room left in bargaining. At the 1921 party congress, which more or less marked the start of NEP, Lenin carried through this course of moderation. In vain, Trotsky advocated the immediate transition of the unions into state agencies dealing with production. On the other side of the issue, a group called workers' opposition wanted to retain or reinforce workers' control and the unions' role in it. This viewpoint was condemned as being an anarcho-syndicalist deviation.

As was the case in the rest of Europe, collective bargaining was dominated by inflation. Cash wages were restored, though at first inflation led workers to press for the continuation of some type of payment in kind.

In 1927 NEP was dropped as a policy, and the country embarked upon a course of rapid industrialization under central planning. Josef Stalin implemented the Revolution from Above. In view of the international isolation of the country (the only Communist bastion in a hostile world), the Soviet Union was to industrialize on its own under a system of central planning. This ran against Trotsky's notion of a Permanent Revolution, in which the Soviet Union would be no more than a link in a chain of international revolution and industrial growth. The first Five-Year Plan went into effect in 1928, the second in 1932. Heavy industry was the main concern. During the years of these plans the nonagricultural labor force increased from 10 to 30 million people. Partly due to official promotion, the share of female workers rose steeply.

The industrialization campaign had important consequences for labor relations and labor conditions. Least affected were wages. Real wages dropped initially, but the larger number of workers per family kept family income rather stable. Wage differentials were widened to encourage productivity. Any opposition to this policy was denounced as petty bourgeois egalitarianism.

Working time was subject to sweeping changes. A seven-hour workday was introduced, that is, forty-two hours a week, accompanied by a three-shift system, which often replaced two shifts of eight hours. The work week was changed from six out of seven days to four out of five days. Sunday, perceived as no more than a religious relict from the past, became just another working day. Since one day off in five was more than one in seven, completely new time schedules had to be created for the three-shift and seven-hour system. Soon, the new five-day week and the three shifts came under attack. It was argued that the shorter period of continuous work depersonalized the labor process, in other words, reduced personal responsibility. The standard week was partially restored, and the three-shift system discontinued. The seven-hour working day remained, representing another major Soviet achievement, after its pioneering role in the introduction of the eight-hour workday. In practice, however, things were different, primarily because of the rise of socialist competition (*sotsialistichesky sorevnovanya*). This new campaign induced individual workers and working teams to increase their output and reduce piece rates voluntarily. The campaign reached its zenith in Stakhanovism. In August 1935 Alexei Stakhanov, a coal miner in the Donets basin, was reported to have cut 102 tons of coal in six hours. The feat triggered the Stakhanov movement, encouraging workers and teams to surpass their daily norms by as much as possible. Indeed, 1,000 percent fulfillment was no longer a rare phenomenon, and photographs of model workers were attached to the factory gate. The movement had its effects on working time. Workers were pressured to work longer than seven hours a day and were denounced as opponents of the production drive if they refused. Another cause of worker resentment was that management increased output norms, based on the higher levels of output, and that longer working days raised the number of work accidents. The campaign was discontinued in 1937, but socialist competition in a more general form remained a lasting feature of the Soviet economy.

Social welfare was another area that saw drastic changes. The tightening of the labor market, in combination with the large degree of protection against dismissal, allowed the Soviet government to discontinue unemployment benefits and even proclaim an official end to the phenomenon of unemployment as such. From then on no official mention was ever made of unemployment. Indeed, if it existed at all, it probably affected only small numbers of workers. In order to tie workers to their workplace, other social welfare rights were made more dependent upon length of employment. Owing to a certain degree of coverage extension the Soviet Union probably compared favorably to the rest of Europe with respect to social welfare, in particular in illness and maternity provisions.

Whatever favorable effects some of the changes in labor conditions may have had, workers were hardly able to benefit. Due to the revived priority of production, the trade unions stressed their role in raising productivity and left the issue of labor conditions to the state and management. Collective agreements closely followed central guidelines and were renewed almost automatically. Union-employer committees met less and less frequently. In such a manner, the unions focused much less on monitoring labor conditions and devoted themselves fully to worker exhortation. This established institutionally the Soviet model of labor relations. The model combined strong state and managerial power over labor conditions and a complete lack of union autonomy. Bargaining had become a mere formality, and work regimentation left workers without any recourse against managerial or state arbitrariness. Indeed, a pervasive trait of Soviet society under Stalin was that complaints could easily be misconstrued as political opposition, and all opposition was severely punished, with or without due process. Noncompliance provided a ticket to northern Russia or Siberia, where millions of people were imprisoned in labor camps and put to work in mines without any labor protection at all. The hardship endured by these prisoners was hardly noticed in the rest of Europe until 1938, when large numbers of leading Communists were sentenced in show trials or just disappeared without any form of trial. The former union leader Mikhail Tomsky was one of them.

CRISIS

Soviet economic performance was all the more astonishing, since the rest of Europe suffered from an unprecedented economic crisis from 1930 on. In most countries, unemployment in the years 1932 and 1933 reached a peak of about one-third of the labor force. Many of those still employed had their work week and wages reduced. In general, clerical workers were affected less than manual workers, but the many unemployed office clerks had almost no futureprospects. After the improvements and the daring prospects of the 1920s, the crisis was a sudden fall into a deep abyss, neither expected nor understood.

At first the crisis did not seem to pose a threat to collective bargaining. Collective agreements continued to regulate labor conditions in a number of industries. They were interrupted by industrial conflict to a lesser extent than in the 1920s. The general decline in the number and scope of strikes was due in part to the unions' restraint in the face of the rapid growth in unemployment. Employers also took a moderate position, since they were rather unwilling to risk their enterprises by staging a lockout.

A major issue was whether wages could be stabilized or should be reduced during a time of unemployment and falling prices. Employers referred to Japan as providing an example of how to overcome the crisis by lower wages. They pressed for wage cuts and sometimes enforced them during the term of a labor agreement. Quite frequently, unions concurred with these developments, basically to keep even more firms from closing down.

Though rather restrained, the unions did raise a new issue: a reduction in working time, initially to a forty-four-hour work week, later to forty hours. In some countries, a shorter work week had already been a demand in the late 1920s as a reaction to rationalization. This kept in motion the spiral: less working time (eight hours a day) led to rationalization, which led to still less working time (forty hours). Unions had supported rationalization because they believed it could improve the working conditions of many workers. According to the unions, rationalization had two additional effects: an increase in work load and a rise in the level of unemployment. Work-time reduction was to provide a solution to both problems. The steep rise in unemployment in the early 1930s made the question more salient. Moreover, because of lack of work many workers were already allowed to work only part-time. Consequently, the main argument for fewer working hours was the battle against unemployment, but in view of the increased work load the unions also presented the other argument, relief for workers. The second argument called for a weekly rather than daily reduction in working time. Interest in a shorter work week was also influenced by the fact that the eight-hour workday had been established, though not always observed, in the years before. Predominant by now was the desire to add free time to the weekend in the form of an English Saturday, already commonplace in craft industries. International contacts within the Second International and the international organization of socialist unions made the demand uniform: a forty-hour work week, preferably consisting of five eight-hour days. The employers were to carry the burden of the shorter work week. Further rationalization and productivity could finance it (and would continue the spiral of working-time reduction and rationalization). The matter was discussed within the ILO, but fascist Italy was the only country taking action in the desired direction. Other nations signed ILO conventions on the principle of forty hours, but due to employers' resistance refused to enforce them.

The central argument put forth by employers was a common one: international competition. According to employers, a shorter work week would inflict a deadly blow to the various national economies, which were already in decline. A second and new argument concerned the relationship between working-time reduction and rationalization. Employers pointed frequently to this relationship. The introduction of an eight-hour workday in the early 1920s had stimulated rationalization and had thus been one of the causes of the crisis. A forty-hour work week would only reinforce the trend toward rationalization and make things worse. Accordingly, employers seemed more sensitive to the effects of rationalization on employment than the unions. However, the latter thought it impossible to stop rationalization anyway, and since it was inevitable, one might as well use it to finance a shorter work week. A secondary argument was the increasing frequency of idleness and work that was paid under the table and evaded safety prescriptions and wage regulations. Employers believed that the eight-hour workday had stimulated this kind of unfair competition and that any further reduction of working time would aggravate the problem. More an expression of employer irritation than a real argument, it was undermined by the large army of the jobless who were able to spend time doing informal circuit work.

The shorter work week did not develop into a source of much conflict. Occasionally, the issue became the unions' counterdemand when employers wanted to cut wages (sometimes in combination with fewer, specifically fewer paid, working hours). Such conflicts could strain labor relations, but to a lesser extent than inflation had in the 1920s. The system of collective labor agreements rarely broke down. One of the largest conflicts involving wage cuts, as well as a reduction in working time, was a general lockout in Norway in 1931, when employers demanded 15 percent wage cuts in new labor agreements. The unions refused and demanded working-time reductions in response. Mediation failed, and economic life was paralyzed for five months. At that point, both sides agreed upon a stabilization of real wages.

Rationalization in itself was a minor issue in labor relations. It was transformed into a full-fledged business in the 1930s and gave rise to a growing number of management consulting firms. The Frenchman Bedeaux led the field. He created a universal yardstick for all work, the so-called Bedeaux Unit, that is, sixty seconds subdivided into a fraction of working time and a corresponding fraction of time devoted to rest. This kind of precision stimulated shop-floor bureaucratization and central allocation of even the smallest work tasks. The system became popular mainly in industries without a craft tradition, like the textile, food processing, and chemistry industries. This prevented strong opposition, although there were some strikes (particularly in Great Britain) against the introduction of this kind of job evaluation and measurement.

The unions' reluctance to organize actions reduced the number and extent of conflicts, in spite of occasional Communist attempts to call strikes. Communists saw an opportunity to denounce those unions accepting wage cuts as being capitalist agents. They were all the more eager to mobilize workers because many of their cells, like the more formal workers' representation within the enterprise, were under heavy strain. The threat of unemployment was not a favorable condition for participation in Communist actions, and workers had become disinterested. In response to this decline, French Communists increased their efforts to organize secret *triangles* (cells). In counterreaction, some enterprises intensified their spying on workers. In general, however, militancy declined wherever social democratic, Catholic, and even Communist unions were well represented.

The scene of strikes moved to other areas. First were regions where the hold of unionism was weak and where traditional anarchism had a relatively wide appeal. Local outbursts of protest occurred spontaneously and would occasionally grow into larger regional strikes or result in local incidents. An example was the 1932 miners' strike in the Borinage, located in Belgian Wallony. The main issue was the linkage of wages to coal prices (gliding scale), which had been partially reintroduced in the 1920s and caused a series of wage cuts during the crisis. The unions complied, but their decision gave rise to spontaneous strikes. Dismissal of strikers expanded the strike movement, and the strikers even besieged the socialist *Maison du Peuple*. An important local incident occurred among unorganized workers in northern Sweden's timber industry. Police shot five participants in the village of Ådalen during a peaceful demonstration against the employment of blacklegs. It was the only bloody incident in Swedish industrial history.

In eastern and southern Europe protests against wage reductions were intermingled with, or grew into, efforts to overthrow dictatorships or the political order. Communists and anarchists were strongly represented in such actions. Examples were a series of Polish strikes in 1932, affecting heavy industry in Upper Silesia and the Łódź textile industry, and a 1933 Romanian revolt in the Givita railway shops near Bucharest. In both cases, the governments responded by imposing restrictions on the right to organize. Wider publicity was given to developments in Spain, where republicans and socialists won the 1931 elections and subsequently declared the Spanish republic. Largo Caballero, leader of the Marxist union, became the labor minister and introduced a series of reforms. The corporate paritary committees were replaced by mixed arbitration boards (*jurados mixtos*). Anarchists accused them of being just another trap to prevent direct action. Anarchist and Communist protests resulted in local strikes and two major insurrections in 1933 and 1934. The second one, in October 1934, was rather general in nature and gave rise to short-lived efforts to establish *comunismo libertario*, especially in the Asturian mining areas. Their program included expropriations, the abolition of money, and a range of social changes. Both efforts were crushed by the police, widening the gap between the republic and the large anarchist workers' movement. Large employers also opposed the republic. They cooperated only unwillingly with the arbitration boards and even set up a new central organization to fight the republican reforms.

IN SEARCH OF NEW POLITICS AND A NEW ORDER

The relative stability of collective bargaining did not reflect the real impact of the crisis. There was a feverish search for new solutions to correct or even to substitute the free market economy. The state was to provide those solutions, and unions and employers increasingly directed themselves to governments rather than to each other. This process of politicization, in other words, the turn from industrial to political action and pressure, to some extent implied a pacification of labor relations. Rather than leading to common political solutions, it increased political tension, not only between conservatives and Catholics on one hand, and socialists on the other, but also between socialists and Communists, and even among socialists.

Some of the economic measures employed to fight the crisis or mitigate its effects were widely accepted, like devaluation and tariff barriers. They were an expression of the trend toward economic self-sufficiency, meant to keep the crisis outside one's country. Another popular measure, the promotion of cartels to restrict production, did not pose large problems either, because it did not affect the state budget. Unemployment benefits did, and that made them a major issue. Because they were facing growing unemployment, most governments tried to prevent a budget deficit by raising contributions or reducing benefits, countering socialist demands to raise benefits. In Germany, the conflict was accentuated by the traumatic inflation that had paralyzed the country during the early 1920s. Bitterness contributed to the fall of the Weimar Republic. In Great Britain the issue caused a cleavage among social democrats, specifically between the TUC and the Labour government. Under the influence of John Maynard Keynes, the TUC not only forwarded the traditional (social) argument that benefits would reduce poverty, but also the new (economic) argument that benefits were an instrument of economic policy, leading to the stabilization of buying power and representing a way to combat the crisis. Not yet advanced as a systematic theory, Keynes's ideas did not enjoy a wide appeal, however, not even among social democrats. The only country where ideas along these lines were put into practice was Sweden. The social democratic government expanded public works and paid market wages to the workers involved. The intention of these wages was to maintain buying power.

Socialists in other nations, in the opposition, argued for more sweeping reforms, carrying on traditional socialist thinking. Their efforts met no success. They borrowed the notion of a national plan from the Soviet Union, though the proposed changes were more limited in scope and left part of the market economy intact. The most influential plan was the Labor Plan (*Plan van de Arbeid/Plan du travail*) developed by the Belgian socialist Hendrik de Man. Its goal was to restructure the national economy, including nationalization and expansion of public works. The plan became a guiding principle for the Belgian socialists and was praised in festive and ceremonious conferences as the only solution to the crisis. Dutch socialists imitated the plan, while socialists in France and Germany adopted some central ideas. Plan socialism never aroused much enthusiasm, however, among the socialist following.

Catholics revived the idea of corporatism. In 1931 the papal encyclical *Quadragesimo Anno* listed the advantages. Italian corporatism remained a major issue in the discussions and festive meetings that followed. Some had put aside their objections under the influence of economic developments and now praised Italy as a model of order in a world of crisis. Others continued to reject it as too statist. Focusing on voluntary corporatist arrangements, they recommended not only legal extension of collective agreements but also new anti-crisis cartel legislation. Holland was the only country that experimented with such voluntary union-employer councils, and they proved to be rather unsuccessful. In practice, only in Catholic dictatorships did a corporatist development seem viable. Rather than promoting voluntary union-employer cooperation, they imposed new structures upon resisting workers and hesitating employers. The goal was to pacify labor relations. As was the case in Italy, such corporate schemes were more an instrument of state rule than an alternative to it. The only lasting example was Portugal. State-controlled unions in that country replaced the existing syndicalist/anarchist union federation and a small Communist splinter group, both of which were outlawed. Within sectoral corporations, the new organizations were to reach collective labor agreements with the employers' associations, the latter being less subject to forced change. Labor courts could impose arbitration where cooperation failed.

The crisis made female labor another popular topic of debate. Catholics were most straightforward in their policy of keeping mother in the kitchen. They desired not only to restore or strengthen traditional family life, but also to alleviate the problem of unemployment among men. The latter argument appealed to socialists as well. Swedish social democrats were an exception in their promotion of outdoor work for women as part of their labor market policy.

LABOR RELATIONS UNDER FASCISM

Most solutions to the crisis, including the socialist plan and Catholic corporatism, emphasized national cooperation. Indeed, like the 1874 crisis, the new crash encouraged nationalism throughout Europe. Since no international cure was readily available, a national solution was sought for an international problem. Nationalism went beyond that, however. The alleged national solutions were embedded in strong symbolism and elaborate rituals. Belief in international economic progress was lost, while belief in a national solution to remedy the crisis and foster growth, as well as belief in the need for a national identity, became a substitute.

In combination with the inability of most parliamentary governments to take strong action, nationalism was at the root of a growing fascination with dictatorial authority in general and fascism in particular. Fascist movements sprang up throughout Europe, engaging in the same kind of street terror that the Italian *fasci* had used before them. The main victims were socialists and Communists. Under the influence of the Nazis, Jews were also increasingly victimized. They became the major scapegoat of the crisis. In spite of the attacks, neither socialists nor Communists worried very much. Socialists responded in a rather resigned fashion. To them, fascism was merely an outgrowth of capitalism (due to the crisis) and would soon wither away. Moreover, they feared increased state repression if they engaged in street disturbances. Since Communists had fewer scruples and less to lose, they were more reckless in their defense. They blamed the socialists (''social fascists'') for their continued support of capitalism.

Fascism turned out to be more than street terror. It represented a mass movement headed by an all-powerful leader and an insistence upon discipline, obedience, and order. These were seen as national duties needed to serve the national community. Although fascism offered employment, the insistence upon order attracted the middle class and clerical workers more than manual workers. Employers welcomed the fascist attacks on socialism and the renewed value placed on discipline and order. At first, the Nazi proclamations in Germany did not seem to offer guarantees of employer autonomy vis-à-vis the state. Even before coming to office, however, Adolf Hitler could dispel the impression among large employers that Nazism was just another brand of socialism. From then on he was supported financially, and the steel magnate Alfred Krupp became his main patron. The stability of traditional politics in other countries prevented the rise to power of fascist movements.

In Nazi Germany, even more than in Italy, fascism implied complete state control of labor relations. Control consisted of three related processes. First, autonomous organizations were crushed by state-dependent organizations. Second, order and discipline within an enterprise were to be enforced by all means as part of a national order. Any infringement or sign of opposition was to be severely punished. Third, the state-dependent organizations were to ensure a more complete integration of workers into the national community. Men were targeted more than women for this. Fascism was unambiguous in its fascination with female family duties and with motherhood in particular.

The obsession with discipline and order was shared by fascists and the system of Communist state control of labor relations. The two differed totally in their aims and the way in which they functioned, however. In contrast to the Soviet social revolution, fascism left free enterprise intact and even reinforced the position of employers. The three processes of state control mainly affected workers. Employers were involved in their application and were especially responsible for maintaining order and discipline. The main difference between fascist Italy and Nazi Germany was the ruthlessness of the latter, expressed in a greater degree of totalitarian control and state terror, and the extermination of various minorities and opponents.

Soon after Hitler's rise to power, German unions ceased to exist. In order to save their organizations, the three union federations engaged in talks with fascist leaders and took part in May 1 celebrations, proclaimed as the new day of National Labor. Nevertheless, the next day the Nazis started the *Gleichschaltung*, the fascist takeover of nonfascist organizations. Union leaders were arrested and their positions occupied by fascists. The organizations were replaced by the compulsory *Deutsche Arbeitsfront*, or DAF (German Labor Front), which organized workers as well as employers.

The second process of state control was imposing order and discipline. Although this was one of the DAF's main tasks, employers were given a free hand to deal with minor incidents of disobedience and discontent. While Italy had developed some corporatist structures as symbols of formal worker-employer cooperation in the 1930s, Germany attached little value to them. A new kind of enterprise council was set up, only to be abolished after a few years. Discipline, the regimentation of work, obedience to the employer, the revival of the idea that the employer was to be *"Herr im Hause"* (master of the house) were not masked but valued as contributions to the national cause. Collective agreements were dissolved and wages fixed regionally by state officials. In practice, wages and working time remained rather stable.

In both Italy and Germany, worker integration was served by an elaborate program of educational, recreational, and cultural services. The fascists emphasized the need for work and for free time (including vacations) as well, but most free time was to be spent in state-controlled centers of activities. The Italian organization *Dopo Lavoro* (After Work), and its German counterpart, *Kraft durch Freude* (Strength through Joy), both very large organizations, were responsible for these cultural and recreational activities. The participants were constantly imbued with a sense of pride to be a worker and the privilege to be able to contribute to the national community. Another contribution was the renewed value placed on manual work. All young men were required to spend half a year doing manual work in road construction, forestry, or agriculture. At the same time, fascism offered to restore white-collar values like hierarchy and loyalty, if not obedience and servility. The fascist new value of manual work as a contribution to the national cause did not affect the appeal of fascism among clerical workers and the middle class, since it took place within the framework of a rigid hierarchical order.

These forms of worker integration would have missed their mark under conditions of unemployment. Indeed, fascists, and in particular the Nazis, could point to a rapid drop in unemployment as a major achievement, due to an ambitious series of public works and a rapid expansion of the war industry. The reintroduction of a compulsory labor book for each worker served labor market policy as well as rearmament. The combination of employment policy, worker integration, and the regimentation of work gave many workers a new sense of belonging within the national community. Many foreign conservatives and Catholics, and even some socialists, were under the spell of this combination of employment and authority, despite the threat posed by German rearmament. German events inspired a number of dictators to impose their own brand of corporatism (for example, in Austria) or a fascist-like pacification of labor relations (for example, in Bulgaria in 1934 and Greece in 1936).

THE POPULAR FRONT

German repression and rearmament finally did start to frighten Communists. They expected not only increasing problems for their organizations but also a major war. It was clear that the Soviet Union might become involved, thereby threatening the new social order brought about by the October Revolution. Under Soviet guidance, Communists outside the Soviet Union gave up their internationalism, which had been characterized by a high degree of isolation from other political organizations. They stressed national cooperation and urged the socialists in particular to assist them in forming a national popular front, partly to remove the international isolation of the Soviet Union. Socialists accepted, though reluctantly, only where Communism represented a sizable movement. The popular front mainly affected the French model of labor relations and added to the force of political action.

The popular front rose to power in both France and Spain. In neither case did it survive long or bring about many lasting changes. The popular front governments attempted to enforce collective bargaining, but the position of the state in French-model labor relations was too disputed to allow any results. Since the state was either an ally or an enemy, it could only alienate the other side, in this case the employers. The importance of the popular front for labor relations was mainly related to the actions from the left and the subsequent reactions from the right. Both popular fronts, once terminated, also became a legend among socialists and communists. They resembled that other legend, the general strike, in that they gained appreciation because of their fighting spirit, rather than their actual success.

The French *Front populaire* was established in 1935. On July 14, the French national holiday, a mass demonstration in Paris celebrated its inception. The CGT-U was allowed to join the CGT again, on condition that it would refrain from forming separate factions or cells. Elections in 1936 brought success. The socialist Leon Blum formed a new cabinet of socialists, without Communist participation but with overt Communist support. During this time, immediately following May Day and the elections, a massive strike movement spread throughout the country. Strikes broke out spontaneously. (Before the formation of the popular front the Communists would certainly have been accused of instigating them and probably would have claimed the responsibility, too.) The strike movement continued into early June, involving 2 million workers. Strikers occupied factories, following the Italian example of 1920, not to continue production as in Italy, but to prevent the employment of blacklegs. In combination with the electoral success, the movement unleashed a wave of unbridled joy among the French proletariat. It provided workers with a renewed self-confidence, of victory over the *patronat* and liberation from the crisis. At last, it seemed, the victory of the popular front and the strike movement would turn the state into a reliable and promising ally in the struggle against employers. Among the demands put forth, abolition of absolute and arbitrary patronal power ranked high, but the demands seemed to matter less than the movement itself. Many thousands of workers rejoined the CGT, including large numbers of clerical workers.

The French patronat, in a state of complete disarray because it faced a popular front government and a nationwide strike movement, asked the former to put an end to the latter. Under the chairmanship of Leon Blum, the CGT and the employers' federation met in his temporary office at the Hôtel Matignon, Rue de Varenne. On June 7 they signed the *Accord Matignon*. It contained a series of employers' grants, including a wage increase and, more important, the pledge to engage in collective bargaining, the right to unionize, and the recognition of workers' representatives within the enterprise. The government promised prompt legislation with respect to the forty-hour work week, two weeks' paid holidays, and collective bargaining. The laws were passed with unprecedented speed, even in the French Senate. The main argument to introduce the forty-hour work week was now less related to curbing the crisis than to giving workers more time off. This was a popular theme by then, introduced from Italy and Germany, rather than from Russia. The issues touched upon by the accord were mainly an overdue recognition of union rights, already practiced to some extent in several other countries. The status of the *délégués* and union recognition were settled in a number of local and regional collective labor agreements, often the outcome of strikes that continued after the accord. A number of other issues were settled as well. The mining industry in northern France agreed to replace the Bedeaux wage system and individual payment by collective agreements covering all mines. Relations also relaxed in the metal industry. Communist groups, operating almost underground during the crisis, came into the open again. Enterprises promised to discontinue the practices of organized strikebreaking and spying on workers, until then recurrent phenomena in the metal industry. Not much of this took root, however. None of the parties were really prepared to engage in collective bargaining, and the employers complied only grudgingly. They regarded the accord and the subsequent agreements as a defeat inflicted by a socialist or Communist strike movement assisted by a hostile government. They blamed their own federal leaders, too, and removed them from office. The employers changed the name of their CGPF, to express more clearly its first priority: Henceforth, the P stood for *patronat* instead of *production*. Employers also evaded or undid other reforms that the popular front had tried to introduce, and a large capital flight was another consequence. Socialists and Communists were divided about this determined resistance, which left the government even less room to maneuver. The suspension of reforms in March 1937 caused a series of protest strikes and some bloody incidents in the Paris region. The front was defeated in elections the next year.

The French electoral success in 1936 was imitated in Spain. Elections in Spain unleashed a wave of strikes and riots instigated by the large anarchist movement.

The turn to the left, combined with strikes and riots, some of them directed against Church property, brought about an early conservative and Catholic response. In the civil war that followed many employers supported Francisco Franco, as did large parts of the state bureaucracy. While Franco marched on and reversed most social legislation in the conquered territories, the threatened republic introduced sweeping reforms, like the expropriation of banks and large enterprises, and union control of communal and state services like transport and electricity. Workers' control spread especially in Catalonia, where the anarchist union coordinated the experiments. German and Italian military support for Franco turned the civil war into an international conflict. An International Brigade, consisting of 40,000 socialists, Communists, anarchists, and left-wing liberals from all over Europe was formed to fight Franco and the Italian brigades committed to his cause. Communists took a leading role in the brigade, as Soviet involvement increased. Several future Communist leaders acted as political commissars, keeping an eye upon the non-Communists in the brigade. The large Soviet and Communist influence in Catalonia caused a split between them and the many anarchists in this region. The Russians and other Communists insisted upon strict discipline and authority in order to be able to stand up to the fascist troops. They also wanted to confine the social revolution to a bare minimum, in order not to lose the support of nonsocialists. Some anarchists agreed, but most of them considered the social revolution to be the very *raison d'être* of the republic, to be stopped neither by outside aggression nor by Communist state discipline. The tension led to a small civil war within the republican area. In May 1937 Communist-dominated police troops started a ruthless campaign in Barcelona to liquidate the anarchists. Many foreign anarchists had already left the International Brigade by then, fleeing from Russian Communists rather than Spanish fascists. In 1939 the war was over. The fascist victory allowed them to impose their 1938 labor charter (*Fuere de Trabajo*) on all Spanish workers. The charter was a mixture of fascist hierarchy and corporatist cooperation.

Popular fronts were also formed in some other southern and eastern European countries, but they were unable to stop the trend toward dictatorship or to survive for long under such authoritarian rule. An example was Poland, where in 1936–1937 a popular front directed the course of a major strike movement and a series of factory occupations. Violent clashes between working-class demonstrators and police troops in Kraków and L'vov resulted in a number of casualties.

TRUCE IN THE SMALLER COUNTRIES

The smaller countries characterized by German-type labor relations were not affected by the trend toward dictatorship. Yet, the rise of German fascism and of national fascist movements made unions and employers more compromising in their mutual contacts, paving the way for a successful and voluntary pacification of labor relations. Because strikes proved to be fertile soil for fascist actions, industrial peace became a growing concern. The rise of the popular front in France and Spain was a second motive. It strengthened the determination to avoid conflicts, notably among employers, who feared an international growth of worker militancy. Their expectations were valid, since the French strikes in 1936 were followed by similar actions in Belgium, where no popular front was involved. The socialist and Catholic unions were unable to stop the spontaneous actions, which started in the port of Antwerp. Consequently, they backed the strikes and transformed them into a single strike movement, the largest in Belgian history. In later years, growing international tension and the threat of war added a third motive for more union-employer understanding.

The trend toward compromise and cooperation was demonstrated in politics as well by the increasing participation of socialists in government. In contrast to what had happened to the popular front governments, socialist participation in government in countries characterized by German-model labor relations encouraged union-employer agreement, first, because the unions did not want to paralyze the socialists in government by calling strikes. Especially in Scandinavia, where socialists were strongly represented or even dominated government, employers considered the government to be on the unions' side. Consequently, a second reason why socialist participation in government contributed to employer-union compromise was that employers complied with some form of mutual understanding with the unions in order to keep government out of labor relations. Although the sense of compromise and cooperation did not totally pacify labor relations (in other words, prevent all labor conflict), it was the beginning of a new stage in German-model labor relations.

In 1935 Norwegian employers and unions took some groundbreaking initiatives after the highly contentious beginning of the decade in that country. They reached a Basic Agreement (*Hovedavtale*), which was reminiscent of the 1899 Danish agreement, expressing their intention to solve labor disputes without recourse to strikes or lockouts. Belgium followed in 1936. A National Labor Conference, resembling Matignon, put an end to the large strike wave. Like their French counterparts, Belgian employers were initially furious about the government's alleged bowing to the unions' intransigence. In contrast to France, collective bargaining was soon resumed on a large scale, often in newly created paritary committees. After union demonstrations, Luxembourg established a National Labor Council in the same year. In 1937, employers and unions in the Swiss metal industry, without any bargaining tradition up to that point, signed a Peace Treaty (*Friedensvertrag*). It stipulated that important changes in wages and any introduction of the Bedeaux system should be dealt with by the organizations, not by the enterprises themselves. The new trend of truces or peace treaties reached a high point in 1938 with the Swedish Saltsjöbaden Agreement, named after the summer resort near Stockholm where the talks took place. Like the Norwegian document, it became the basic agreement for national labor relations. It contained detailed procedures to be followed in case of labor market problems (that is, labor disputes). A Labor Market Committee was set up to take charge of central-level negotiations between the federations. In several other German-model countries, bargaining was encouraged by novel legislation in the late 1930s (for example, Luxembourg in 1936, Holland in 1937, and Iceland in 1938). It was especially an expression of growing government involvement in wage bargaining in Holland. It set the country apart from most other small nations, where the truces were reached to prevent such involvement.

The labor truces, most of them concluded between the national federations, set the German model of labor relations (no longer applying to Germany) apart from the French model. In the latter, conflicts and political strikes (against a new conservative government) continued to characterize labor relations. Fascism, a popular front, and even the threat of war were too far off in the British Isles to have much impact on the British labor relations model. Even where they were interrupted by the war, the German-model truces represented important starting points of postwar union-employer relations.

8

The Second World War and the Period of Recovery

THE SECOND WORLD WAR

The Second World War provided the Nazis with the opportunity to impose their order and their theories of race in large parts of Europe. Both within Germany and in the occupied countries, workers of different nationalities were treated according to their "race." The Germanic people in the Low Countries and Scandanavia, as well as the French, were less well off than the Germans themselves, but their treatment compared very favorably to the fate of the Slavs, especially Poles and Russians.

In Germany the conditions of German workers were stabilized. Although labor discipline was tightened, it stopped short of full work mobilization. The thousands of Dutch, Belgians, and French, most of them unemployed, who went to Germany voluntarily worked under comparable conditions, though they put in longer hours and were subject to a stricter labor discipline. To cope with labor motivation problems, especially among foreign workers, labor camps were set up to punish (officially to "educate") people by assigning them very heavy work for ten to twelve hours a day. The Poles and the Russians, who were deported forcibly, had to work under such conditions permanently. They remained in camps and were left to their fate if they became exhausted or ill.

German policies in the occupied countries varied markedly. Poland and the occupied part of the Soviet Union were subject to full colonial exploitation. Industry was expropriated and dismantled. Moreover, the extermination of Jews affected Poland the most. The Danube countries and the Balkans were slightly better off. Outside the Soviet Union, eastern European labor, already more militant than in the western part of the continent, became the core of national resistance movements. The course of the struggle contributed to a further radicalization. Many employers in eastern Europe tried to flee before the arrival of the Germans. Some of them even were successful at sending parts of their plants abroad.

The Germanic countries and France were treated better. They were allowed some autonomy and could retain their national industries but had to attune them to German needs. The Germans even introduced some improvements in labor conditions in western Europe. Their first concern was unemployment, which plagued several countries as a consequence of wartime disruption. Public authorities were pressed to take appropriate measures, for instance by improving labor exchanges, public works, and extensions of social welfare. A second concern was the introduction of a national minimum wage, which could be advantageous to rural labor in particular. For this reason, rural labor supported the Germans in some countries, at least for a while. A statutory wage policy, replacing collective bargaining, stabilized the rest of the wage structure.

Elements of a corporatist order were introduced in western Europe, either under German pressure, or as a homemade brew of fascist, Catholic, and right-wing social democratic ideas. The unoccupied part of France, fascist Vichy France, promulgated a labor charter in October 1940. Though it provided for mixed councils, not much came of this initiative. French industry also reintroduced its own methods of control. like spying on workers and employing individual piece rates. Such actions had been discounted in 1936, but evidently there was no commitment involved.

Unions and employers' organizations in western Europe were left with little other choice than to adapt to fascist supervision or dissolve. The outcome was basically dissolution, but there were some efforts in the Low Countries, mainly by socialists (less by Catholics) to retain their organizations under fascist control. Some leading socialists were concerned that the Catholic organizations would be allowed to continue and usurp the socialist following. A more positive motivation was that collaboration at last offered the opportunity to establish one national union movement, to be dominated by socialists because of their larger numbers. Others simply admired the way that German workers were integrated into society, conveniently overlooking the degree of repression involved. Employers' associations were dissolved either as part of the corporatist framework, like that in Vichy France, or by the employers themselves. Employers in Holland no longer saw a function for their organization after Catholic and Protestant unions had been dissolved. During a later stage of the war, representatives of employers and labor in the Low Countries resumed mutual contacts in secret talks, focusing on postwar labor relations. In contrast, the war increased the distance between employers and labor in France, where overt collaboration of employers was rather widespread, if only because collaboration offered the opportunity to fight union militants.

Initially, Communists were shocked by the 1939 German-Soviet pact. In France, the CGT asked all its members to condemn the pact openly in order to prevent anti-Communist feelings from turning into anti-CGT measures. This resulted in a factual split. Communists left the organization and revived the semilegal network of *triangles*, now spread more widely among the new union recruits of 1936. Communists played a prominent role in resistance movements not only in France, but throughout Europe after the German invasion of western Europe (April–May 1940). They became even more committed after the German invasion of the Soviet Union (June 1941). They were also very influential in the strikes that were called in the occupied territories, in spite of heavy reprisals. Most of the actions were aimed at wage adaptation, commonly in combination with protests against poorly functioning food supply programs. Such strikes rarely exceeded one working day in order to prevent repressive countermeasures. In May 1941, however, thousands of miners in the north of France and in Wallony held out for more than a week.

The transition to total war in 1942 changed German policy toward the occupied territories. It imposed labor mobilization, but also a massive deportation of labor in Germany. In light of fascist ideas surrounding a woman's place in the home, foreign labor rather than women had to fill the vacancies. The Sauckel campaigns, named for the German official responsible, forced 650,000 workers to leave France, while Belgium had to send monthly quotas of 10,000 during 1943. Under total war conditions, the Germans also became more interested in exploiting the Poles and Russians than in exterminating them. Jews could sometimes even prolong their lives for some time by working in factories within or near the extermination camps. The camps were the domain of the paramilitary SS organization. Despite the low productivity of the prisoners, due to bad physical conditions and early exhaustion, their sheer numbers provided the SS with a large economic potential. German industrialists opposed the economic power and cheap labor that these camps enjoyed. They received permission to set up their own enterprises within or near the concentration camps, where SS prisoners were subjected to forced labor. IG Farben, a chemical giant, even saw fit to establish a subsidiary in Auschwitz. Instead of wages, the firms paid a small amount to the SS for each prisoner-worker.

The Soviet Union and Great Britain also converted to a full-fledged war economy. War preparations in the Soviet Union led to renouncing the seven-hour work day. The eight-hour workday was restored in 1940. The Soviet Union also officially returned to the work week of six days. The German attack in 1941 caused enormous social upheaval. While the Germans forced a migration, the Russians themselves retreated while dismantling complete industrial plants and infrastructural works, some of them constructed shortly before. They were moved to the Urals and rebuilt. Most workers moved as well. The upheaval involved 10 million people, for whom new living space and other provisions had to be created almost overnight. A total mobilization of labor was in force during the war. New labor camps were set up to punish truancy and any lack of labor discipline. Mobilization affected women most of all. They soon formed the majority of the industrial labor force.

The Russian efforts to mobilize women for industrial work were even surpassed by the British. Various devices were tried, like deliberately keeping soldiers' pay low, campaigns of voluntary mobilization, and support services like day nurseries. Due to union and employer resistance, equal pay did not constitute part of the measures. Ernest Bevin, labor minister and former secretary of the dockers union and the Transport and General Workers' Union, was responsible for these policies. The TUC was also actively engaged in the government campaign to buttress labor discipline and productivity. Order 1305 declared strikes illegal, and a National Arbitration Tribunal was set up to issue binding decisions with respect to labor conditions. The influence of shop stewards (and their numbers) increased again, but production was their major concern. Together with management they took part in Joint Production Councils. Because of the rise of semiskilled work before the war and the ample availability of skilled workers, dilution was felt to be less of a problem than during the First World War. Therefore, unions rather readily gave up restrictive trade practices, the more so because the government pledged to lift the wartime measures as soon as the war was over.

In Britain, the growth of female employment in industry and the hardship caused by German air raids contributed to the popularity of welfare provisions and of social security in particular. Two plans for a more active social and economic policy stood out and provided two major themes of postwar labor relations that would influence not only British but also continental social and economic developments.

First, a report was issued by William Beveridge in 1942 on social insurance. The report proclaimed war against the Five Giants (Idleness, Ignorance, Squalor, Disease, and Want) by means of an extensive system of social welfare and health care. Maternity grants, sickness benefits, industrial injury and unemployment benefits, retirement pensions, widows' benefits, and death grants were to be made available to the whole population. They would secure at least a subsistence-level living for everyone, and ultimately these programs were to put an end to traditional poor relief. Benefits and contributions were to be equal for all. The proposals differed from the continental tradition, which was influenced by Bismarck's social insurance, consisting of income-related benefits and contributions confined to workers. To the liberal Beveridge, income-related insurance was to remain the realm of private initiative and additional individual or collective arrangements.

Second, the 1944 White Paper on Employment Policy advocated Keynesian economic policy and demanded that management maintain full employment. Beveridgian social security fit well into this framework.

In the small neutral countries like Switzerland and Sweden there was less state involvement. The prewar truces remained in force. Finland added a comparable wartime truce in January 1940, when the country was under Russian attack. In contrast to most prewar truces, this January Engagement (*tammikuun kihlaus*) of employers and unions did not build upon a previous tradition of collective bargaining. Like those truces it provided a base for postwar bargaining.

The previous observations point to the conclusion that the effects of the war on labor relations differed along the lines of the existing models. Governments within the British model had to bring about the wartime pacification of labor relations. This took the form of imposing arbitration in Britain and a statutory wage policy in (neutral) Ireland. In line with the British model tradition, the Irish unions opposed the 1941 Wages Standstill Order. Apart from Germany, Austria, and Czechoslovakia, where any attempt at autonomous unionism was suppressed by every means, the German model continued its tradition of adaptation and truces, mostly between the national federations. The agreements were concluded overtly in the neutral countries and in Denmark, which escaped occupation, while they were the result of secret talks in the Low Countries. In France, both labor and employers used the war almost as an extension of politics to continue their conflict. In the rest of Europe, labor relations were pacified forcibly, under corporatism, fascism, or the Soviet model.

THE PARTICIPANTS IN POSTWAR LABOR RELATIONS

The most profound feature of postwar labor relations was the degree of direct state involvement. The enormous destruction caused by the war and the resulting expectation of a long process of reconstruction were the central motives for this increased governmental role. Most governments took for granted that they had so much control over this process because of their wartime residence and their composition. First, a number of governments had spent the war in exile. They had become acquainted with Keynesian and Beveridgian ideas in London, good remedies, it seemed, to prevent new growth of unemployment. Leading Communists from central and eastern Europe had been exiled in Moscow and returned with the urge to revive a national or popular front consisting of all progressive forces. Second, conservatives and Catholics had not been very firm in their opposition to fascism and now for some time left initiatives in the political arena to the Left. Moreover, German policy had implied the disappearance of large employers in the occupied countries of Eastern Europe. This provided social democrats and Communists, the latter quite prominent in the wartime national resistance movements, an opportunity to set the agenda.

Communists could retain their positions of power in the countries liberated by the Red Army and now under Soviet supervision. Elections decided on their fate in western Europe. They needed to be content with a minor role alongside the social democrats and later the reactivated conservatives and Catholics as well. Only in France and Italy were Communists able to remain in the forefront of politics.

A new phenomenon in unionism was the rise of a unified or unitary union movement (*syndicalisme unifié, Einheitsgewerkschaft*) in many countries. It was rooted in the resistance movement or even represented a direct continuation of it. Leadership was in the hands of Communists and other militant members of the prewar labor movement. At its inception at least, unified (or unitary) unionism was the expression of popular mood. This mood favored national unity after so much common suffering and hardship. The Communist-promoted national or popular front offered it the brightest future and was in line with the general political perspectives of the movement. In the countries under Soviet supervision, the unified union movement became a centralized force under Communist guidance in politics and labor relations. Traditional organizations had been relatively small, except in Czechoslovakia, and opposition against the unified movement could easily be construed as opposition against national unity and the Communist liberator.

The stronghold of unified unionism in western Europe was Italy. The movement's rise in that country was encouraged by the early elimination of socialist organizations and by the remaining organizational network of the Communist movement. The increasing opposition to fascism and to the forces that had supported it (like the Church and employers' organizations) represented another contribution to its growth. Communists were especially active in creating the new union movement. The new organization was no more than a loose confederation of member unions, which organized Communists and socialists as well as Catholics. Before the rise of fascism, Italian unionism, in particular in the industrialized northern part of the country, had shared some characteristics of the German model. The long absence of social democracy and the rise of the Communist-dominated unified movement meant a shift to the French model of unionism. The CGT in France also integrated socialists and Communists again. However, they also remained rather autonomous within the confederation. The small Catholic union continued its existence alongside the CGT. Unified unionism also became a force of importance for some time in the Low Countries. Initially, socialists and Catholics favored some form of unity, but both rejected the political priorities of unified unionism and soon revived their own unions. The socialist union movement maintained its strong cooperation with the Socialist party, while Catholic unionism again revealed its heavy promotion and domination by the Catholic Church.

Germany was divided. The Russians promoted an *Einheitsgewerkschaft*, with rapidly increasing membership. The British and Americans valued grass-roots activities as part of the process toward democracy in their zones. They opposed heavy centralization in any domain, because they believed it would lead to strong state power and facilitate another takeover of such centralized organizations by the state. As a consequence, they allowed local initiatives, except those aimed at a national *Einheitsgewerkschaft*. The British Labour government sent TUC representatives in an advisory role. In line with the recommendations of American unions, they advocated a return to industrial unions. The federation that would coordinate their activities was to be a very weak one, like the TUC itself. Accordingly, a new union federation, *Deutscher Gewerkschaftsbund* (DGB), was set up in the British zone in 1947. Later it became the new West German union federation. In accordance with the German-model tradition the DGB redeveloped an extensive network of social provisions, including a very large housing fund called *Neue Heimat*. Power in the federation rested with the sixteen member unions, which were organized along sectoral lines. The new organization thus carried on the principle of industrial unionism, not that of unified unionism, in spite of the earlier plans for strict centralization, developed by the first DGB president Hans Böckler. Nevertheless, the DGB was a unified organization in two respects. First, it became the only general union federation without Catholic or other rival organizations alongside it. The DGB adhered to formal neutrality in politics, in order to prevent the rise of such rival federations, though there were intimate informal links with the Socialist party. Second, the DGB did not admit any separate white-collar organizations.

As was the case at the end of the First World War, the Second World War unleashed a wave of organizational activity among clerical workers and state employees. New organizations arose, coordinating existing and newly created associations, both within and outside the major union federations. As a formative stage, the period resembled the one that gave rise to national union federations at the turn of the century. Three types of unions came to represent clerical workers and state employees as a result of this process of expansion, amalgamation, and organization.

First, separate clerical unions within the larger federations were a continuation of prewar organizations and were predominant in the British model and in a few countries, like Belgium, characterized by the German model. There were still a large number of status-based unions in the British model, while the organizations increasingly amalgamated into one or two unions in the German model (one for clerical workers and one for the public sector). Second, the new DGB explicitly carried on the principle of industrial, or sectoral, unions. Separate white-collar unions were no longer admitted. The new sectoral unions organized both manual and clerical workers, without any status distinction. They were dominated by manual workers in manufacturing and by clerical workers in the service industry. In other countries, such mixed unions, which recruited manual as well as clerical workers, existed side by side with clerical organizations.

Apart from a few countries like Austria, Belgium, and Ireland, where the major federations had a virtual monopoly, a third form of clerical workers' organizations came into existence after the war. This form consisted of large independent federations, coordinating existing or newly created unions of clerical workers and state employees. Consequently, separate or mixed organizations within the major federations often faced a new and independent federation, specifically directed at clerical workers and state employees. In France, the *Confédération générale des cadres* (CGC), created in 1944, was a reaction against Beveridgian social security proposals, which were deemed too egalitarian. In general, it organized technicians and lower and middle management instead of white-collar workers. More than in other countries, this category was subject to the patriarchal authority of the corporate elite in the centralized French companies. It was therefore more willing to organize. In Sweden, a union federation not related to the general socialist federation started to organize state employees and clerical workers (*tjänstemännen*). It was to become the largest white-collar organization in Europe. Similar union federations were created in the rest of Scandinavia and in Finland. At a later stage, these Scandinavian organizations were followed by smaller federations that were exclusively involved in organizing associations of academicians. In West Germany, two independent organizations were set up, one for clerical workers (*Angestellte*), and one for state employees (*Beamte*). State employee organization addressed primarily civil servants and clerical workers in public services. Manual workers in the public service sector remained a part, or even the backbone, of the major federations. Consequently there was almost as much variation within as between the distinctive models of unionism in the structure of clerical unionism.

The position of employers as an organized party in labor relations was weakened by numerous charges that they had complied quite readily with German orders or had supported the fascist cause outright. Even where most charges were dismissed, employers themselves preferred to remain in the background for some time. On the other hand, employers had also been engaged in wartime talks with unions about postwar reforms. They therefore became involved in direct negotiations with government and unions in several countries. To indicate that they had distanced themselves from wartime events and that they supported an increase in decisionmaking at the central level, employers' organizations were reorganized and renamed. A new French organization, *Conseil national du patronat français* (CNPF), was established in 1945. The employers' organizations' fresh start was motivated by a need to extend their sphere of influence. They would have more say in issues that might be raised in central-level contracts (relating to the larger domain of state policy). The separation between employers' organizations and economic or trade associations was often continued, for instance in West Germany. Large enterprises were nationalized at once in Eastern Europe, which left virtually no room for employers' organizations. The same applied to the Russian zone in Germany. Initially, employers' organizations in the other zones were allowed at the local level only, in order to prevent the revival of big industry as a political pressure group. The foundation of the DGB was followed by the rise of a new employers' federation, *Bundesvereinigung der deutschen Arbeitgeberverbände* (Federal Union of German Employer Federations). In contrast to the prewar VDA, the BDA organized employers not only in manufacturing but also in banking and insurance, transport, and other service industries.

Relations between the three participants in labor relations developed along diverse lines. In the German model, prewar and wartime truces and contacts with the government facilitated postwar mutual understanding. Belgian talks in 1944 resulted in a Concept Pact of Social Solidarity, in which a state wage policy for the reconstruction period was outlined. Also included were a system of social security and several institutions devoted to employer-union contacts. Most of the proposals of the pact were implemented. Dutch employers and union representatives had also agreed to cooperate, but they had to give in to a returning government that favored more state control. The prewar and wartime contacts created the basis for a series of postwar settlements, which ranged from an extension of an existing truce in bargaining (for example, in Switzerland) to full-fledged and formal settlements involving national governments (in other nations). In the latter case they could cover a range of subjects, like reconstruction policy, Keynesian economic policy, wages and prices, social welfare, state consultation by unions and employers, and union-employer relations. Indeed, the postwar economy and the reconstruction period was envisioned as one of consultation and negotiation instead of strike and strife. The process of reconstruction and the introduction of Keynesian economic policy in a number of countries were considered to be a shared responsibility of the governments, unions, and employers, thus requiring common efforts and mutual contacts. Some of the postwar settlements were translated into official agreements, while others consisted of a number of related formal or informal arrangements.

The formal or informal links in the German model between the social democratic and Catholic unions and the social democratic and Christian democratic parties in government favored state support for the settlement and their implementation. The participation of Communists in government silenced opposition within the unions. The settlements and the revival of bargaining contributed to a reduction in the number of labor conflicts, setting the German model apart from the other models, characterized by higher strike rates.

The other models lacked this kind of coordination. There was only a limited mutual understanding that central coordination of wage talks should be continued in the British model. Postwar talks pertaining to economic policy in France and Italy took place between the governments and employers. The Italian union confederation and the CGT were excluded from such contacts but were also not very eager to become involved. Nevertheless, as was the case in the British model, unions and employers in both countries felt the need for a system with a central coordination of bargaining. Such a system would be part of or an alternative to a statutory wage policy. There was less room for autonomous decisionmaking outside the state in the rest of Europe. The Iberian Peninsula continued its corporatism, and the Soviet Union the Soviet model. In the countries under Communist influence, the Communists only reluctantly allowed some deliberation. Communist control of the (unified) union movement, their hold on government, and the nature of such control impeded discussion, however. It also stifled any opposition to state measures. The absence of employers' organizations further reduced the need for discussion.

In short, the prewar models of labor relations were revived, with more state involvement and centralization than before the war. A few countries shifted from one model to another. In Finland, the wartime truce became the basis for the adoption of German model labor relations. In Czechoslovakia the German model was deserted. This country joined the other nations of Eastern Europe and came under Soviet influence. Italy had combined characteristics of the German and the French models before the rise of fascism. The rise of Communism made the country shift to the French model, in which high priority was given to political action. The link between the union movement and the Communist party was far less binding than in France, however, and bargaining was more acceptable to employers and unions.

THE ISSUES

Reconstruction

The nationalization of crucial sectors of the economy, for example, mining, railways, parts of banking, and heavy industry, became a common feature of economic policy in Europe. As in the period after the First World War, nationalization was carried out to a lesser extent in the German model. In the rest of Europe the absence of private entrepreneurs or private investment funds and the central role of these sectors in reconstruction policy facilitated nationalization trends. The contribution of these private sectors to warmongering in the nations that had supported the Germans (and in France) provided an additional argument here. In Germany itself, only the Soviet Union introduced nationalization in its zone. After nationalization, industrial enterprises were dismantled and transported to the Soviet Union as reparation payments.

Most countries heavily affected by the war also started to experiment with some type of state planning of the economy. Central planning represented either a completely new course, as in France, or just a temporary measure to allocate scarce raw materials during the reconstruction period. Industrial production was the top priority, and coal mining was especially targeted for stimulation in any way possible.

More generally, the need to prevent a new rise in unemployment transformed Keynesian state intervention into a dominant trend in economic policy. Social security expansion was one of its components. Social democrats were the most devoted advocates, but Catholics and liberals heartily accepted it as well. Communists favored more direct state control of the economy and had less concern for purchasing power or for consumer goods.

The reconstruction efforts caused a number of changes in the nature of employment and the composition of the work force. By far the most important development was the recruitment of women. Though the war had enhanced the appreciation for family life and the role of women as housewives, women became involved in the reconstruction of industry throughout Europe. Since industrial employment offered higher wages and more freedom, it almost put an end to the domestic service industry, probably the largest single employment opportunity for women until the Second World War. The increasing numbers of female workers in manual and clerical jobs did not alter their inferior position. They had to settle for the lower wage scales in all sectors of the economy and were paid less for the same work.

Wages

Socialist and Communist participation in government and the expectation that great societal change was imminent, convinced the continental unions to put the wages issue into governmental hands. The most immediate state concern during this period of ever-rising prices was wage control. Wages were to be stabilized, fluctuating only slightly with price increases. Inflation was not to get out of hand under any circumstances. The relation between wages and prices was at the heart of an almost general and rather extensive wage policy, which continued during the 1950s in some places. This would also have effects on wage determination in later years. Employers and unions were just as determined to prevent a wage and price drift. They supported the more general features of this policy and were commonly involved quite directly in its formation or implementation. Price stability proved to be an uphill struggle, however. In countries where food rationing continued, a black market also continued to exist. The end of rationing did not solve the problem, because officially fixed prices made the black market flourish once again. The high prices paid there represented a constant challenge to wage policy.

After the war, several governments initially reenacted the wage decisions that had been taken just before the war or under German occupation. A one-time and fixed wage increase, ranging from 10 to 50 percent, was meant to offset the deterioration during the last months or immediate aftermath of the war. It was intended to provide some breathing space until a more systematic wage structure could be introduced. New systems were designed, consisting of separate wage scales for each industry, taking into account the traditional differentials between skilled and unskilled, male and female, urban and rural wages. Higher wages were to remain at the same level; the lower scales were increased slightly. Another small step in the direction of more equality was the introduction of a national minimum wage in some countries. It applied mainly to women and children, since they were at the bottom of the wage scales or had their own (low) scales. Commonly, the minimum wage was combined with a compulsory forty-eight-hour work week and sometimes also with a ban on dismissals. The goal was to provide all members of the national work force with at least minimal living conditions. Even if the measures applied to clerical workers, the latter could evade a wage policy rather easily, due to their career prospects and their long road to a maximum salary.

In the German model (apart from Germany) and the French model, wage policies took the form of collective bargaining under state supervision. This implied bargaining within the limits set by the government, sometimes in co-ordination with central employers' and union representatives. Governments preferred and promoted sectoral bargaining because it was easier to control than enterprise bargaining. The latter was often restricted to the detailed application of sectoral agreements. Central unions and employers' organizations only rarely engaged directly in sectoral bargaining, but when this was the case they were deeply involved. They either had previously reached an agreement with the government regarding the maximum wage increase to be allowed, or else they advised the government whether to approve sectoral agreements. Sometimes they did both. In Belgium, the government, unions, and employers' organizations met several times at National Labor Conferences to discuss the wage structure and the size of wage increases to be allowed in the paritary committees. The Dutch and French governments used their right to extend collective agreements as an instrument to impose their wage policies. The spread of bargaining in France was due in part to government pressure and to the Communist participation in reconstruction policies. This particular combination made employers and unions comply with bargaining under supervision.

In the British model, and in the German-model countries less affected by the war (like Scandinavia and Switzerland), unions and employers' organizations confined themselves to voluntary wage restraint, sometimes after government appeal. Labor courts were set up in some of these countries to facilitate nego-tiations, solve disputes, and impose discipline. In contrast, wage policies were highly centralized in the countries under Communist influence, though informally some room was left for decisions within nationalized enterprises.

Two developments hampered attempts to restrain and to systematize wages. First, the almost universal need to establish or reestablish heavy industry and mining made a major issue out of wages in these sectors. The issue demanded immediate solutions, without awaiting the creation of more elaborate wage sys-tems. Various solutions were attempted, including wage increases exclusive to those sectors, enterprise-related fringe benefits such as free coal supplies, and special bonuses for new workers.

The second development disturbing the creation of elaborate wage scales was the rising cost of living, due to the failure of price controls. Countries that had a more stringent wage policy, like France and Holland, allowed normal wage increases under strict supervision in order to offset rising prices. Countries that had earlier gone or returned to employer-union bargaining preferred premiums (to supplement wages) as a temporary device, leaving the recently introduced wage scales intact. Italy introduced a gliding scale (*scala mobile*) to adapt wages to prices, but this step did not prevent new premiums. Most premiums missed their goal of being temporary. On occasion they would even surpass regular wages. Unions consequently exercised pressure to include them in regular wages. Once such wage adaption had taken place, ongoing inflation led the unions to ask for new premiums, to be included in wages later on. The lag in wages caused discontent among the unions' following and gave rise to spontaneous strikes, in particular in busy sectors like mining, ports, and heavy industry. The unions tried to stop such strikes. Communist leaders even condemned strikers as being supporters of big business and held to a very strict wage policy in the countries where they exercised or shared state power. Nevertheless, the strikes caused tension within the unions. While Communists tried to reinforce the existing measures, socialists and Catholics advocated a return to collective bargaining.

In Western Europe state control was soon reduced and rationing given up. Only in Germany did the allied powers adhere to it until 1948 and refuse to allow bargaining, prolonging wartime wage measures instead.

Social Security

The popularity of Keynes's and Beveridge's ideas was instrumental in making social security one of the major topics of employer-union (and government) contacts and of political debate. The Beveridge proposals were in line with the traditional socialist preference for more unification and for compulsory socialist security. After the war socialists readily took over these ideas. Although the Communists were less devoted to the issue, they did not want to be outdone in Western Europe. Key issues were the degree of central control and of uniformity. Socialists favored a compulsory, centralized, and uniform system, without the traditional inequalities in benefit rights. The unions could remain administrative agents within the new system, but overall responsibility would reside with the state, which would raise funds through progressive taxes. In contrast, employers, Catholics, and conservatives tended to prefer some extension of the traditional system. Such a system was to retain differences in social welfare for the various categories of workers and nonworkers and leave the administration in the hands of employers and unions. Since Catholics and conservatives were unable to regain strength until some years after the war, the subject was not a hot issue at first. Socialists could pass some of their own proposals as part of the more general postwar settlements. In later years, conservative and Catholic opposition removed opportunities to take such actions, and the return to traditional social welfare schemes reinforced differentiation again. Without exception, clerical workers could retain their privileges (for example, earnings-related old age pensions rather than flat rates).

Even when traditional elements of the Bismarckian system were retained, social security was often completely recast. In accordance with previous legislation, and in line with governmental makeup, the new systems differed to some extent along the lines of the distinct models of labor relations. Social welfare in Great Britain conformed to the Beveridgian ideas, and the same applied more or less to Scandinavia, where social democrats were in power. In the other countries characterized by the German model, social welfare became a mix of Bismarckian and Beveridgian elements. In France, a *Caisse unique* was introduced in 1946, but the French system continued its differentiation. Gender differences in treatment were common to most systems, since both the Bismarckian and the Beveridgian schemes applied mainly to male workers, who were regarded as the wage earners for their families.

Consultation Institutions

Wage policy, social security, and the Keynesian government involvement in the economy made German-model countries look for formal and informal devices of union and employer advice. Institutions for such common advice already existed in a number of countries, but none of them had gained importance and they advised only rarely if at all. Consultation and deliberation institutions were a topic of discussion in tripartite government-union-employer or bipartite employer-union contacts. They were a central component of the postwar settlements in the German model.

On occasion, such institutions were referred to as corporatist. Indeed, they were a form of corporatism, since they gave employers' organizations and unions a central role in the making and sometimes also in the execution of social and economic policy. But they differed considerably from traditional corporatism, which had been regarded as an alternative to state policy, and even more from fascist state corporatism, which had been an instrument of state oppression. The introduction of a strict wage policy especially created an immediate need for consultative committees or councils. Legal enactment of such institutions was often retarded by two developments. The first was disagreement on the number of organizations to be represented, especially with regard to the union side. Not until the unified union movement had broken up or had been isolated by the traditional organizations was the issue solved. The second was the expectation that such advisory bodies might interfere with the role of parliament in politics at a time when parliamentary activity was being resumed. Legislation was often postponed until the end of the 1940s or even later. Meanwhile, advice was given in formal or informal meetings, for example the Belgian Labor Conferences or the Swedish Thursday Club, involving the government, employers, and unions.

Union and worker representation within enterprises represented another problem to be solved through legislation or union-employer agreement, though the nature of such representation was a hotly debated topic. The role of union representation within corporations had been developed quite thoroughly in the British model, but the British shop stewards remained a rather exceptional case. Representation had already been given a formal status in Scandinavia, but its position was very modest, limited by all kinds of guarantees against independent action. Although the nature of the French model ruled out any formal regulations, it also gave union activists considerable informal freedom of action. The absence of unionism in the occupied countries during the war had encouraged the rise of illegal enterprise unionism. On the continent, however, this type of unionism had been heavily prosecuted by the Germans and by many indigenous employers as well. After the war, enterprise unionism was extended and was given a formal status in some countries characterized by the German model (for instance in Belgium in 1947). Both unions and employers made great effort to keep such enterprise unionism in check. The former feared that it would interfere with union-employer bargaining; the latter feared interference with employer decisionmaking in technology and work processes. Unions in Holland even explicitly refrained from establishing any type of representation within enterprises.

During the period of reconstruction (and in some nonoccupied countries during the war) raising productivity was the main reason for establishing official employer-union institutions or employer–work force cooperation within enterprises. In addition to productivity, a second motive in several countries on the continent was the reaction against fascism and the fascist reinforcement of entrepreneurial power. The support of the fascist cause by German employers and others gave rise to a notion of power sharing or at least of worker consultation. This would supposedly prevent any repetition of such war support.

Two developments in the postwar period encouraged the spread of consultation as a tool. First was the nationalization of large enterprises, and second was the introduction of a new school of management from North America. The nationalization of large enterprises had only limited effects on labor relations, since production, not worker control, was the first priority. To some extent nationalization improved the position of the unions, in particular in Great Britain where some union leaders were appointed as the managers of nationalized firms. The novel North American ideas in labor psychology and sociology stemmed from the human relations school. It advocated worker consultation and more generally a revaluation of human relations in the firm. Both were seen as remedies against worker desinterest or opposition.

The particular shape that the institutions of cooperation and consultation took depended on the nature of union representation within the enterprise. The shop stewards and the employers in Britain continued the wartime practice of raising production (Joint Production Councils). This extended and formalized the position of the shop stewards. The three Scandinavian countries had laid down the functions and the limits of enterprise representation in their prewar basic agreements. From 1945 on they also introduced something similar to joint production councils, or cooperative councils, in which at least all union representatives participated.

Other countries characterized by the German model followed a different course: Representation of the enterprise work force as a whole took place in a works council or enterprise council. Works councils implied a clear distinction between union and work force. The distinction was popular among employers, and among Catholics and conservatives in politics, because it stabilized the (generally low) level of union activities within the enterprise. Work-force representation in Germany and Austria had already started with the *Betriebsräte* of 1918. France also opted for it and introduced the *conseil d'entreprise* in 1945. In theory, works councils or enterprise councils could function independently of the unions. In practice, the councils came to be dominated by the unions, if only because in most countries concerned the unions had a monopoly when nominating candidates, making them more similar to Scandinavian councils. The functions of the councils were the same throughout Western Europe: consultation on matters of general enterprise policy. Formal arrangements prevented the influence of works councils on the enterprise's economic affairs for several reasons. First, in most countries the manager was also the chairman of the council, and he more or less decided the agenda in order to ensure that the advisory body did not raise subjects that the chairman did not want to discuss or turn into a kind of institutionalized opposition to management. Second, the economic information to which the councils had access to had to be provided by management. The nature of this information, relating to production and investments, became one of the central issues in the legal foundation of the councils. It was a battle especially between the socialists on the one hand, and Catholics and conservatives on the other. This discord was also one of the reasons for creating a distinction between an enterprise council and union representation. Despite the importance of the issue, in practice most councils confined themselves to social affairs, concerning, for example, the use of enterprise-based social funds and specific social welfare provisions.

Throughout Western Europe, the councils would remain of secondary importance in labor relations for a long time. They occupied a place in the shadow of collective bargaining or informal contacts between employers and union representatives. In Eastern Europe revolutionary enterprise councils had sometimes taken the place of prewar management and even gained control of industrial plants. They were heavily dominated by the unitary union movement (under Communist control), which favored the centralization of decisionmaking.

THE BEGINNING OF THE COLD WAR

Relations between Communists and non-Communists became increasingly strained. In Western Europe, tension stemmed from increasing employer self-confidence, the restoration of capitalist free enterprise, and the failure of Communists to obtain more than a small minority position in elections. In Eastern Europe, in France, and in Italy non-Communists took offense at the leading position Communists claimed in the national front. The Communists, on the other hand, regarded their allies as being too weak in almost all fields of government policy. The Communists, however, encountered problems in obtaining full workers' support for wage restraints in the large metal and steel industry, traditional Communist strongholds in some countries. Whereas Communists supported most strikes before the war, they now tried to stop all actions, straining relations with enterprise militants. Only the Italian Communists felt free to support larger wage actions, but Italian wage policies were less strict than elsewhere. In France, a strike at the nationalized Renault factories in April 1947 represented a turning point. Initially, Communist militants and leaders criticized the non-Communist strike leaders and even demanded their dismissal. As the movement expanded, the Communist leaders, more or less forced by their following, started to back the strike. In May, the Communists in government denounced the government's wage policy, and before they realized it they found themselves thrown out of the government.

In the same year, the Marshall Plan led to a more definite breach between Communists and non-Communists in Europe. Though one of the aims of the plan was to contain the influence and the spread of Communism, Communists initially welcomed the plan as a valuable contribution to production. The Soviets later rejected the plan as imperialist and summoned all Communist parties in Western Europe to break with the socialist "servants of imperialism" and to discontinue the national front strategy. The Communist parties followed the new guidelines, and Communist unions resumed their roles as transmission belts of the Communist parties. To their relief they could again support or lead spontaneous (or other) strikes against national wage policies or against any other pertinent issue.

The CGT could hardly wait to get involved again. It had reached an agreement with the employers' organization just before the conference about a general wage increase. Now it encouraged a general strike wave, most of all in the coal mines. Demands included wage revision, in light of rising prices and a minimum wage, and the Marshall Plan to a lesser extent. The strikes had one basic result: a new schism within the CGT. The reformist wing under confederate leader Jouhaux saw itself plunged into an undesired adventure and split off. It established the CGT-*Force ouvrière* (CGT-FO or just FO), named after a reformist periodical in the confederation. The third time the organization broke up, after the split in 1921 and the unofficial breach of 1939, was again partly due to international developments. This time the Communists retained a large majority. They had built up a strong organization during and right after the war and could now lead the opposition against wage policies. The split contributed to a rapid decline in overall French union membership, leaving only a small following for the new confederation. The socialists resumed their anti-Communist stance, and the Communists their reviling, calling the socialists fascists once more. Although the Italian Communists were expelled from the government, too, the socialist and Catholic participation in the Italian union confederation did not allow for immediate political action. Nevertheless, Communist support for spontaneous strikes gave rise to an open quarrel within the Italian union organization.

After the Marshall Plan, a second major event, the Communist coup of March 1948 in Prague, closed the curtain across Europe more definitely. The Communist-dominated (unified) union movement and the works councils (*zavodni rady*) played a prominent role in the coup and in the developments leading up to it. One of the first issues involved was the close alignment between the union movement and the Communist party in Czechoslovakia. It made Catholics and socialists look for some form of political representation in the union. The union leadership granted some concessions in the system of enterprise council elections, but the councils were of minor importance, since they were heavily dominated by the union delegation. Subsequently disputes arose over an extension of nationalization, a Communist demand, and the implementation of larger wage differentials in the public sector, a Catholic concern favoring their backers among clerical workers. In the hope of new elections, Catholic and conservative ministers resigned as a protest against the replacement of high police and security officials by Communists. In response, both the Communist party and the union movement called for massive demonstrations and strikes in support of the government. A works councils' congress backed the Communist stand with respect to the issues at stake and called for a one-hour support strike, in which 2 million workers participated. Before and during the strike police forces occupied strategic areas in Prague, assisted by a large workers' militia, rearmed shortly before. Under Soviet pressure and the pressure emanating from the Prague Coup, the president decided not to call for the elections. Instead, he accepted the replacement of the Catholic and conservative ministers by Communist ones. The coup was one of the most powerful acts of legal works councils ever. In combination with the Soviet influence it provided the Communists with a monopoly of power.

The Prague Coup increased the fear of Soviet expansion and of an imminent Communist takeover in countries not under Communist control. Distrust between Communists and non-Communists became open hostility. Wherever Communists occupied high official functions in Western Europe, they were removed. The breach between Communists and non-Communists in Italy and France became total. In Italy, a failed attempt on the Communist party leader's life in July 1948 caused a series of spontaneous strikes and local uprisings. The union confederation called a general strike to gain control over the movement. The action became a trial of strength between the union and the government. It ended after two days, but for the Catholic part of the union that was too late. It left the confederation and created its own, predominantly rural union confederation. Socialists followed the Catholic example.

In France, the CGT, intimately linked to the Communist party, fiercely opposed the country's internal and foreign policy, including the founding of NATO in 1949. Once the CGT had assumed a leading role in strikes, it introduced political demands or protest and calls to support the Soviet Union, as the true defender of peace. A prominent example of this position was a major miners' action in October 1948. The strike started as a more or less spontaneous action against social policy, but the CGT took control and made the Marshall Plan a main target. This allowed the government to treat the action as a political strike and to commit troops in order to resume production. In the following years, the confederation called some other strikes with specific political aims, like colonial policy. The only other country outside the new Soviet bloc where Communists dominated the union movement was Greece. In response, the Greek government silenced the union government, imposed a new leadership, and established more state control. The latter would last for over two decades.

The position of Communists was much weaker in the nations characterized by German- and British-model labor relations. This allowed Catholic and socialist unions and political parties to isolate the Communist parties and the Communist-dominated unified union movements. Even the TUC became involved in a struggle against Communist leadership in member unions, in particular the electricity workers' union. There was no formal tie between a union movement and the Communist party in any single Western European country, however. Formally, the CGT (Amiens 1906) and the remnant of the Italian confederation remained independent. The strong personal ties of leading unionists and the Communist party and the idea of unions functioning as transmission belts allowed the Communist party to exercise factual leadership. The socialist and Catholic unions also had personal ties with the respective parties, and union leaders sometimes had a seat in parliament. But social democracy, with its relatively lively internal discussions, did not allow such direct party leadership over the unions. There was less need for it among Catholics, since Catholic union restraint suited the Catholic party (or the Christian democratic party, dominated by Catholics), which was strongly represented in various governments. Communist party dominance of unionism was thus much heavier and more clearly visible. The cold war reinforced the ties between political parties and unions, however, whether characterized by party dominance or not.

The cold war also affected the international union organizations. In 1944, under the auspices of the American, Soviet, and British unions, a World Federation of Trade Unions (WFTU) was founded. The social democratic unions left the organization in 1949 to create the International Confederation of Free Trade Unions (ICFTU). Henceforth, the WFTU only organized the unions based on the Soviet model, plus the Communist-dominated federations in France and Italy. The Christian (that is, mainly Catholic) unions revived their own organization. The Belgian Catholic federation was by far its largest member.

DIVISION AND STABILIZATION

The division of Europe into East and West and the cold war between the two sides reinforced the process of stabilization already under way. Eastern Europe followed the Soviet example and implemented Soviet-model labor relations. The capitalist order was restored in Western Europe, and free enterprise was cherished as a basic human freedom. Planning, now considered to be a temporary reconstruction device only, was given up, except in France. Yet, the state remained involved in the economy in a number of countries. It applied Keynesian principles to influence the economic cycle and Beveridgian or more traditional principles of social welfare. Germany shared the fate of Europe and was divided into two separate countries. Most governments in Western Europe that had not yet done so presently discontinued their direct or indirect control of wages and encouraged a transition or a return to collective bargaining.

A main reason for this retreat was the consideration that recovery had been completed. The worst scarcity had passed, the black market had disappeared, and prices had become more stable. Union restraint kept wage demands from surpassing price fluctuations by very much, and bargaining could take place without state supervision. Great Britain was an example of this, where a formal agreement between the government, the unions, and the employers replaced earlier wage policies.

The second reason for governmental retreat was the amount of protest it had sparked. This protest, directed either at wage policies as such or against their application in specific cases, was a destabilizing force in politics. It could be prevented by taking the more normal course of union-employer bargaining, which affected politics less directly. The cold war and the expectation of Communist strikes only hastened the end of wage policies. Communists, however, were not the only ones to protest against the freezing or slow adaptation of wages. In France, the Catholic union and the new FO called a one-day protest strike in November 1949 against wage policies and in favor of collective bargaining. The action, supported by the CGT, was probably the last opportunity for the government to retract its wage policies and to allow free bargaining. A law was passed in February 1950 regulating collective labor agreements. It opened the possibility of extending such agreements and also introduced a nationwide minimum wage, called SMIG (*salaire minimum interprofessionel garanti*). This minimum wage was to be incorporated into all collective agreements. Belgium gave up its wage policies in 1948 and reinstalled the index, that is, the indexing of wages. In Italy wages were adjusted in central agreements.

The cold war also provided a third reason for ending wage policies: the urge to limit state power as a reaction against the Communist concept of a powerful state. Bargaining was now called free bargaining and treated as another human freedom not to be curbed by the state. The new trend was visible most clearly, as most trends at the time, in West Germany. During the occupation, wages, or more accurately rations, had been fixed by the allied powers. Collective bargaining was allowed to a certain extent after the currency reform in 1948. When the employers did not offer a high enough wage increase, the unions called another one-day protest strike. One of the largest single actions followed, mobilizing 9 million persons, but without much result. The new Federal Republic established free bargaining as a sacred principle and instituted an explicit right to negotiate collective agreements, totally independent from government intervention (*Tarifautonomie*). The new and cherished right was a sequel to the policy of the Western allies, intended to reduce the power of the central federations in German labor relations. Prevention of another fascist takeover was a major reason for such developments. By now, the danger of a Communist takeover loomed even larger, and the right to bargain became a product of the cold war. Due to factors such as late independence, the close proximity of East German Communism, and the absorption of millions of forced migrants and fugitives from the Communist countries, the new right was defended more fanatically than in countries more accustomed to such bargaining. An extensive body of labor legislation (*Arbeitsrecht*) and jurisprudence was developed to establish formal equality between the bargaining partners and to prevent disorder. It contained detailed regulations with respect to strikes and lockouts.

The isolation of Communists facilitated legislation on consultative institutions, since there could no longer be any doubt about which organizations should be represented in paritary councils and other similar organizations. The recognized or representative organizations might dispute the number of the seats assigned to them, but they were determined to exclude any other organization. Several countries now created paritary or other central-level councils, regulating and sanctioning institutions that in practice had already started before, albeit more informally. Belgium instituted a parity advisory council for economic affairs and another one for social affairs in 1951. The Dutch combined them into a single Social and Economic Council (*Sociaal-Economische Raad*, or SER). It was intended to be the apex of an all-encompassing corporatist structure, but in the end it became almost its only remnant. The council consisted of fifteen employers, fifteen union representatives, and fifteen appointed experts, and its president was another expert. It was the heaviest body of its kind in Western Europe and advised on all social and economic bills. The council derived its importance in part from the very strict and long-lasting Dutch wage policies. It was supposed to give advice in these matters and demonstrated the very close relationship between unions, employers' organizations, and the government. Within the German model, Switzerland remained exceptional in its lack of such cooperative institutions.

The West German reinstitution of free enterprise was demonstrated by the introduction of *Mitbestimmung* (co-determination), a hot issue for a number of years. It implied the appointment of half of the supervisory board by the unions and enterprise workers and also of one of the (usually three) managers. The demand was rooted in the same background as the one for work councils and was related to the tradition established during the Weimar Republic. The new constitution contained a vague notion of *Mitbestimmung*, but the new Christian democratic government did not like this limitation on free enterprise. The employers' organization and the government complied only after being threatened with a strike. A law enacted in 1951 confined *Mitbestimmung* to the large enterprises of the steel industry and mining. There was to be no parity in other sectors; unions and workers would be entitled to appoint only one-third of the supervisory board. A major strike in the printing industry in 1952, aimed at having the original scheme introduced, failed.

In sum, the three models of labor relations in Western Europe became more uniform right after the war. The major causes were state involvement, centralization of employer-union contracts, and the institutions of employer–work force cooperation within the enterprise. The cold war disrupted this trend toward uniformity to some extent. The Soviets imposed their model in Eastern Europe more definitely, and the differences between the other three models returned in Western Europe. West Germany joined the German model again, but without the consultative institutions and corporatist arrangements that became characteristic of the smaller nations. The state was regarded as a possible danger to society and democracy rather than as a partner in bargaining in West Germany. It was better, many agreed, to keep the state at a distance.

9

Bargaining in the 1950s and 1960s

After the period of recovery, economic growth remained a central concern and soon overrode other political issues. Common interest in growth transformed productivity increase into a major yardstick of improvements in labor conditions and allowed a voluntary pacification of labor relations. Conflicts in the 1960s were regarded as impediments to growth and to material improvement.

THE STRUCTURE OF BARGAINING IN THE 1950s

The cold war continued to isolate Communists in Western Europe during the early 1950s. It mainly affected the position of the French CGT, which saw several union leaders arrested. The Italian Communist Union, less dominated by the party, was less suspect. The cold war did not bring socialists and Catholics together, however. Catholics saw a Communist danger everywhere, while socialists were disappointed about the total return to free enterprise. In the second half of the 1950s there was widespread Communist disorientation after the Soviet invasion of Hungary and de-Stalinization. In combination with peaceful coexistence between East and West, this reduced tension in Western Europe.

Political strife notwithstanding, there was a general consensus regarding the need for further economic growth after the Marshall Plan had contributed to the successful completion of reconstruction. Indeed, the 1950s was a decade of growth, though there was much variation. At the beginning of the 1950s the cold war stimulated rearmament and industrial development. The war in Korea even caused a short boom in prices and profits. Governments frequently urged wage restraint, but the appeal was ignored by both employers and unions, the former under the spell of growth plus willingness to pay high wages in order to attract workers and prevent labor disputes and the latter bent on a larger workers' share in the growing national income. When prices dropped again after the Korea boom, the unions refused wage cuts and soon demanded new increases. Low unemployment gave them firm ground to stand on.

Only a few countries, in particular Holland and Finland, still practiced a comprehensive wage policy, in which wage adaptation to prices rather than a larger workers' share in national income was at stake. The Dutch guided wage policy (*geleide loonpolitiek*) spanned the entire decade, almost without opposition or interruption by wildcat strikes. The process of policy formation and implementation was very intricate. A private and paritary Foundation of Labor, consisting of union and employers' representatives, gave formal advice. The national government tended to follow such advice and would issue guidelines. Sectoral organizations would then initiate negotiations and submit their agreement to a Board of State Mediators for approval. The board would again ask the central organizations for advice. Thus, the board prevented or at least concealed direct government intervention in the approval procedure. Finnish policy was less intricate and less effective. It was hampered by rather frequent wildcat strikes, some of them secretly supported by the unions. Union discontent increased during the first half of the 1950s, partly due to the official price level of agricultural products. In March 1955 the problem led the union federation to call a general strike. After nineteen days the employers granted a wage increase, but they were compensated by a tax reduction. The strike more or less put an end to official wage policies.

Most other countries had abandoned official wage policies by the end of the 1940s. Governments couldn't help interfering in some of them, however, for instance by issuing incidental warnings or unofficial guidelines. The French government tried to influence the wage level and reduce the national deficit by imposing restrictions on wage increases in the large public sector, followed later by cuts in employment. It canceled the measures in August 1953, under pressure of a general strike called by the socialist and Catholic unions. The Fifth Republic, starting in 1958, intervened more directly in wage formation by prohibiting automatic adaptation of wages to prices. The government made an exception only for the SMIG, indexed since 1952. In West Germany *Tarifautonomie* did not leave any room for such intervention, although state governments mediated upon request in larger disputes.

Indirect state involvement did not affect union-employer contacts. Collective bargaining gained in popularity, even among very large enterprises. Nevertheless, the three models of labor relations retained their distinctive features.

Industrial bargaining within the German model fixed labor conditions in meticulous detail. Its coverage was nationwide in the smaller countries, while in West Germany negotiations took place within each of the federal states. On both sides of the bargaining table the central federations to some extent coordinated the demands and counterdemands without being involved in bargaining directly. As had been the case before the war, agreements in metallurgy and the steel

industry paved the way for negotiations in other sectors. In West German metallurgy, the national union *Industriegewerkschaft Metall* (IG Metall), by far the
largest member of the DGB, was such a *Schrittmacher*. Large enterprises had
their own agreements, negotiated by management and union officials. Such
enterprise agreements often set the tone for industrial bargaining in the same
branch. In other instances they surpassed the outcome of industrial agreements
in case the latter preceded them. Collective bargaining was slow to develop only
in clerical work. It seemed that clerical workers in most countries were attempting
to keep ahead of manual workers in the area of labor conditions and requested
the same wage increase and working time reduction as manual workers, in order
to retain their privileged position with respect to both wages and time off. This
motivated novel claims by manual workers, which again gave rise to similar
demands by clerical workers. Within the category of clerical workers, some
branches and sectors (for example, technologically advanced industries and banking) acted as pilot branches for other sectors (such as insurance companies). The
German model continued its low strike profile during the 1950s, which had been
a distinctive feature since the postwar settlements and a striking contrast to the
other models. Lockouts had become rather exceptional after the war. Only in
West Germany were they still a common response to a major strike. West German
employers attached great value to this legally sanctioned equality in weapons.

British industrial bargaining was still confined to dispute procedures and some
basic labor conditions. Actual wage decisions were left to the informal contacts
between management and shop stewards. This decentralization of bargaining
and the continuity of craft unionism caused a number of interunion demarcation
conflicts, in particular where new technologies were introduced and work processes changed. Such disputes were at the heart of, or at least a major issue in,
a number of British labor conflicts during the 1950s (for example, a general
railway strike in 1955). In these actions, craft unions tried to enforce the exclusion
of less skilled workers organized in other unions, to the astonishment of the
unions on the continent.

In France, the scope and effects of industrial bargaining remained very limited.
In that respect the law of 1950 shared the fate of the 1919 law pertaining to
collective agreements. Both laws contributed to short-lived spurts in collective
bargaining, but they failed to bring about more lasting results. A new phenomenon suddenly appeared in 1955, however—formal enterprise bargaining. This
type of bargaining replaced the highly informal agreements between unions and
employers at the enterprise level. Renault, the nationalized *usine pilote* of French
industry, introduced formal bargaining under the pressure of strikes and violent
riots which took place at the shipyards of St. Nazaire and Nantes. This step was
taken to prevent the strikes from spreading to the easily inflammable Renault
plants. The time needed for the agreement, a single day, demonstrated the lack
of a bargaining tradition. In other countries at least one day was required for
shaking hands and setting the agenda. Some fifty large companies followed
Renault's example. The CGT continued to have doubts about formal enterprise

bargaining and did not sign until it had held a referendum for approval. The Communist-dominated confederation in Italy had the same objections against enterprise bargaining. It feared a loss of revolutionary zeal and national fighting spirit, but it eventually gave in after Catholic and socialist unions started negotiations at the enterprise level.

A common trait of the three labor relations models in Western Europe was by now the interplay between enterprise, sectoral, and central-level employer-union contacts. The importance of each of the levels and the nature of contacts varied among the three models. Occasionally, parties would shift from one level to another when disagreement occurred, thus postponing the rise of industrial dispute. Ireland represented a curious example of this kind of mobility. Central bargaining and local or sectoral bargaining were successively used in the process of bringing about wage adaptation. Every other year rather informal wage rounds, alternately at the central level or in pilot industries, gave rise to a nationwide round of bargaining.

The importance of bargaining was recognized in the public sector as well. Though no government was yet prepared to grant formal bargaining rights, some nations explicitly recognized union rights and started or extended union consultation.

THE ISSUES OF THE 1950s

Only in Great Britain did raising productivity by means of new technologies become an issue in employer-union contacts, sometimes in combination with demarcation disputes between various unions. The unions on the continent lacked control over new technologies, but that did not bother them. On the contrary, to them productivity growth seemed to be the clue to steady wage increases, and they were thus quite devoted to it. The Scandinavian unions had already reaffirmed their lack of control in the basic agreements and their devotion to productivity growth in the postwar agreements on joint production councils. In 1954 the Belgian unions participated in a common employer-union Declaration on Productivity, explicitly promising to assist in raising productivity. Indeed, the unions on the continent regarded the British strikes against new technologies as marginal actions, preventing progress. Increasingly, the British unions were regarded as old-fashioned organizations fighting an irrelevant battle against material improvement. The British unions could point to the fact that they had a degree of control over technology that the unions on the continent lacked and to the high level of grass-roots activities within their organizations. During this time of increasing consumption (owing to productivity growth), both arguments seemed obsolete on the continent.

The union interest in productivity, especially pronounced in the German model, increasingly made unions use productivity increase as a yardstick for wage increases. During the 1950s the unions were no longer content with the adaptation of wages to prices, in other words, stability of real wages. They also wanted to see a link between the growth of productivity and wage increases. Sometimes their demands even surpassed productivity growth. In West Germany, IG Metall called a strike for that purpose in Hesse (1951) and another one in Bavaria (1954). They lasted four and three weeks respectively and were settled by state mediation.

To various national governments, creating a link between wages and productivity growth had the advantage of keeping down inflation, a major state concern during this decade. Inflation fears motivated repeated calls for wage restraint, especially when low productivity sectors followed in the footsteps of the wage raises of high productivity industries. The Swedish unions tried to put an end to these appeals by designing a new wage policy. They regarded high wages as conducive to productivity growth and combined the two concerns with the wage equality of a solidaristic wage policy. The combination implied a more active promotion of productivity, rather than a passive attitude toward changes in technology. In order to apply this Rehn-Meidner model, named after its authors (both of them union economists), the Swedish union federation supported central wage bargaining. The model rejected wage restraints, including productivity-linked wage increases, as a means to curb inflation. In their opinion, such steps could not stop unofficial wage drift. Instead, the lower-wage groups were to be brought on a par with the higher paid. That would force less productive sectors and firms to close, raise the general level of productivity, and reduce inflation. The disadvantages of unemployment could be offset by an active labor market policy, consisting of intensive retraining and additional social welfare benefits during the period of retraining. Instead of subsidizing low productivity by means of low wages, as was done in Dutch wage policies, this line of thinking stressed high productivity as a condition of full employment. Obviously, Swedish employers did not share union enthusiasm for high wages. They were also in favor of central bargaining, however, since they believed it would prevent wage drift. In actuality, they were the driving force behind the first central negotiations, which resulted in a settlement in 1956.

No agreement could be reached with regard to the second part of the Rehn-Meidner plan, a public investment fund. In order to prevent wage drift in the most productive sectors, towering profits there had to be taxed away. Since heavy taxation might reduce the amount of investment capital, capital was to be provided out of public funds. An obvious means to bring that about was to extend the Beveridgian old age pension system by providing everyone with an earnings-related pension. The pension funds were to be administered collectively and be available for investment in industry as a public fund, in addition to private investments. The pension reform was a very hotly debated issue in 1957, even among socialists, but the proposals passed Parliament. This allowed the Rehn-Meidner ideas to be put into practice, though in a less strict form than advanced in the original model. Swedish developments deliberately ended the almost universal combination of full employment and recurrent pressure for wage restraint. To leftist critics they represented Fordism in due form, adapting everything in life to mass production and mass consumption. The other unions on the continent looked on with envy. To them the Swedish unions became a new example for their own activities. The Swedish situation constrasted in particular with the non-solidaristic wage bargaining characteristic of the British model. Together with the Renault agreement of 1955 it seemed to open a new era of bargaining for great improvements in labor conditions without too many labor conflicts. Nevertheless, no union on the continent dared to follow the Swedish example. Most of them continued to subscribe to wage demands within the limits of productivity increase, rather than make them a separate issue, as the Swedes had done.

Union efforts to secure a larger workers' share in the growing national income not only found expression in wage increase demands, but also in negotiations about giving workers more time off. Since the argument of sharing work did not apply, the unions preferred a shorter work week and longer holidays to a return to the eight-hour workday. They started exerting pressure for a reduction to at least forty-four or forty-five hours in the mid–1950s. Such a setup would provide workers a free Saturday afternoon or even a complete Saturday off. In addition to the increase in productivity and work load, the spread of the automobile as a means of transportation was one reason to implement a five-day work week, allowing one to spend Saturday under the car and Sunday in it. The tight labor market and favorable economic conditions and prospects made the employers give in almost at once, but the unions kept the issue on the agenda. In some countries adhering to the German model, work-time reduction was translated into wage costs, as part of agreements on wage increases. Part of the increase was allocated to work-time reduction and the rest to raising real wages. An example of this was the agreement reached in West German metallurgy in 1956, which reduced the work week to forty-five hours nationwide. This *Bremer Abkommen* contained an 8 percent labor cost increase, of which 6.7 percent was spent on work-time reduction. A similar agreement in 1957 led to a further reduction to forty-four hours. The Belgian union federations called the government to their support. Employers and the government reached a consensus in a series of top-level meetings in 1955. First they promised to investigate whether the forty-five-hour work week should be introduced, then where and when to introduce it. In a later meeting, the focus was limited to why some sectors were still lagging behind. Elsewhere, holidays were generally extended to two weeks. Sometimes partial holiday pay was included to cover extra holiday costs. Holidays were especially an issue in France. The main subject of the Renault agreement and of the other enterprise accords reached in 1955 was the introduction of a third week of holidays.

In part, the demands for less work time were aimed at reducing the inequality between manual and clerical workers, since the latter already enjoyed a work week of forty-two hours or less. The culture of mass consumption blurred the differences in living conditions, at least superficially. Union concern for productivity growth increased manual workers' responsibility as well. Employers still believed quite strongly in preferential treatment for clerical workers, due to patterns of enterprise hierarchy and worker loyalty. Like the white-collar workers themselves, they opposed the trend toward more equality. Employers often gave in under union pressure, but they were able to undo leveling measures by offering clerical workers new advantages. Most clerical workers (paid each month) were entitled to continued pay during illness or other circumstances that prevented work. They also had better guarantees against arbitrary dismissal. In contrast, most manual workers were paid each week, had such guarantees for two weeks at most, and had to rely on social security benefits from the very onset of an illness. This difference led unions to demand additional sick pay for manual workers, which would guarantee the worker 80 or even 100 percent of the normal wages, at least for one or two weeks. In 1956, one of the issues in a metallurgy strike in Schleswig-Holstein, Germany, was the introduction of additional payment for six weeks. (Other issues were longer holidays and more holiday pay.) The strike was a partial success (though overshadowed by a fine of 100 million marks that was meted out because IG Metall had called the strike before bargaining procedures had been concluded and in doing so had violated a peace clause). The inclusion of additional benefits in industry agreements led to the creation of sectoral social welfare funds. The construction industry pioneered in this area. Before the war it had already started to pay construction workers benefits when bad weather prevented normal work. Now additional sick pay, maternity leave, and additional pension benefits were covered as well. In large enterprises, such benefits were sometimes rooted in an earlier paternalistically patterned employers' concern, later turned into a corporate concern. What was initially a favor later became a right, something clerical workers had enjoyed for some time.

Socialists were unable to bring about more equality in social security legislation. New systems or additions to existing ones, for instance in West Germany, deviated considerably from the Beveridgian ideals. Yet, only rarely were they an issue of parliamentary debate. Social democratic unions were quite content that at least, and at last, their members were covered by obligatory provisions. Swedish pension reform, greatly reducing inequality between manual and clerical workers, was by far the most marked. In France, central agreements in 1958 and 1961 covered additional old age pensions and additional unemployment benefits. They also reduced the gap between provisions for manual and clerical workers.

Enterprise reform was no longer an issue, either. Socialist and Communist union programs still contained demands like worker control, but the practice rather than the program mattered. And the practice meant raising the level of consumption and extending the amount of free time devoted to it. Works councils had been instituted by law in most countries, though they had a difficult start. Employers hesitated to provide the necessary information about the financial side of the enterprise. However, unions were more interested in their workplace delegations and were rather indifferent about financial information during this period of continuing growth. The negative employers' attitude also applied to German *Mitbestimmung*. In 1955, a Ruhr industrialist thought it fit to label it a form of union blackmail, and other employers took his side. In protest, 800,000 workers in the Ruhr coal mines and steel industry participated in a one-day strike. The protest also focused on the employers' efforts to evade the obligatory *Mitbestimmung* regulations by creating holding companies outside the sphere of mining and steel, to which the principle was confined. Within the larger companies, the *Arbeitsdirektoren* took their work very seriously and in some cases spoke out against strikes. *Mitbestimmung* aroused no interest at all in other countries. Employers opposed anything resembling it, and unions feared that they would be saddled up with responsibility without any real influence.

PRODUCTIVITY AS A COMMON PRIORITY

National political conflict declined even further with the end of colonial policies in the early 1960s. Ironically, two French political strikes in 1960 and 1961 were called to support a conservative government in its policy of decolonization. Only one topic of interest remained: economic growth.

The transition from coal to oil as the prime fuel constituted a major economic change. Mining areas were in decline, while complete new industries arose, especially near the large oil ports. The rise of the latter was also due to the emergence of the Common Market and the enormous growth of international trade. Automation, the almost natural reaction to the tight labor market of the 1950s in the richer parts of Europe, caused a shift from manual to clerical work. A large immigration movement from the Mediterranean countries (including southern Europe) and former colonies filled the vacancies in manual and especially in unskilled work. Great Britain recruited immigrant workers mainly from former parts of the British Empire and France from its former colonies in northern Africa. The *Gastarbeiter* (guest workers) in Germany tended to come from southern Europe and from Turkey.

Labor relations in the 1960s were influenced by this shift in the composition of the work force. Three other related developments affected them more directly, however. First was the extension of Keynesianism to a form of indicative planning. Second was the general attachment to labor peace as a condition for growth and, third was the extension of central-level negotiations.

The popularity of national planning in the early 1960s stemmed from a number of factors, including the undisturbed flow of crude oil which replaced irregular coal supplies, the general extension of enterprise planning, international economic cooperation, and a growing appeal to and ability of the government to deal with small disruptions in the economy. The only country that had continued a planning tradition since liberation was France. The absence of unions in this *économie concertée* made this country irrelevant for the planning experiments in other countries, where union participation was deemed crucial. In Belgium, a programming office was set up in 1959, and both employers and unions were represented on the board. A British conservative government founded a National Economic Development Council (called "Neddy") in 1962. After some hesitation, the TUC decided to participate, thereby joining the government and the employers. Later in the decade (in 1967) even West Germany, more than other countries devoted to free enterprise, obtained its *Konzertierte Aktion*. All these experiments were a more active variation of Keynesian economic policy, but they stopped short of real planning. In Italy, as in France, the Communist-dominated union confederation refused to participate in planning. It justifiably feared some form of official wage restraints.

The second development, besides planning, that had a significant impact on labor relations was the commitment to labor peace. This commitment was related to the generalization of the productivity formula, that is, the link between wages and productivity. In light of the Scylla and Charybdis of inflation and unemployment, wages were a major concern to governments. Indeed, they were also a central object of indicative planning. Continuing economic growth reduced the potential dangers, because it facilitated employer-union agreement with respect to an important parameter of wage increases: productivity growth. The link had been applied only partially and cautiously in the 1950s. Now, however, its use became more common and widespread. To the government it solved the problem of inflation. To employers the predictability of productivity growth under planning allowed projections of future labor costs. And in light of continuing growth, the unions could guarantee their numbers a constant and fixed wage increase. Labor conflicts would only endanger planning and ultimately also progress (that is, economic growth), considered to be the base of the burgeoning welfare state.

The productivity formula was the expression of a pacification of labor relations, and it contributed further to stable labor conditions in the mid–1960s. Employers' organizations and unions were transformed from bargaining parties into social partners (*partners sociaux, Sozialpartner*), stressing common interest rather than conflict. The trend was most pronounced in the German model, though it also affected the other models. Labor peace in West Germany was interrupted by only one major strike, in the metal industry in 1963. After the strike, however, IG Metall signed an agreement with the metal employers to prevent future strikes (in return for the employers' pledge to forget about the remaining DM 38 million of the DM 100 million fine imposed in 1956). Labor disputes were also rather rare in the public sector, despite the fact that several governments extended the bargaining rights of public sector unions.

Automatic wage increases and the unions' renunciation of strikes posed the problem of how to keep union membership satisfied and how to attract new members. Union work increasingly consisted of calculating entitled wage increases and participation in committees, processes rather removed from everyday reality for union members. Employers profited most according to the unions, because they no longer had to face union demands. This led some unions that were especially devoted to a harmonious bargaining relationship to request (rather than demand) special advantages for union members or employer contributions to union services. In West Germany, the construction industry union was severely rebuked by its fellow unions for making such an appeal, which was considered to be a breach of traditional claims to represent not just union members but the working class as a whole. The Belgian Catholic union federation also requested such advantages, as well as employer subvention of specific union activities like vocational training. The main result in Belgium was an annual union bonus, which was paid by the employers to organized workers in both large union movements (Catholic and socialist). The bonus more or less covered the costs of union membership. Typically, payment was withheld when there was a strike in that year, which created a true predicament when a union planned to call a strike.

The link between wages and productivity was applied especially in countries embracing German-model sectoral bargaining, with the exception of Sweden. Its application and interpretation in West Germany remained a bone of contention only in metallurgy. In 1960 the director of the national bank advocated the link in his Blessing Memorandum. But by the way of exception this warning against inflation was not taken too seriously, since the prediction concerning productivity growth was far too conservative. The federal government itself proposed a wage increase surpassing productivity growth in 1963 in order to put an end to the metalworkers' strike and lockout in that year. Meanwhile, the productivity link had come to be generally accepted. In 1965 another mediator (Meinhold) advised applying it in the steel industry, in combination with compensation for increasing prices. This Meinhold formula (wage increase equals productivity rise plus inflation) subsequently became an accepted base for wage bargaining under the *Konzertierte Aktion*.

Unions and employers stressed the central level of bargaining in the smaller countries characterized by German-model labor relations. Coordinated wage bargaining would curb inflation and allow some leveling of wages in favor of lower-paid workers. In line with the need for planning and predictability, wages were preferably fixed for two years at a time. Wage increases in both years were either fixed in advance for these years, based upon expected productivity increases, or left more open (yet still dependent upon productivity). Central wage coordination was already a tradition by the 1960s in Denmark, and in 1960 employers and unions renewed their nonsubstantive basic agreement of 1899. Within a year, however, coordination failed again, and workers from all branches of transport went on strike for higher wages. The government solved the conflict by imposing arbitration upon the unwilling employers. The dispute did not detract from the peaceful character of labor relations during the following years. The national federations in Belgium started to bargain for themselves in 1960. They reached two-year social programming agreements, related to the attempts to program the economy. The agreements, reached in 1960, 1963, and 1966, contained improvements in secondary labor conditions and served as guidelines for sectoral bargaining. In Holland, the productivity formula was applied to save the strict national wage policies. Upward pressure on wage rates became too strong, however, and soon the government was approving any agreement, with or without the link. This resulted in a wage explosion during the mid–1960s.

Contacts at the central level increased in Great Britain, but they had less impact on sectoral bargaining, let alone on informal bargaining at the level of the shop floor. Pressed by high inflation, the government tried to impose wage restraints. In 1965, a Labour government first drafted a Declaration of Intent with employers and the TUC to restrain wages and prices. Then it introduced a voluntary early warning system for wage and price increases. When that failed, the Prices and Incomes Act was passed in 1966, which imposed a wage freeze. It was the first nonvoluntary, statutory wage control since the 1940s—and it was imposed by a Labour government. Wage policies failed, however, due to the frequent changes in economic policy (the stop-go cycle) and the predominance of informal shop-floor bargaining. The British wage policies did not contain any reference to productivity growth. On the contrary, these policies were undermined by the first enterprise agreements containing such a link between wages and productivity. Under pressure from American firms like Ford, shop stewards and unions accepted the link. Industry agreements in metallurgy followed this example and related wages to productivity in 1964 and 1968, raising wages more than wage policies allowed. The agreements also denounced workers' opposition to measures that improved productivity like rationalization and changes in work organization, a deviation from traditional British union practice.

Wages were not the only issue at stake in planning and in more general tripartite contacts. Employers and unions were invited to give their advice on the entire range of economic and social policies, including housing, education, and finance. This extension of contacts between the national federations was a third feature of labor relations during the 1960s, related to planning and to the centralization and pacification of wage bargaining. Employers' organizations and trade union federations became expanding bureaucracies, employing increasing numbers of staff to fill the committees. The combination of consultation and centralization was especially pronounced in the German model. It represented the apex of what might be called neo-corporatism that had started after the war. The growing participation of social democrats in governments facilitated neo-corporatism, which pressured the unions to moderate wage demands in bargaining. By doing so, employers were also attracted.

Austria was the most prominent example of corporatism. In 1957, two years after the end of the allied occupation, a paritary committee on prices and wages was set up, called the *Paritätische Kommission für Preis- und Lohnfragen*. Labor was represented by the trade union federation and by statutory chambers of labor, dominated by the union. Employers were represented by their own statutory chambers, more or less relics from traditional corporatism. The prominent role of the chambers was facilitated by the importance of nationalized large enterprise. It reduced the importance of the employers' organization with its membership of small firms. The prime minister presided over the final meetings of the committee, and other cabinet members participated as well, but without affecting its autonomy. The committee dominated collective bargaining. Sectoral organizations required committee consent before they were allowed to engage in negotiations, and they subsequently had to submit their agreement for approval. But the committee also had to be consulted on all social and economic bills. It more or less decided the contents of policy in those fields, monopolizing the role of expert adviser to the government and sometimes preparing bills itself. This dominating position was facilitated by the strong links with politics. The unions remained in close contact with the socialists, and the employers' chambers were in contact with the Catholic party.

No other country reached this degree of policymaking by unions and employers—not in Scandinavia, where social democratic government power favored the trade unions, nor in Belgium, where the large Catholic union movement left Catholic-dominated governments a greater freedom of action. Still, consensus rather than conflict was the rule everywhere. Even the decentralized labor relations in the British model and the contentious relations in the French model were affected, without the development of similar forms of consultation. In 1958, the Fifth Republic reinforced the position of the *Conseil économique et social*, but in practice consultation was confined to large enterprises. Switzerland remained an exception within the German model. As a last vestige of classical capitalism, it valued labor peace, but it lacked any significant state involvement or central consultation.

Of course, pacification was not complete, least of all outside the German model. However, apart from Italy, the rate of conflict declined throughout Western Europe. Two sources of conflict did remain: the change from coal to oil and efforts by governments to keep their budgets in check. In both instances, governments, because of their central role in the economy, were heavily involved. The major scenes of conflict were the coal mines on the continent, where miners protested mine closures or the supposedly preferential treatment of new sources of energy. Closures seriously affected inland regions traditionally devoted to mining and now deprived of their main source of living. Fearing social upheaval and drastic changes in a traditional social climate, regional authorities joined miners in their protest. Even if governments were not involved directly, they were addressed as being responsible for energy policies. In 1962, miners in Saarland (West Germany) demanded both a wage increase and more state subsidies for mining in order to improve coal's competitiveness with other energy industries. Miners in Decazeville, in southern France, occupied their mines in the same year. They celebrated Christmas underground, enjoying the wide support of the entire region. A general miners' strike hit France the next year. The goal was to assist mining in its struggle to close the gap that had been forged with other industries. The strike started in the North and the Lorraine region and lasted for over a month. The French government first responded by calling a general mobilization of all miners, but later agreed to study the wage differentials.

A second source of conflict was the need that governments felt to gain more control over their own budgets and the rising costs of social welfare. This issue was related to mining's fate, since unemployed miners were a heavy burden on the state budget. Successive French governments tried to economize partly by limiting wages in the public sector as it had done in the 1950s. This policy caused strikes in the railways and in public administration within several years. A major Belgian strike was called in the winter of 1960 to oppose stricter government control of social welfare spending and mine closures in Wallony. The latter had already been a source of strikes the year before. The strike was directed against a law (*Eenheidswet/Loi unique*) that combined a series of social security measures relating to increased spending on jobless miners. It was concentrated in Wallony, lasted three weeks, and almost gained the character of a regional uprising. It failed it its main aim, to keep the bill from passing parliament. Nevertheless, strikes supporting mining seemed to be marginal actions by that time. Though the government was the major target of such action, its role in coordinating the national economy went unchallenged.

REDUCING INEQUALITY

The generally shared expectation of continuing growth and the rather easy transition by workers from manual to clerical work encouraged the trend toward more wage equality between industrial branches, manual and nonmanual work, male and female workers, and across industrial regions.

Wage inequalities were reduced where the productivity formula was applied in central bargaining. In many countries, this promotion of equality was a main union motive for central bargaining or the central coordination of sectoral bargaining. Although Swedish wages were not linked to productivity, the union federation focused on reducing the clerical-manual wage gap. A three-year agreement, reached in 1966, seemed a step forward, until the employers granted the white-collar federation a wage increase almost twice as high. The latter agreement caused much friction between the general union federation and the employers. Relations improved again after general talks about a coordinated procedure, involving the white-collar organization. The unions rejected strict application of the productivity formula, as advocated by the employers, but they agreed to link wages more directly to productivity growth in that part of the economy that was subject to international competition.

Inequality between male and female wages also became a major issue during the 1960s. A first step had been taken in the early 1950s when the ILO adopted Convention 100 in 1951, stipulating equal remuneration for work of equal value, a definition that had a wider application than simply equal work. Though some countries changed their legislation accordingly, the practice was more difficult to change. A second step, of more importance to women in Western Europe, was the Treaty of Rome. This treaty was signed in 1957 to establish the Common Market and not only provided for the principle of equal pay for equal work, but also fixed a timetable for its introduction. France was the major force behind this provision. It had enacted equal pay in 1946 and wanted Holland and Belgium to follow suit, thereby ending what was perceived to be unfair competition. The Low Countries complied, but were able to prevent any implementation of the wider definition employed by the ILO convention, that is, equal pay for work of equal value. The adaptation of legislation and practice was very slow, and the deadline was shifted to 1965 in the early 1960s. Sweden, which was not a member of the Common Market, remained ahead of Europe with respect to equal payment because of the union's solidaristic wage policy and day-care provisions allowing mothers to work outside the home. Previously, women had only occasionally called a strike for more equality, and their low rate of organization had kept the unions from pressing too hard for increases. Employers opposed more equality because they feared a new wage drift by male workers trying to maintain their privileges. Actually, women profited more from the reduction of sectoral wage differentials, for instance between male-dominated high-paying metallurgy and female-dominated textiles, but such reductions were hardly a general trend.

A pattern of regional inequality was at stake in Italy, between the industrialized North and the Mezzogiorno. In 1961 the central organizations reached a three-year agreement to reduce the number of wage zones from thirteen to seven and the regional wage variation from over 30 to 20 percent. During the mid-1960s the leveling of wages became part of a more all-encompassing national effort to promote the industrial developments of the South.

The trend toward more equality in wages was far from universal. The reduction of inequality was more prominent in the areas of working time and social security coverage.

In several nations characterized by German-model labor relations the two-year central or sectoral agreements allowed a transition to a forty-hour work week, with one or two hours less for clerical workers, in several stages. The growing need for objective measures of new labor conditions was expressed in the calculation of the costs stemming from work-time reduction (as labor costs) in increasingly greater detail. West German metallurgy pioneered the forty-hour work week. The national Bad Homburg Agreement in 1960 provided for its gradual introduction in metallurgy within a five-year period. Later, the tight labor market was used twice as an argument to postpone the implementation of a new stage, but in 1967 the forty-hour week became a reality. Other industrial sectors and countries followed suit. France pioneered again in the area of holidays. Renault granted a fourth week of paid holidays in a new enterprise agreement, paving the way for other large enterprises.

The 1960s also witnessed an enormous rise of social welfare expenditures, in part financed by the state. Social security expenses almost doubled in several countries, from about 10 percent to 20 percent of the national income. The increase affected all areas of social welfare and was due to both a rise in benefits and an extension of categories involved. In general, the changes favored manual workers and reduced manual-clerical inequality. Countries that had not yet done so introduced minimum benefits related not only to price levels but also to the national minimum wage. Benefits were also to be increased to match wage increases. Where the unions were actively engaged in social security administration, as in Scandinavia and Belgium, the increase contributed to a further rise of the organization rate of manual workers. This rate increased to over 80 percent, compared to 50 percent or less in other countries.

Less attention was given to the inequality between indigenous and immigrant workers. For a long time the unions saw the migrants as a threat to the long-standing union achievements, rather than as a potential force to be organized. Indeed, the newcomers were hard to organize and ready to evade collective agreements that applied to them. They had little choice. Many legal migrants were interested in returning to their home country with large savings or in transferring money to family members in their country of origin. Illegal migrants feared dismissal and a forced return if they protested too loudly against any encroachment upon labor agreements or social legislation.

10

Revolt and Recession

Large spontaneous strikes brought an end to the period of relative labor peace from 1968 on. Worker participation became the catchword of the 1970s, even under less favorable economic conditions. After the 1974 oil crisis it changed from an offensive union demand to a defensive item, aimed at saving employment.

CRISIS OF AUTHORITY

In early May 1968, French students started a protest movement against traditional authority in university education. For several days the students' quarter in Paris, the Quartier Latin, was the scene of heavy rioting and street fighting, and a disputed territory between students and police. The CGT condemned the leftist intransigence (*gauchisme*) of the students, but to protest police violence, it called a general strike on May 13. The strike paralyzed the country and culminated in a large mass demonstration in Paris. Workers also imitated the students' occupation of a number of universities. They occupied the large automobile and aircraft factories in a wave of spontaneous strikes, sometimes locking managers in their offices. After hesitating for a long time, the government engaged in talks with employers and unions. During a long weekend of bargaining at the government office (rue de Grenelle), they reached the *Accord de Grenelle*, which resembled the 1936 accord. It included a large general wage increase, the gradual introduction of the forty-hour work week, and the introduction and legal sanctioning of union enterprise representation. The CGT hesitated to sign the agreement officially. Indeed, the CGT leader Georges Seguy was jeered when he came to explain the terms of the accord in the occupied Renault plant. The

CGT organized another mass demonstration in Paris under the pressure of the ongoing strikes, but the day after the demonstration twice as many people demonstrated in support of the government. The government resumed power with new self-confidence. By mid-June the largest strike wave ever, involving 8 to 10 million workers and 150 million working days, was over.

Other countries followed the French example. Workers challenged employers and union leaders in a large number of spontaneous strikes. The wave of actions put an end to the period characterized by the relative absence of labor disputes and appeared to usher in a new era of worker militancy.

The May revolt and the wave of strikes throughout Western Europe were not so much a resurgence of class conflict, however, as an expression of a crisis in traditional authority. Whether exercised by parents, priests, political leaders, employers, or union leaders, traditional authority had been affected in a number of ways. Increased consumptive spending and media exposure had undermined traditional nonconsumptive values. Geographic mobility, the spread of the automobile, and housing in new suburbs had upset traditional patterns of social contact. In part, these developments were due to the increasing scale of economic life and to Fordist mass production, accompanied by rationalization and the concentration of production.Traditional values, as well as the Fordist adaptation of social life, were the first targets of attack. Soon, capitalist society itself was under attack. Even Sweden had difficulty maintaining its position as the example for labor relations in the rest of Western Europe. In the spring of 1968, the Prague Spring served as a model for many young people, since it lacked both the elements of capitalist exploitation and the very strict authority of Communism.

Within the industrial world, a "new working class" set the strike train in motion: young workers employed in semiskilled work, with some degree of technical training (for example, assembly-line workers in automobile factories). To many of them, the years of general and vocational education were not valued in that kind of employment, and strict authority and work pace did not correspond with the degree of freedom enjoyed outside the factory gate. The rise of new technologies created the idea that new social relations were possible, but young workers found themselves subject to traditional discipline and authority. Moreover, rising unemployment during the late 1960s made them victims of the new technology they admired. They became subject to greater mobility because it was difficult to find jobs.

The rationalization and concentration of production reinforced the feeling that employer authority was rather arbitrary, while it also affected union appeal. Rationalization was the reaction to an overcapacity in sectors like steel, shipbuilding, and artificial fibres, caused by increased overseas competition and European overinvestment. Mergers reduced the number of companies, especially in France. The older plants were either reduced in size or closed within the new conglomerates. The process disproportionately affected traditional industrial regions dominated by steel factories, like Wallony and Lorraine. As with the mine closures in the past, it disrupted existing communities and life-long social contacts. High wages had served as a compensation during the golden 1960s. The student revolt meant the end of easy compliance. The old term alienation was again used, this time implying the loss of individual self-determination. This loss was perceived to be due to decisions by monopoly capital and the state, the latter being dependent upon the internal logic of the former.

The waning of authority accelerated in 1967 and 1968. A brief economic setback persuaded the unions that they had to be content with small wage increases, putting an end to the lavish compensation given to offset the effects of rationalization. In the meantime, expectations were still rising, as was inflation. These developments, in combination with a rise in unemployment, affected the authority of employers and unions. Toward the close of the decade, improving economic prospects added to worker resentment. Soon workers competed against each other for large wage increases.

In addition to France, where worker activism decreased after June, Italy was a major site of militancy for a number of years. Semiskilled migrants from the South became the most active. They represented the Italian version of the new working class. The Italian strike wave consisted of a number of general political strikes and spontaneous workshop actions. The former were organized by the three union confederations who were responding to successive Catholic-socialist coalitions' failure to bring about effective social reforms (for example, in the area of old age pensions) and general government impotence. Spontaneous shop strikes took place in the Fiat factories and other large factories in northern Italy. In contrast to France, the unions used the mobilization for political reform to gain control over such shop actions. The combination of political actions and organized shop-floor actions culminated in the hot autumn (*autunno caldo*) of 1969. The confederations cooperated closely and placed housing and health policies high on the agenda. These issues thus became the foci of general strikes. The unions even engaged in direct negotiations with the government, using this as an alternative political circuit, bypassing the political parties. At the same time they were careful not to impede the shop actions. Instead, they stimulated such actions and raised their effectivity by calling articulated strikes (*scioperi articolati*): short work disruptions shop by shop instead of shutting down the whole factory at once. The effect was comparable, however. As such, the strikes were almost an extension of the earlier spontaneous actions, but they were planned in advance. The main demands in these strikes were wage increases, more equality in wages, and more worker control of work organization. The various types of strikes continued into the early 1970s. The unions were involved in bargaining at all levels, but support for their political demands died away slowly.

In 1969 and 1970 spontaneous actions broke out in several other countries on the continent, often when collective agreements were renewed. The unions tried to gain control of the strikes, but they did not express political demands as in Italy or France. This pattern fit the German model. However, the rapid sequence and size of the spontaneous actions, and of organized strikes later on, gave them a more general and political nature. Even countries where spontaneous strikes had been rare in the past now had their share of them, a sign of widespread and intense discontent and a decline of traditional authority.

The unions in West Germany started to regret their modest claims of 1967–1968. They demanded a new round of negotiations in 1969. When the employers in the steel industry refused to negotiate, a series of spontaneous September strikes broke out in the Hoesch works in Dortmund. These strikes proceeded to spread throughout the country. In the winter of 1969, miners in Sweden and Belgium engaged in spontaneous actions directed against collective agreements that had been reached in 1968. Similar actions took place from 1970 on in other countries. Except for France, the wave of strikes continued into the early 1970s. The unions desperately tried to reestablish control by recognizing strikes. Strikes and lockouts in several West German automobile factories (in 1971 and 1973) ranked among the larger actions of the early 1970s. The strikes aimed at securing higher wages and involved several hundreds of thousands of workers. Factory occupations like those in France and Italy also occurred in other countries. The most spectacular example of such an occupation, arousing wide publicity, took place in the Lips watch factory in Besançon, France, in 1973. In contrast with most other occupations, it was started not so much to enforce wage claims, as to continue production in spite of the employer's decision to close the gates. Over 1,000 workers participated in an effort to continue production under worker control. The workers withstood all government (and CGT) efforts to compromise, but the police evacuated the factory after two months.

WORKER PARTICIPATION AND MISCELLANEOUS ISSUES

The spontaneous start of most actions demonstrated that discontent was directed not only at employers and the state, but also at the unions. Indeed, the three of them responded to the actions by changes in policy and in their mutual relations.

Employer Concessions

The most common demand and outcome of the actions was a large wage increase, a common device used to silence other claims as well. Union restraint in response to the recession of the 1967–1968 was overcompensated by general improvements. The productivity formula was set aside for several years as the unions inflated their wage demands in new or additional bargaining in order to reaffirm their control of the strike movement. As before, not only a wage increase but also wage equality was at stake. The general mobilization for spontaneous strikes and later for union-organized strikes involved groups traditionally less inclined to action, like women and clerical workers. The latter sometimes even agreed to synchronize or coordinate bargaining with manual workers, in order to put pressure on the employers and to globalize or generalize improvements in labor conditions. This new feature in labor relations was encouraged by the threat of rationalization, equally affecting manual and clerical workers. In Italy, agreements resulted in a unitary framework for manual and clerical wages (*Inquadramento Unico*) and the gradual abolition of geographical wage zones.

Wage claims were sometimes an expression of discontent regarding rationalization and its effects on working conditions and social life. Apart from wage demands, this discontent gave rise to two other claims: work-time reduction, and more importantly, the extension of worker influence within the enterprise. The first demand continued the spiral of rationalization and work-time reduction. Indeed, reducing the work load rather than unemployment was at the heart of the most general demand, the forty-hour work week (already enjoyed by most clerical workers). The trend toward the forty-hour work week had already started during the late 1950s, but it had been toned down to prevent the labor market from being tightened any further. The demand was reintroduced during the setback of 1967–1968 and was one of the main points in the 1968 Grenelle Accord in France. It was also a source of friction between the CGT and automobile workers, who demanded its instant introduction. The course of its introduction remained gradual, and the reduction in work time was partly reversed by overtime work.

The forty-hour work week represented no more than a minor issue when viewed as a compensation for rationalization and alienation. A second issue, more worker influence within the enterprise, was far more important. It was argued that more influence would improve the workers' position in the face of rationalization. Workers would have more information about a company's policies and prospects, plus better protection against layoffs. Rationalization and concentration of production were not completely new issues, but they had previously been easily translated into wage claims and work-time demands.

Rationalization appeared as a major problem for the first time in Sweden. The Swedish unions' solidaristic wage policy had deliberately encouraged productivity growth through rationalization and labor mobility. They became more active in response to disadvantages like massive layoffs and social problems during the mid–1960s. Two central agreements in 1964 and 1966 addressed the new interests. The first extended the term of prior notice with respect to dismissals. The second reinforced the position of the works councils in matters of technological change.

The setback of the 1967–1968 aroused union interest in West Germany. IG Metall and the metal employers reached an agreement offering workers a certain degree of protection against layoffs that resulted from rationalization. The agreement applied especially to older workers, who experienced greater difficulties when leaving their jobs, and even more difficulties in finding new employment.

Participation (in enterprise decisions as well as in national politics) rose as a powerful slogan in the French May events. In various countries, shop-floor delegates, who had traditionally confined themselves to social complaints, increasingly demanded or took the right to discuss economic matters as well, for example relating to technology, investments, and concentration. The broadening of interests was also due to the rise of younger union militants who belonged to the new work force and lacked deference to traditional authority. The unions adapted to this development and demanded more competence for union delegates and works councils.

Union representation on the shop floor was especially at stake in the French model. Enterprise activism had a long tradition in that model, but it had remained a source of conflict between employers and unions. The French government adopted participation as a device to silent revolt. Toward the end of 1968 a law was passed on the *sections syndicales* of the Grenelle Accord. These sections ranged from one to five workers, who enjoyed some protection against dismissal. Changes in Italy were more sweeping. Employers accepted the rise of *delegati* as new and rather informal delegates, but at the expense of the internal commissions. Nationwide agreements sanctioned the position of the delegates, a change from a system of rather passive complaint settlement to more militant complaint raising in matters of working conditions. An official workers' statute in 1970 (*Statuto dei Lavoratori*) improved the unions' position in collective bargaining and indirectly also the position of union representatives.

Works councils rather than union delegates were involved in the German model, and in some countries both institutions could be found. The emergence of works councils had reflected the pacification of relations within the enterprise, but they were upgraded under pressure of the actions. To some extent they became a new forum of employer-union contacts and a new arena of conflict. Traditionally, the councils had been entitled to discuss information on the economic functioning of the enterprise. In practice, however, this right had not been exercised very actively. Employer resistance had affected the workers' willingness and the postwar boom had reduced the workers' desire to discuss economic and financial matters. Now the general demand for more influence in matters affecting one's own life led the unions to demand an extension of council rights. They argued in particular for an end to the widespread managerial practice of hiding behind the excuse of lacking knowledge about company plans that were decided upon in multinational headquarters elsewhere. Not only was the competence of the councils extended, but their character was also changed. The union militants elected in the councils strengthened the position of the union vis-à-vis the council. Reinforced union influence and the militant mood of these years transformed the works councils more into an arena of dispute between employer and workers than the instrument of harmony they had previously been. Councils became accustomed to expressing more openly views deviating from the employer's views and to requesting outside advice or public support.

In addition to new obligations to provide information in advance about the introduction of new technology and changes in work organization, employers also had to grant more protection against dismissal. Advance notice time was prolonged, and the obligation was introduced that employers find alternative employment for workers who were laid off. Employers opposed such new measures as being detrimental to their flexibility in international competition. And as a matter of principle, they opposed them as representing an infringement upon their prerogative. Employer resistance was strongest in Sweden, where the employer prerogative constituted part of the statutes of the employers' organization (par. 32) and also a clause in all collective agreements since the general agreement reached in 1906. However, after their major priority shifted to worker protection, the Swedish unions (assisted by social democratic government domination) were able to extend worker participation. The reforms restored the Swedish position as an example for the other unions in Western Europe. A series of laws strengthened the position of union delegates and extended the term of prior notice when workers were dismissed. The unions also obtained the right to select two members on the boards of large companies. In contrast to the West German *Mitbestimmung*, they had the right to inform the unions about the firms' policies. Other nations characterized by the German model also extended the competence of works councils and introduced forms of codetermination.

The many improvements in the area of workers' and union rights did not satisfy the more ardent advocates of workers' self-determination. They demanded complete workers' control or *autogestion* (self-management), another powerful slogan of the May movement. Self-management was considered to be a more complete remedy for alienation than participation. The union role in the self-management philosophy ranged from taking over management to acting as a countervailing power opposite management, if the unions had any role at all. The Catholic or former Catholic unions especially had loosened their relations with the Church, had broken adrift, and had adopted some of these ideas. The CFTG in France provides an illustrative case. It had changed its name to *Confédération française démocratique du travail* (CFDT) during the process of deconfessionalization in 1964. During the 1968 strike wave it supported all spontaneous actions and became a main advocate of *autogestion* and participation. The CGT remained loyal to its preference for wholesale social transformation. As Lenin had done in the early 1920s, the CGT regarded self-management as a left-wing deviation (*gauchisme*). To others the Prague Spring in 1968 had lowered the threshold with Eastern Europe, allowing Yugoslavia to serve as a possible model. Several union delegations journeyed to observe the Yugoslav system of workers' control function in practice. Most of them returned subscribing to the conclusion that the idea might be good, but that conditions in Yugoslavia were so much different. Occasional Western European examples of *autogestion*, such as in the occupied Lips factory in France, also gave rise to a new élan of workers' control.

Union Changes

Whether they were correct or not about their own role in the ongoing crisis of authority and in the generation gap, union leaders accurately perceived the threat to their position. They discovered an effective response to spontaneous militancy. First, they turned general grievances into specific demands. They demanded the recognition of enterprise level union activities in the French model, whereas in the German model they extended activities within the enterprise. In both cases the change implied employer concessions. Second, in combination with this partial shift, they also modified their own internal organization. As part of a general trend toward decentralization and democratization, grass-roots activities were given more room and more influence. The process was especially visible in Italy, where new structures and procedures were created for member consultation. The three metalworkers' unions (Communist-dominated, Catholic, and socialist) started the trend by turning the new enterprise *delegati* into the core of their organization. Rank-and-file initiative was revalued, even in those places where *delegati* were not union members. The common support for shop-floor militancy led to more unity among the unions, and the three confederations followed that example. They loosened their relations with the political parties and practiced unity in action in political strikes and demonstrations. In 1971 the new unity was formalized in a new confederation, without the three-member confederations having to give up their own identity. The new federation also followed the transition to enterprise-based rather than locally based unionism. There was a priority shift from industry to enterprise bargaining. The shift implied concessions by employers as well as by unions, since both had often opposed bargaining at the plant level. This mobilization and adaptation increased membership in the Italian union movement by more than 20 percent. The French CGT was almost as successful. Union growth in other countries was more modest and only partially affected a longer trend of stabilization or slow decline.

State Involvement

The state provided the protest movement with an even more important target than employers and union bureaucracy. Major complaints related to its bureaucratic functioning and the limited room for nonparliamentary political participation. It was argued that political participation, whether directed at parliament or not, needed to be increased and that economic democracy should be its base. Although the new ideas were too diffuse to result in a new political design, they did raise the workers' level of interest in politics and also the number of claims on the government. State funds were not only to benefit monopoly capital but also workers. Not all union shared this criticism of the capitalist state completely, but all of them adopted the new claims. Two of the more prominent demands were the expansion of state investments to maintain or restore full employment and the extension of social security rights for those who were unable to find employment.

The first demand, concerning state investments, was primarily voiced to assist industrial sectors in trouble, like mining, shipbuilding, and the steel industry. Workers in the affected industries asked the state to improve plants owned by the large steel concerns but in danger of closure. The threat of unemployment for thousands of workers in regions reputed for their traditional militancy lent force to the arguments. The second demand, involving improvements in social security coverage and benefits, served the goal of more equality. The movement for more distributive justice was general during the 1960s, but it gained strength after 1968. Governments complied by increasing the level of benefits and extending social security coverage to new groups, like the disabled, who had been unable to pay any contributions to the system. Increased social security spending not only served the cause of equality, but was also meant to facilitate rationalization and worker mobility. One of the more popular measures was the introduction of early retirement (pre-pension) schemes, which removed older workers from the labor market. The German reforms of unemployment insurance in 1969 and old age pension insurance in 1972 combined equality and worker mobility. Holland went to great lengths to guarantee a general minimum income for all citizens. Stressing equality rather than mobility, it linked minimum benefits to the minimum wage in 1974.

Union-employer-state Contacts

Throughout Western Europe, state spending provided unions and employers with a motive to continue tripartite contacts. The unions could ask for more, and employers could try to counter such demands. Both sides were also well aware of the disadvantages associated with top-level meetings. For the unions such contacts posed a threat to the closer contacts between the top and the rank and file, while the employers feared early government compliance with militant union demands. These considerations cooled the zeal to maintain German-model corporatism. Corporatism was either in trouble or given up completely to make room for less obliging forms of contact. Belgium exchanged its traditional central-level contact for two larger conferences, held in 1970 and 1973. The first one dealt with democratization and social security, and the second with employment and the necessity of state investments.

Governments still tended to favor corporatism, or simply central-level contacts, if only to raise another subject: inflation. The enormous rise in wages had induced employers to increase prices, since other forms of compensation, such as rationalization, had only given rise to new conflicts. Inflation reached double digits in several countries and became a major state concern in all three models. The West German government put great effort into retaining the wage moderation contained in the *Konzertierte Aktion*. In Ireland, the government urged for more obliging national wage agreements, which would then replace the system of informal two-year wage rounds. Faced with the threat of state intervention, both the employers and the union complied. From 1970 on, employers and unions negotiated National Pay Agreements in the Employer-Labour Conference. The agreements provided for fixed wage increases. Guided wage policy had been given up in Holland, but a law was passed in 1970 endowing the government with the power to prohibit any wage increases. For the unions this provided a motive to stop corporatist cooperation in the Social and Economic Council and to call a highly exceptional one-hour general protest strike. The French government prevented a large wage increase in 1969. A general strike involving 5 million people was the consequence. These actions indicate that interests diverged more than before 1968, when inflation and unemployment had been either a common concern or less of a problem.

During this same period, Great Britain became the scene of a new and highly disputed form of state intervention in British-model labor relations. While the unions on the continent were extending shop-floor control and grass-roots activities, their British counterparts were busy defending them against the government. In 1964 a Labour government installed a committee under the leadership of Lord Donovan to investigate the disputed power of the unions, especially in matters of technological innovation. The Donovan report, published in 1968, did not lay the blame on the unions but pointed to the existence of two rather independent systems of labor relations in private industry as the main shortcoming of British labor relations: A formal system, encompassing formal union-employer contacts, and an informal one consisting of shop stewards–management contacts. To overcome this duplicity and to inject more unity into bargaining, the committee recommended a voluntary transition to more formal factory agreements covering all workers within an enterprise. It also advised such legal steps as registering unions, allowing public control of internal union rules, but above all of closed-shop regulations. A bill was prepared but was withdrawn after protest demonstrations and strikes. These developments widened the gulf between the TUC and the Labour government. In 1971 Conservatives withstood union protests and passed the Industrial Relations Act. The law encouraged unions to register and imposed some general rules on union practices. It transformed written collective agreements into legal contracts, which guaranteed the right of individual dissenters who opposed a closed shop. It also required strike ballots when larger disputes took place. Though some of the ideas were adopted from the United States, many were already rather common in the German model. The unions rejected state regulation of labor relations and refused to cooperate. The effort to bring British labor relations more in line with the German model failed.

To some extent, state intervention in Ireland served the same purpose, but was less far-reaching. In addition to the National Pay Agreements, the government made it more difficult to establish new unions and encouraged the amalgamation of unions. It did not attack the position of the shop stewards as such, since the latter were already less autonomous than their British counterparts.

THE OIL CRISIS AND STATE INTERVENTION

The international monetary system came under increasing stress during the late 1960s. Large deficits in the American balance of payments, due to the Vietnam War, and a shift in the balance of industrial power from the United States to Europe and Japan, undermined the position of the dollar. Partly in response to repeated devaluations of the dollar, the oil-producing countries raised oil prices in 1973 to four times their previous level. This oil crisis had deep and lasting effects on the Western European economies. It had an extremely negative effect on their budgets and contributed to a further rise in inflation and unemployment.

The inherent difficulties of attempting both to curb inflation and to reduce unemployment made economic policy a bone of contention again. Right and Left, employers and trade unions, drifted apart more irreconcilably in their economic analysis and policy priorities. Employers attributed increases in unemployment to changes in the economic structure rather than to the trade cycle. Continued restructuring and rationalization were perceived to be the answer. Such a move would stimulate technology and reduce dependence on oil. An absolute precondition for greater competitiveness, however, was a reduction in the inflation rate. Social democrats recognized the structural nature of some of the unemployment, for instance in the steel industry. However, to them unemployment was predominantly cyclical in nature. It could be reduced by a continuation or even a reinforcement of Keynesian demand management. The effects of anti-inflation policy on unemployment and of labor market policy on inflation made governments try a mixture of both or made them shift from one to the other. Great Britain was the only country that let things run their course. Governments in this country were paralyzed by their new relationship with the unions.

While governments on the continent were preoccupied with the new combination of stagnation and inflation (stagflation), rationalization continued, whether state-supported or autonomous. The main victims of these developments were women and the recent migrants from the Mediterranean, the former employed in the textile industry and the latter in steel and metallurgy. The unemployment rates for female workers did not initially arouse much interest, if only because they did not lead to massive protest actions or demands on the government. In contrast, the growing unemployment of immigrant manual workers gave rise to rather quick action. Governments put an end to official recruitment practices in the various source countries and imposed—or more accurately, tried to impose— more control on the influx of immigrants and *Gastarbeiter*. Their redundancy during this period of recession made them an easy scapegoat.

The decline of traditional industry and the rising unemployment affecting women and migrants popularized the notion of a segmented labor market. According to this idea, national labor markets were not characterized by a continuous range of supply and demand, but were divided into two or more distinct sections, each having divergent entry requirements and career prospects. The first, including the public sector, financial services, and technologically advanced industries, had the features of an internal labor market with highly standardized rules and a great degree of stability. Jobs had high employment security, high wages, and favorable career prospects. The better functions were mainly filled through internal promotion. In contrast, a small part of the first segment and most of the second, including traditional industries, only offered lesser jobs with low wages, limited prospects, and high instability. Women and immigrant workers tended to populate the second segment and the less well-off part of the first (for example, in lower administrative functions). Still worse, they had little access to the better part of the first segment, because they were perceived to lack adequate work values and an interest in a long-term career.

Besides the more formal labor markets, the unofficial and invisible economy expanded rapidly during the 1970s. This informal (grey or black) circuit offered part-time or occasional work to both the employed and the unemployed. Income generated in this invisible economy escaped taxation and social security contributions, but most governments felt unable to influence this situation, even though they deplored it.

The growth of direct state intervention in the economy, designed to curb inflation and stop the rise in unemployment, gave the state a central role in labor relations. Governments imposed limits on wage increases, or at least tried to influence the course of bargaining. Corporatist union and employer consultation was continued or revived, providing governments and employers with the opportunity to press for wage restraints, while unions could issue demands for employment programs. Priority differences, in combination with increased pressure by members of unions and employers' organizations alike, hardly allowed for agreement. The same applied to central-level collective bargaining and allowed room for government interference.

Only in Holland, with its tradition of a state wage policy, did the government interfere right away. In most other countries, the rise in oil prices at first only added fuel to worker militancy. Large wage increases seemed to be eroded by inflation and high gasoline prices. Wage explosions exceeding 10 percent in 1974 and 1975 were the result, but the effects on inflation and labor costs hastened state interference. State intervention in Denmark and Belgium followed the failure of central-level bargaining, intended to bring about some moderation. In Denmark, the two-year central agreements increasingly met with difficulties. Some 300,000 strikers, the largest number in Danish history, stopped work in 1973, when the agreement was supposed to be renewed. In 1975 the Danish government prevented a new dispute by extending existing agreements for an additional two years. It overrode employer opposition to a new agreement in 1977 by incorporating the agreement into a law. The Belgian government broke with a tradition of nonintervention spanning more than twenty-five years by imposing a 100 percent tax on any wage increases agreed upon for 1976, partly to finance an early retirement system. Though these interventions were thought of as incidental, they set a precedent and hung over later negotiations like a sword of Damocles.

Governments also had at their disposal more indirect means to influence union-employer bargaining or to alter its effects. In West Germany money circulation was tightened to enforce restraint. The measure prevented employers from translating increased wages into higher prices and induced them to seek alternative solutions through rationalization or layoffs. A rare non–Social Democratic government in Sweden even devaluated the krone as an explicit means to rectify a wage increase. The promise to reduce taxes for the lower income categories was a more positive government sanction for union restraint. In the central bargaining process, unions and employers would sometimes refer to taxation policy and general budget decisions (for example, in the Irish National Pay Agreements in the late 1970s). Governments would also invoke the relationship between wage restraints and tax reduction in tripartite contacts as the Swedish government did in 1974 and 1975 in two Haga agreements (named after the place where the talks were held).

Union protests against state measures usually did not go beyond issuing protest statements or organizing an occasional demonstration. Unions more or less accepted state-imposed moderation not only in the German but also in the French model, especially when they were able to exercise influence on social policy. In 1978, the Italian unions formulated this influence as a priority in the EUR-Line (named after a conference center in Rome). It was facilitated by the historic compromise between Christian democrats and Communists. Soon, however, disappointment led to the revival of political disputes. Even French unions were rather moderate in their protests. From 1974 on the CGT and CFDT coordinated their protests in a so-called unity in action. Sector-based action days, initiated during the 1960s, culminated in two nationwide action days in 1976 and 1977.

In contrast, two British governments were defeated because they failed to stop unions from securing big wage raises. A new Conservative government combined the Industrial Relations Act of 1971 with a strong state wage policy. Frequent short protest strikes in public services culminated in major strikes in electricity and in mining during the winter of 1973, right after the height of the oil crisis. Fuel shortages led the government to ration electricity and even shorten the work week to three days in December. Both the government and the miners saw the strike as a political trial of strength reminiscent of the Great Strike. This time, however, it was the government that tried to change the British model of labor relations and was defeated. In the meantime, the Labour party and the TUC had signed a Social Contract, covering democratization of the economy, wage restraint, and tax deductions for lower-income groups. The new Labour government immediately repealed the most fiercely opposed provisions of the Industrial Relations Act, but also issued stricter wage guidelines. The TUC initially accepted them, but being unable to put an end to protest strikes, it reversed its position. Ford Motor Company went against the guidelines, in company-wide bargaining for more than twenty plants. This was a new feature in Britain, which was enforced by the unions. As was the case during the 1960s, when Ford had introduced productivity bargaining, company-wide bargaining solved what the Donovan report had considered to be a central problem in British labor relations: employer acquiescence in shop-floor bargaining. Both Ford initiatives conflicted with a strict income policy. During the winter of 1978, strikes resulted in another wave of actions and a new test of strength, this time between the unions and a Labour government.

Employers throughout Western Europe tried to restrict the level of wage increases to the rate of inflation or less as the various governments were also attempting. They raised objections to institutions like the Italian *scala mobile* or the Belgian index, which linked wages to prices. Though the unions remained stubborn, wages were scarcely keeping pace with inflation at the end of the decade. Real wages stabilized or even declined. Investment wages, in the form of nonmarketable shares, would sometimes serve to compensate workers in the more productive firms. This kind of indirect wage, however, remained an exception.

Other issues high on the agenda were similar to those in previous years: work time and worker participation. More than before, these issues were related to unemployment. Work time was generally reduced to forty hours during the first half of the decade. Some unions had already started to demand a thirty-five-hour work week by that time, motivated by the need to reduce unemployment. This demand was not pushed far, however.

PARTICIPATION AS A DOUBLE-EDGED WEAPON

The energy put into the issue of participation was a consequence of efforts earlier in the decade and, as before, the efforts were prompted by rationalization. More than in the early 1970s, when it constituted a concession to workers' interest, participation was also introduced as an employer device to combat disinterest and lack of motivation among workers caused by the combination of alienation (relating to the crisis of authority) and the demoralizing effects of rationalization and plant closures. Increasing absenteeism due to sickness was one of the signs of disinterest, if not of worker protest. Novel forms of work organization were intended to counter this development. They ran counter to the general trend of centralization and lack of interest in shop-floor activity during the mid–1960s. Experiments had already started in Norway, designed by social scientists from the human relations school and consisting of the formation of rather autonomous small working groups. Workers within such groups no longer had fixed jobs, but they were allowed to change tasks assigned to the group. In the 1970s, the growing rate of absenteeism in several countries induced managers to introduce such self-governing groups. But rationalization and growing unemployment made such groups unattractive to employers and workers, and their spread remained rather limited.

Increased worker influence on enterprise decisions was also at stake. There was a great deal of activity surrounding forms of *Mitbestimmung*, West German-style, which was encouraged by the European Community. The community's executive agent, the European Commission, formulated a proposal in 1970 providing for equal representation of shareholders and workers on the supervisory boards of large companies. Arrangements of this type made their debut in a number of countries, both within and outside of the European Community. A new West German law, implemented in 1976, raised the proportion of workers' representatives on the supervisory board in large companies from one-third to one-half. (This ratio had existed in mining and the steel industry since 1951.) Nevertheless, parity continued to cause conflicts between socialists and liberals in government. Therefore, provisions were made for a second vote by the chairman, who was a shareholders' representative. In Great Britain and France, the Bullock committee and the Sudreau committee respectively (both named after their chairmen) advocated similar schemes, but nothing came of it. In Britain the TUC and the employers changed their views during the course of the debate. The TUC, traditionally opposed to union responsibility at the top of the enterprise, was now in favor. The employers preferred this kind of worker participation over shop-floor militancy, but feared a cumulation of union and worker activities. French unions were not in favor of such union responsibilities, and employers were even more hostile in their reaction than their West German or British counterparts. Switzerland, the least participation-minded of the German model countries, arrived at its own solution. A referendum was held that led to the rejection of any kind of *Mitbestimmung*.

Works councils and union representation within the enterprise had already been covered by union-employer agreements reached or legislation enacted between 1968 and 1973. Therefore, there was less initiative on this point. Some countries introduced reforms, though none were as sweeping as those in Sweden. In 1976, Swedish legislation reinforced the bargaining position of the unions, already occupying an unequaled position in the German model. The Act on Employee Participation in Decision Making (*Medbestämmandelagen*, or MBL) put a formal end to the employer prerogative (Par. 32). The law required employers to negotiate not only in the area of social affairs but to negotiate all major changes in working conditions, including questions of what to produce and how to produce it. To that end, they had to give the union access to almost all of the company's economic information. The extensive union rights were used primarily to negotiate employment levels and the timing of dismissals, however.

Indeed, the main source of union anxiety and increasingly also a bargaining topic was the dwindling labor force through massive layoffs. Unions and works councils, usually working together, were determined to exercise influence on the size of the company work force. They used their influence to seek advice from outside experts, request state support, contact members of parliament and the press, and occasionally also to occupy plants while continuing production. This especially affected factories of large multinationals, since such companies could more easily shift production between plants and countries. Unions also started to bargain for employment guarantees. In Holland, negotiations concerning the exact number of jobs to be maintained in the next years even dominated yearly bargaining toward the end of the 1970s. Elsewhere, employment bargaining was often confined to companies in trouble. Agreements either specified employment targets or the amount of new investments as an employment guarantee. However, the importance of employment agreements was reduced by their lack of success. Employers could postpone layoffs or carry them through after a corporate reorganization that was not covered by the agreement.

In sum, the participation drive in the second half of the 1970s was characterized by divergent motives and effects. The major union goal was still related to the militant emancipatory efforts of the early 1970s. Participation was to form the base of more equal relations between employers and workers. Most actions were defensive, however, with a focus on saving jobs rather than implementing new ideals. Employers favored participation in forms that contributed to productivity, but they were quite defensive or even recalcitrant when it affected their decision-making powers. At the same time, the recession favored the employers' own offensive in values. They stressed the value of profit making and social hierarchy instead of equality. Leadership and authority within the firm were advanced as the very foundation or at least as preconditions for free enterprise and employment. In their opinion, profit making needed to be reemphasized as the motor of economic growth, rather than denounced as the cause of environmental pollution and social problems. Their growing fighting spirit was sometimes demonstrated when employers rejected as too indulgent central agreements reached by their organizations. Another sign of growing combativeness was the increasing efforts to withstand union actions. The West German lockouts in 1978 in the metal industry of Stuttgart and Mannheim, the steel industry, and printing were examples. The lockouts took place to counter union demands for more control of technological innovation and work-time reduction. Lockouts remained quite exceptional in other countries.

The effects of the participation efforts and the oil crisis on the labor relations models were not uniform. Despite the major strike movements in France and Italy, the German model was affected most. Unions and employers stressed the importance of the enterprise as a place for labor contact. From a pacified forum it sometimes changed into an arena of conflict. The shift to a more decentralized level reduced the importance of the central level, but left the dominant position of sectoral bargaining intact. The British model underwent modifications that propelled it closer to the German model, but the British government's intervention to accomplish this failed. Its main effect was a politicization of labor relations, pitting the state against the unions. The frequent large actions in the French model strengthened the position of the unions and buttressed the formalization of union representation within the enterprise.

During the mid–1970s the French model also reinforced its own position in Western Europe. Somewhat separately from the rest of Western Europe, political developments changed labor relations in the dictatorships of southern Europe. After decades of fascist-like corporatism in Spain and Portugal and several years of military dictatorship in Greece, major strike waves accompanied the rise of parliamentary democracy. The strikes amounted to a kind of popular revolt intended to enforce more sweeping changes. To some extent the former Communist networks turned the strikes into a form of political mobilization. Workers' committees (*comisiones obreras*), for instance, played a prominent role in Spain. They arose in the 1960s and early 1970s and engaged in enterprise bargaining, bypassing the official vertical unions. The committees became the core of a new union movement in the course of the strike wave in 1976. They also came increasingly under Communist domination. Toward the end of the 1970s the socialist union and the employers reached a basic agreement, laying down guidelines for collective bargaining and union representation. At first, the committees rejected the agreement, but they soon joined the socialists in collective bargaining. A new official Labor Statute, enacted in 1980, sanctioned the rights of the basic agreement. In Greece, the main target of the strike wave was a government policy restoring traditional labor legislation, state supervision of unionism and restrictions on the right to strike. The state-supervised union organization opposed the strike wave, but was not able to stop it.

Developments on the Iberian Peninsula brought into existence a revival of the French model of labor relations. The absence of bargaining, the rise of Communist movements with a longstanding underground network, and the important place of politics in the transitional period characterized political and social life. The same applied to Greece to some extent, but state control of the unions was continued in this country. The unions initially had high hopes in this period of democratization and hectic political activities, while employers feared the worst. However, state policy offered moderate reforms at most in these three countries, which increased the tension between governments and unions. The main priority of state policy was economic, rather than social, development because economic development was regarded as a necessary condition to gain entry into the European Community.

11

Labor Relations in Eastern Europe Since 1948

THE INDUSTRIALIZATION DRIVE

After the Prague Coup in 1948, the Communists used their power monopoly to impose the Soviet social and political system upon Eastern Europe. Most nations became "people's republics" or "people's democracies," behind the Iron Curtain and under the tight control of the Soviet Union. Part of the new order consisted of imitating the Soviet model of labor relations. Only Marshal Tito's Yugoslavia was able to follow a national "road to socialism," different from the one in the Soviet Union.

All states created their own heavy industry under a system of central planning. Everything else was secondary, including the workers' councils that had sprung up after the war. The new priority continued to gain momentum during the Korean War. As was the case in the Soviet Union, a combination of nationalization, industrialization, and central planning was aimed at achieving extensive economic growth. The targets of the five-year plans were actually targets of physical output, stressing quantity rather than quality or productivity.

The priority given to heavy industry implied a massive migration. Large numbers of agricultural workers crowded existing, as well as new, industrial and mining centers. The labor market was subjected to central planning in order to guarantee a constant labor supply. Women were encouraged, or pressed, to seek industrial employment. In addition to the regular work force, Communist brigades were set up to work in the construction industry and in road construction. They were made up of enthusiastic young workers and students. The Soviet example of state terror also caused a rapid rise in the number of labor camps. The prisoners, representing more than 1 percent of the population, were set to work at various infrastructural projects.

Restrictive measures were also applied to the regular labor force. The Eastern European governments were especially concerned about the high rate of labor turnover. Workbooks were introduced as a remedy, and sometimes unauthorized leave became punishable. Both the extensive use of labor in industry and the restrictions placed upon labor turnover caused an almost permanent labor shortage. The new policies provided for the abolition of unemployment, following the Soviet example. Consequently it became extremely difficult for industrial managers to fire workers. Workers enjoyed a very high level of job security in this system, probably the major official concern with respect to working conditions.

Eastern Europe also followed the Soviet example regarding other working conditions, such as wages and work time. Uniform systems of wage grades were centrally devised as part of the plan. Wage levels were linked to the job qualifications, regardless of age, sex, or worker qualifications. There was little room for enterprises to make autonomous wage decisions. The number of manual workers, clerical workers, and technical staff within each enterprise was incorporated into the plan as three separate categories. The plan prescribed the average wage for each category and the total wage fund available to each enterprise.

The high degree of equality associated with the wage levels was countered by some opposing trends. First, wages were related to productivity, but this relation was more a general aim. In practice, some margin existed between the state planners, who attempted to keep wage increases below productivity growth, and individual enterprises, which were eager to solve the problem of labor shortages by finding ways to increase wages. The high priority given to heavy industry and mining allowed even larger margins in those sectors, since output counted more than wage costs. In 1949 wage rates in the Czechoslovak mines increased by 50 percent. This wage differentiation among industrial sectors soon became a general practice. Second, the actual amount of pay varied with labor performance as a result of an almost total shift from time rates to piece rates and an elaborate system of bonuses. The bonuses were part of the wage fund assigned to each enterprise. Though assigned centrally, they could be administrated separately. Resulting wage inequalities, though smaller than in Western Europe, were hailed as a progressive characteristic of the road to socialism. This situation was believed to contrast with petty bourgeois egalitarianism. In general, wages more or less stabilized during the first years of the industrialization drive.

As was the case in Western Europe, the length of the work week had been set at forty-eight hours. Overtime was probably far more widespread, however, due not only to the spread of piece rates and bonuses, but also to stakhanovism and socialist competition. As a rule, two hours of overtime a day were a legal limit. Work time was often extended to this limit, creating a sixty-hour work week. The increase in wages that could have resulted from this was often nullified by a concomitant decline in piece rates.

When the Communists took over, labor discipline and exhortation became the first task that the unified trade union movement took upon itself. The unions also engaged in collective bargaining with enterprises, but contracts only repeated plan guidelines. Within the enterprises, the unions solved individual complaints on a very limited scale. The unions did offer their membership material advantages, however. In addition to educational, cultural, and recreational facilities, membership was an important advantage when securing housing and social welfare. Housing facilities were one of the few subjects covered by collective agreements that allowed for some variation between enterprises. Social security benefits ranged from 50 to 90 percent of previous wages, but only union members were entitled to such rates. Nonmembers received half the benefits. As a work incentive, benefits were not only generalized, but also made dependent upon the length of previous employment. In the early 1950s social welfare provisions, union activities, and the primary labor conditions were laid down in national Labor Codes, which were usually imitations of Soviet regulations.

The right to strike was outlawed, either explicitly as part of such formal regulations or more implicitly. Strikers in Czechoslovakia could even be punished by up to ten years of prison. Nevertheless, there were several strikes and slow-down actions in the Czechoslovak mines in 1950. Apart from the threat of heavy penalties, the unions probably also contributed to the relative absence of labor conflicts. The organization rate was very high (close to 90 percent), mainly due to strong social pressures. In combination with the various union facilities, the almost total coverage reinforced the unions' role as transmission belts of the Communist party. It allowed the unions to integrate the many rural migrants into urban social life and get them accustomed to industrial discipline. The absence of unemployment, the high degree of job security, and the general egalitarian nature of Eastern European society may have been positive inducements for union membership. The appeal of this system was probably lowest in East Germany, because of its exposure to West German media, and in Poland. The latter country was less egalitarian than the rest of Eastern Europe, had a long history of Russian occupation, and a tradition of labor revolt. The forced absence under Communism of rival organizations left labor turnover as the only viable form of protest for discontented workers. Any other form of protest was severely punished. East German workers had the opportunity to migrate to West Germany until the construction of the Berlin wall in 1961 completed the Iron Curtain.

NEW COURSE AND DE-STALINIZATION

Stalin's death in 1953 and the end of the Korean War allowed some relaxation of control in the Soviet Union. The new leaders disagreed rather openly about the uncompromising priority of heavy industry. They were also concerned about food supply shortages in the rest of Eastern Europe as peasants resisted the collectivization of agriculture. In order to solve the problem, East Germany took recourse to the reduction of industrial wages; the specific measure was a 10 percent rise in output norms. The supply shortages and wage reductions called forth worker protest. Construction workers in East Berlin went on strike in June 1953, and strikes and riots spread throughout the country. Demands initially focused on the wage decrease but soon also incorporated political change, such as freedom and free elections. The Soviet army stationed in the country suppressed the revolt. There were thousands of arrests and forty-two death sentences.

Another country that tightened up economic policy was Czechoslovakia. A currency reform not only reduced the amount of money in circulation, but also eliminated private saving accounts. These steps caused a small protest movement at the Skoda works in Plzen and in Ostrava's heavy industry. Demands also extended from income to political change, in particular free elections. The movement was suppressed.

The protest actions in East Germany and Czechoslovakia led the new Soviet leaders to intensify their pressure on the rest of Eastern Europe. The national party leaders complied, and in July and August all openly confessed to their failures, admitting their responsibility for the excessive acceleration of industrial growth and the neglect of consumer goods and agriculture. The trade unions were blamed for their disinterest in workers' living conditions. From the second half of 1953 on, Eastern Europe followed what was called a New Course, with more official interest in agriculture and consumer goods. Wages were increased, most of all in Czechoslovakia, to compensate for currency reform. Restrictions on labor mobility were lifted, and other regulations were applied less strictly, if they were still in force. Many labor camps were closed, and some of the huge infrastructural projects that employed camp inmates were discontinued.

In 1956 Nikita Khrushchev defeated his competitors at the top of the Soviet Communist party. He put an end to the New Course and reinstalled heavy industry as the central concern of economic policy. At the same time, the de-Stalinization campaign of February 1956 set in motion a movement of economic and political reforms. It resulted in a thaw in public life, which undermined the party's hold on public life and caused a crisis in politics in several countries. The rapprochement between the Soviet Union and Yugoslavia also acted as a catalyst, and it had the effect of popularizing Yugoslav self-management. The combination of a certain degree of intellectual freedom and the specific aim of self-management especially affected Poland and Hungary in 1956.

In Poland anti-Soviet sentiments and feelings of loyalty to the Catholic Church were voiced rather openly. Intellectuals discussed new prospects for social and political life, while workers envisioned the introduction of workers' councils (rady robotnicze). The Zera automobile factories in Warsaw were a center of such discussions and a leader in the movement toward workers' councils. The thaw also allowed specific grievances to become the starting point of more general protest. A rise in output norms and deficiencies in food supplies were the focus of protest in the locomotive factories of Poznań. A strike broke out, and a protest movement spread throughout the city. Initial demands were confined to lower prices and higher wages. At a later stage, however, the issue of more freedom was added to the demands, and anti-Soviet slogans were heard. More than fifty people were killed in fights between demonstrators and the army, and hundreds of ''agents of imperialism'' were arrested. Discussions and the spread of workers' councils went on for some time in Warsaw, even under the threat of Soviet intervention.

In Hungary workers' councils were not formed until the end of October, when a general strike took place in Budapest. In contrast to their Polish counterparts, the Hungarian councils even tried to act as a rival political power, thereby carrying on the tradition of the Russian soviets of 1905 and the Hungarian councils of 1919. Not only more autonomy for workers' initiatives was at stake, but also the Communist power monopoly as such (that is, the core of the Soviet model). The protest movement resulted in a national revolt against the Soviet Union. When the party leadership promised to end the Communist power monopoly and announced the country's neutrality, the Soviets invaded the country and crushed the revolt in a fortnight. Workers' councils that had sprung up within enterprises were allowed to continue for some time, but their functions were limited, while party and union leadership was restored. The workers' councils were then phased out.

Because they were less of a challenge to the party, the Polish councils were allowed to continue and were even legalized. Rules were drawn up for their election and their functioning, and provisions were made for a certain degree of economic decentralization. The councils were granted the right to establish work norms and wage rates within the limits of collective agreements. They could also determine the allocation of that portion of profits that had been put aside for social purposes since 1955. However, the party soon tried to reduce their influence again, because it regarded the councils as strongholds of anti-Communism. Fearing spontaneous elections, it took steps to coordinate or organize the elections by refusing nonparty candidates. In 1958 the councils were made part of larger conferences of self-management, also including enterprise union committees and party cells. This put an end to the councils' autonomy, and soon afterwards, they fell into decline.

Other Eastern European countries were less affected. Attempts to set up workers' councils in East Germany failed. Romanian railway workers in Bucharest participated in demonstrations. The government prevented the spread of actions, however, by raising the minimum wage and by referring to the possibility of using Soviet troops—in sharp contrast to the new Polish leadership, which had done everything to prevent Soviet intervention. Throughout Eastern Europe, wages were raised under the pressure of recent events, and enterprises were given more freedom to pay bonuses.

Soviet intervention in Hungary did not cause a complete return to Stalinism. Communist control in Poland remained especially relaxed. Western nonintervention in Hungary and peaceful coexistence favored the introduction of reforms in the Soviet Union. This was also to some extent a reaction to the Polish and

Hungarian events of 1956. The reforms decentralized party control of economic and social policy, although they did not affect the subordination of labor relations to Communist party politics, the central characteristic of the Soviet model.

Part of these Khrushchev reforms in the Soviet Union involved discontinuing the system of central control by ministries for each industrial branch in 1957. Responsibility shifted to a number of economic regions and to regional economic councils. Regional trade unions negotiated collective agreements with regional and local councils in order to determine labor conditions. Although they had to observe central regulations, they were rather autonomous in interpreting the central guidelines, and in developing detailed specifications. The unions were summoned to pay more attention to labor conditions and social provisions. Plan fulfillment, however, remained the primary concern.

In 1956 labor mobilization, which dated back to the war, was abolished completely, and absenteeism ceased to be a criminal offense. The introduction of permanent production conferences in 1958, probably influenced by the Polish workers' councils, encouraged worker participation. These conferences covered a range of topics, including enterprise performance and a variety of social matters. Decision-making power remained with management, however, and the system of one-man management was left intact. Moreover, the factory union committee had to take a leading role in the conferences, which guaranteed strong party leadership and party representation. The spread of such committees remained rather limited.

Though the opportunity for regional and enterprise wage differentiation increased, the Soviet government also tried to reduce the general level of wage inequality. It introduced a minimum wage for industrial workers, introduced uniform wage scales, and reduced the relative weight of bonuses. A further transition from piece rates to time rates was meant to improve the quality of work output. A new form of socialist competition fostered wage variation again from 1959 on. Brigades of Communist labor and shockworkers of Communist labor did their utmost to raise the level of production and involved 5 million workers within a year.

Work time, less affected by this new competition, was reduced in the early 1960s. The workday was set at seven hours, implying a forty-two-hour work week. Soon, forty-one hours became the official norm. The norm was undercut by a trend toward a 5×8 hour work week in advanced industries characterized by continuous work, such as petrochemistry and machine construction. In practice, work time remained above the new norm. It was also still subject to rushing (*shturmovshchina*), in other words, the speeding up of work during the last week of the month, in order to fulfill monthly plan quotas. The unions consented to this type of overtime concentration, though they became more active in their efforts to enforce existing collective agreements. The union role in social welfare and social legislation was also extended during this period. In 1960 the unions were officially given the right to take legislative initiative in such matters. Social security was recodified and extended in 1956.

The rest of Eastern Europe followed the Soviet example and reverted to assigning renewed priority to heavy industry without adding many new reforms to those secured in 1956. Czechoslovakia was the exception in that in 1958 it introduced a more direct link between wages and enterprise performance. Such steps were meant to provide an incentive for both workers and management to increase productivity. The slowing down of economic growth in the early 1960s made the country return to a more central regulation of wage levels. In short, the period of 1957 to the mid–1960s was one of stabilization rather than reform outside the Soviet Union.

THE YUGOSLAV SELF-MANAGEMENT

The breach with the Soviets in 1948 reinforced Yugoslav determination to seek its own course toward socialism. According to the Yugoslavs, the large bureaucracy, closed elite, and fusion of party and state power in the Soviet Union distorted the Soviet views on deviating developments in other countries. In contrast, the Yugoslavs came to stress the role of the Communist party in developing a socialist democracy, which was to be characterized by worker initiative. Factories were to be managed by their employees in name of the national community, instead of simply by a state and party bureaucracy. To some extent, the focus on the national community contrasted with the Eastern European class-based dictatorship of the proletariat. The Communist countries' economic blockade against Yugoslavia in 1949 probably speeded up developments. A rather sudden appeal was made to start implementing workers' control, or self-management (*samoupravljanje*). Self-management was enacted by law as early as the summer of 1950, and preparations were made for its implementation in manufacturing, agriculture, and the service industries.

This formal introduction of workers' control was an exceptional event in European labor relations. Until that time it had been attempted in short-lived experiments imitating the Paris Commune. Examples were the Russian soviets in 1905 and 1917, the soviet republics in the aftermath of the First World War, and the Spanish Civil War. Instead of being a popular movement, it was a deliberate policy in Yugoslavia under firm state guidance. Initially, it aroused only a limited amount of interest in the rest of Europe, however. Any reference to the movement was prohibited in Eastern Europe and among Western European Communists, since it was considered a detestable and nationalistic deviation from the correct course being pursued by the Soviet Union. In Western Europe, the Yugoslav experiment was denounced as just another Communist device of political and economic mobilization. Indeed, Communist rule in Yugoslavia tended to be just as harsh as in the rest of Eastern Europe, and party tolerance of public debate was confined to matters of self-management. Frequent changes in policy, as well as new experiments, increased the autonomy of self-management, however, all without giving up overall party control. More specifically, reforms were aimed at strengthening the position of worker's control vis-à-vis enterprise management and the autonomy of the enterprise vis-à-vis state organs.

The 1950 law introduced two distinct types of councils within enterprises, a workers' council (*radnichki savet*) and a management board. The workers' council, the locus of self-management, was supposed to consist of fifteen to one hundred members. The average size was approximately twenty, and in smaller plants the council tended to comprise the entire work force. Members were elected for one year, and the trade unions organized the elections. Several characteristics of this system deviated from Eastern European practice. The slate could include more names than there were council seats, there was some degree of work-force consultation in the enterprise, and elections took place by secret ballot. The workers' council elected the management board, consisting of anywhere from three to eleven members. These members came out of the council's own ranks, and the elections also took place by secret ballot from a slate made up by the workers' council. In order to allow for the necessary rotation—a cherished practice of the Paris Commune—the management board was also elected each year and was allowed two consecutive terms at most. At least three-fourths of its members were supposed to be production workers. The enterprise director was an ex-officio member of the management board, and he also attended workers' council meetings. He was not elected but was a state-appointed official.

Workers' councils, which met at least once every six weeks, had to approve the enterprise's economic plan, as well as the general regulations pertaining to labor conditions and safety. The management board acted as its executive. The main task of this board was to check the director, who had the actual executive power within the enterprise. The most frequent topic of council discussions during the 1950s were labor productivity, wage payments, and social benefits, but also sales and investment. However, major decisions were prescribed by centrally framed plans and were subject to intricate procedures of approval by higher-level agencies. When the council disagreed with the director, lengthy procedures followed. Most directors had become accustomed to the highly centralized nature of planning and decisionmaking prior to 1950 and therefore had difficulty adapting to the encroachments upon their authority. Moreover, by preparing and coordinating discussions within the council and the board they (like their counterparts in the Western European works councils) were able to continue their authority. Council independence was also limited by trade union control of the candidate nomination procedure and by party control of the union organization. Still, compared to the rest of Eastern Europe, self-management at least added the council chairman and the trade union representative to the enterprise's power circle. Elsewhere, the manager and the head of the party cell were the only persons involved. The composition of self-management boards made labor conditions a central concern within this circle.

The influence of the enterprise and of the workers' council within the enterprise was gradually extended during the course of the 1950s. The scope of central planning was reduced in 1952, and the enterprise wage fund was made dependent upon sales. At first, councils easily agreed to layoffs in order to increase the opportunity for wage increases for the remaining work force. This aggravated the problem of unemployment (a phenomenon that was not denied in Yugoslavia). Later, a profit tax led enterprises to raise the number of workers, in order to reduce pretax profits. Another means to evade the new tax was to lift all wages, a kind of enterprise egotism frequently criticized in the Yugoslav press. Union branches intensified their efforts to keep the councils in check, advocating lower wages and longer working hours. In this manner, they even became a counter-vailing power to the workers' councils.

The unions' position regarding the workers' councils transformed Yugoslav unionism into a distinct, fifth type of model, distinct from both the Western European models and the Soviet model. The unions functioned far less as transmission belts of the Communist party than in the Soviet model. They stressed productivity and wage moderation, but they did so rather autonomously. In contrast to the Soviet model, their main partner in decisionmaking with respect to wages were their own members, which became a distinctive feature of the Yugoslav model of labor relations. The model shared with the Soviet model the Communist monopoly of power and party control of labor relations, but the two models differed in the nature of control. There was far more room for union and worker initiative in Yugoslavia, even room for power sharing at the enterprise level.

Union efforts to keep wages down affected their role as a place to lodge complaints. Workers with individual complaints preferred to address the workers' council, rather than the union branch. Indeed, one of the main council activities in the 1950s was handling complaints (a union function in the other types of unionism). Council work was not confined to acting as a place to deposit complaints, however. The councils tackled more questions than any device of workers' control or workers' consultation in the rest of Europe, and they involved a larger proportion of the national work force. Due to the official rules on membership turnover, about one-third of the members regularly took part in council activities. As was the case in Western European union activities, unskilled workers and women were underrepresented. Although they comprised a small minority of the total work force, members of the Communist party occupied one-third of all seats, reinforcing the position of the enterprise's party boss vis-à-vis nonparty members and management.

The rise of the Polish and Hungarian councils in the mid–1950s added to Yugoslav self-confidence and pride, even after the experiments in the rest of Eastern Europe had been discontinued. In 1957 a general congress held by the councils in Belgrade proudly made up the balance. It also provided an opportunity to raise the issue of extending enterprise autonomy and workers' control. In the same year various reforms met these demands. The reforms coincided with those taking place in the Soviet Union, but were carried out in complete independence. One of the changes widened council autonomy in allocating money from the profit funds. As a rule, the councils took into account what part of an enterprise's profits were due to economic circumstances and marketing performance, and what part to increased work efforts. Funds were allocated accordingly, going into enterprise funds and to improve personal income. The reforms also enlarged the workers' councils' influence in determining wage scales. Within the limits of existing regional collective agreements, reached by the unions and regional economic councils, enterprise workers' councils were able to make decisions autonomously but only after obligatory consultation of the union branch and the local council. The objection that the wage system failed to motivate workers led to the spread of payment based on results, countering the trend in the rest of Eastern Europe. This was accompanied by a decentralization of wage determination within the enterprises. Decisionmaking shifted to the level of enterprise departments, whereas it had taken place at the enterprise or plant level at an earlier stage. As a result, wages became dependent upon individual performance, the performance of the specific economic unit, and of the enterprise as a whole, "complex payment," as it was aptly called.

The councils were blamed for increasing inflation during the early 1960s. Allegedly, they diverted too much money into personal incomes, rather than other funds. Sweeping reforms in the mid–1960s tackled this and other problems more profoundly. The reforms were carried through autonomously, though they resembled changes that took place in the rest of Eastern Europe.

THE REFORMS OF THE 1960s

Capital and labor shortages in the early 1960s plagued the more industrialized people's democracies. Labor supply problems also arose in the richer countries of Western Europe, but there they were solved by the influx of immigrants from the Mediterranean countries (including Yugoslavia). The shortages directed attention to the need to raise productivity and were at the root of a shift from extensive growth, stressing output rather than input, to intensive growth. A series of reforms during the second half of the 1960s introduced the planning of intensive growth. The reforms were the cause of increasing differentiation in economic policy among the Eastern European countries. In general, they consisted of two major changes in the fields of economic planning and control: decentralization and a growing role of demand and supply considerations. Decentralization went beyond the Khrushchev reforms, which had partly decentralized economic decision making along regional lines. The new reforms consisted of a partial decentralization to the enterprise level, along functional lines, which implied the substitution of detailed central planning by plans with a much smaller number of output targets, leaving more room for enterprise decisions and for horizontal relations between enterprises. Changes in price policies, and the emphasis on profits (based on sales) as the main indicator of enterprise performance, reflected the growing importance of supply and demand conditions as determinants of enterprise behavior. The decentralization of decisionmaking was partly offset by a wave of enterprise amalgamations, which increased the scale of industrial enterprise. On the other hand, the greater role of market forces gave rise to new small private enterprises in retail trade and in catering and tourist services.

There were wide national variations in the actual outcome of the reforms. Yugoslavia implemented the most sweeping changes. It almost gave up central planning and replaced it with a new course of market socialism in 1965. The purpose of this turn to more enterprise and council autonomy was to facilitate efforts to link the Yugoslav economy to those of Western Europe. Decentralization also affected the internal organization of enterprises. Larger enterprises, or at least their administrations, were split up into basic organizations of associated labor, which elected their own workers' councils. The basic organizations' autonomy reduced the influence of enterprise management and transformed enterprise decisionmaking into a process of bargaining between the basic organizations involved, which were coordinated by the enterprise's central workers' council. Wages were made dependent not only upon enterprise performance, but to an even larger extent on the results reached by the basic organizations. As a consequence, wage differentiation increased.

The Yugoslav reforms widened the gap with the rest of Eastern Europe, where the party control of labor relations shifted somewhat to the enterprise level but remained very strict. Hungary was the only country that approximated the Yugoslav example. It introduced a system of New Economic Mechanisms in 1966. Planning was retained, but it changed to a stricter kind of indicative planning. In some countries, notably Czechoslovakia and Poland, discussion focused on the advantages and disadvantages of market socialism. The ideas soon extended to political and social life and included democratization demands. Only Albania continued to adhere to Stalinism, remaining suspicious of any new developments.

A chief aim of the reforms was a more productive labor input. Since one of the means to that end was greater labor mobility, the reforms did not meet with overt worker enthusiasm. The Soviet Union started experiments in 1967 that constituted a deviation from the traditional commitment to job security. In some factories, management was given the right to lay off workers without the responsibility for finding alternative employment. The chemical giant Shchekino, located near Tula, was the first to apply the new policy. This Shchekino system spread to other enterprises. Despite savings in labor costs and the concomitant rise in efficiency, the expansion of the new system was very slow. Moreover, most workers, at least in the Shchekino factory, were not removed but were employed in marginal activities. In this way, the system primarily extended an enterprise's influence in engaging in new activities and shifting labor accordingly. This policy aimed at increasing labor mobility conflicted to some extent with the determination to reduce labor turnover. Czechoslovakia had abolished the labor book and was now attempting to cope with labor turnover by extending the term of notice for workers where higher wages constituted the main motive to move.

One of the main effects of the reforms was the growing wage differential both within and between enterprises, as was the case in Yugoslavia. Under the new system, wages became dependent upon enterprise performance, specifically on profits. To encourage high-quality work, piece rates were increasingly replaced by time rates to reduce the link of wages to individual output. Rather than individual performance, enterprise performance became the new parameter for wage determination and a new cause of wage differentiation. Especially in Hungary negotiations (under the New Economic Mechanisms) became a two-party affair rather than just the elaboration and copying of government guidelines. Unions in other countries also shifted their attention to labor conditions, but this did not lead to a change in the nature of bargaining. Governments made efforts to prevent large wage cuts by guaranteeing not only a minimum wage but also a standard wage. In Czechoslovakia, this amounted to 92 percent of previous average wages, while in Hungary, the level depended upon a worker's category. Manual workers were guaranteed full wage rates, middle ranks 85 percent, and top-level personnel 75 percent. This created a situation in which the entire enterprise work force shared high profits, while only middle- and higher-echelon workers suffered if there were losses or low profits. Despite the taxation of enterprises, intended to prevent large wage increases, wages rose throughout Eastern Europe in this period.

The pressure to work overtime ostensibly declined during this period. Nevertheless, especially in Poland and in the Soviet Union workers, most of them women, still spent much of their time in queues in front of retail stores. The queues left the impression that there was very little consumption and even outright poverty.

Czechoslovak reforms marked the end of de-Stalinization in that country and gave rise to a democratization movement, which was initially confined to intellectuals. From 1966 on, there were also various scattered experiments with enterprise self-management. In general, however, workers did not become involved until the party leader's removal from office during the first months of 1968. At that time the Prague Spring spread to factories and to the trade unions. It included an autonomous movement toward self-management, accompanied by lively discussions about the functions and influence of workers' councils. In contrast to the Polish councils of 1956 and to Yugoslav self-management, workers elected mainly technicians to take positions on the councils. The trade unions became involved in setting up councils but were unable to keep pace with developments. They were soon overrun, and union elections were used to remove Communist *apparatchiki*. The new party leadership was unwilling or unable to stop these developments. It gradually moved in the same direction, and soon found itself heading toward a type of "Communism with a human face." This democratization process even impressed Western Europe. The party allowed more room for other organizations such as the unions to operate, without giving up its leading role in society. The surrounding Communist countries increasingly regarded the Czechoslovak experiments as a threat to their own political order and invaded the country in August 1968 to restore the Communist power monopoly and international Communist unity. At first the invasion did not stop the spread of self-management or other reforms and even gave a new impetus to the movement. However, the new enthusiasm was not given much time to ripen. Under pressure by the Soviets the party carried through purges within the trade unions and imposed a ban on union and workers' council meetings. After a change in the party top in 1969, most reforms were turned back, and the Soviet model was restored.

The Prague Spring forced wages upward in the rest of Eastern Europe but did not lead to comparable movements of democratization. On the contrary, apart from Yugoslavia reforms were slowed down and economic control was partially recentralized. In wage matters, efforts were exerted to reintroduce more uniformity by issuing more elaborate central directives.

LABOR REVOLT IN THE 1970s

The stabilization of economic policy was temporary in some nations, and Hungary especially resumed its reforms in the 1970s, though on a more modest scale. The general renewed emphasis on consumer goods in Eastern Europe was one of the motives to expand trade with Western Europe. To some extent this trade continued the traditional nature of exchange. Eastern Europe imported advanced technological products and exported agricultural produce and consumer goods. The intensification of economic relations made Eastern Europe more susceptible to the vicissitudes of the world market, with respect to both prices and wages. Price increases and wage reductions were a central cause of revolt in the 1970s. Again, Poland became the main scene of revolt.

A first revolt broke out in 1970 when the Polish government, with a poor sense of timing, announced a rise in food prices a week before Christmas. The reason given for the decision was the need to boost food exports to pay for industrial imports. The rise in prices added to other uncertainties, such as less job security and impending wage reforms, which were generally regarded as a way to decrease wages. After extensive discussions about the new wage system, workers of the large Lenin shipyards and other dock workers in Gdańsk initiated a protest movement. Their protest demonstration was violently put down, resulting in more than twenty casualties. Szczecin was another scene of riots and bloodshed. When riots spread to several Baltic ports, the Polish government canceled the price increases and dismissed the Communist party leader. Gdańsk and Szczecin were again the scene of strikes and demonstrations in January 1971. Demands now included the release of arrested strike leaders and the discontinuation of a campaign encouraging voluntary overtime work. The strike did not end until the new party leader himself met with the strikers—an act unheard of in all of Europe. The party leader spent most of his time explaining Poland's economic situation, but he gave in on the issue of overtime. The next month, the prime minister traveled to Łódź to meet female workers who had gone on strike in the textile industry. In the course of these various protest actions and outbursts of discontent, the government temporarily reactivated the workers' councils dating from 1956. Informal groups in some of the large metallurgy enterprises and in the shipyards remained poised to challenge such official structures by organizing strike committees.

The 1974 oil crisis did not pass unnoticed. Western Europe increased its exports, but it also made life difficult for its trade partners by refusing new credits and restricting imports. This transferred part of the blow, caused by the high oil prices, to Eastern Europe. Price and wage policies in Eastern Europe were under great stress. In Poland a new governmental attempt to increase prices in 1976 met again with labor opposition. This time large armament works in Radom, south of Warsaw, were the scene of action. Party functionaries tried in vain to stop a protest demonstration. As was the case in the Baltic ports in 1970, the local party building became the main target in the subsequent riots. Troops were sent in, and fighting caused some fifteen casualties. Rioting also broke out in the large tractor factories located in Ursus near Warsaw. Price increases were again canceled, but this time a number of rioters received long prison sentences. The actions, and especially the prison sentences, caused a reactivation of Catholic and intellectual opposition despite the fact that the strikers themselves had not expressed any demands of a more political nature.

In Romania food supply shortages and pressure to work overtime caused a work stoppage in August 1977. More than 30,000 miners in the Jiu Valley stopped working for two days. The national party leader himself interfered. In spite of promises that no action would be taken against the strikers, some of them were arrested and large numbers fired. A campaign was started in 1978 to give more autonomy to work councils, which had been introduced in 1971. This step was probably a means to prevent further actions.

Other countries also experienced their share of workers' protest. In Hungary, labor unrest toward the end of the decade focused on the decline of real wages. There were some short strike actions, which were concentrated in the industrial area south of Budapest. In 1972, strikes and riots were even reported from a Soviet city, Dneprodzerzhinsk, a center of heavy industry in the Ukrainian Donets basin. The background of these developments remained obscure. Strikers and rioters received severe sentences.

Job security was at stake more directly in a labor dispute that took place in Györ, Hungary, in 1980. The protest concerned forced labor transfers. Indeed, a number of countries were attempting to increase labor mobility at that time. The Soviet Union supported the Shchekino system more emphatically and introduced a change in planning, which left the size of the enterprise work force out of the planning procedures. Wages and work force became subject to the firm's influence, representing a further decentralization of control. Increasing labor mobility also encouraged more labor turnover, a matter of concern for the party and the government. While transfers by enterprises were generally supported, workers were discouraged from changing jobs. In 1979 the Soviet Union extended the notice that workers had to give from two weeks to one month, while leaving the term that the enterprise had to give unaffected. This trend contrasted with that in Western Europe, where the term of notice was extended for enterprises but not for workers, in order to improve job security. In general, however, job security was still much higher in Eastern Europe. It was only in Hungary that frictional unemployment became a topic of discussion.

Taking place after the extension of enterprise autonomy in the 1960s, the revolts of the 1970s were an expression of increased worker participation. Governments made further concessions under the pressure of the protest movements. They were also quite aware that workers' participation, being the only means to express discontent (with the exception of labor turnover) had a high revolt potential. Any attempt to extend worker participation beyond the enterprise met with heavy reprisals. This restriction enlarged rather than reduced the gap with Yugoslavia. Not only was worker participation far better developed in that country, but so was union autonomy, at least at the local and regional level. On the whole, the unions were not involved in labor conflicts or in any conflict settlement in the rest of Eastern Europe. They became more interested in matters of labor conditions, but remained rather passive in expressing or handling complaints or discontent. Only Hungary made a step toward union autonomy. The Hungarian Communist party played down the notion of unions being a transmission belt and favored more union autonomy (at the central level, instead of the enterprise level as was the case in Yugoslavia). Increased union autonomy remained a taboo subject in the other countries characterized by the Soviet model. Statements in that direction were occasionally voiced, and in 1978 and 1979 there were even some scattered attempts to set up independent unions in the Soviet Union. These attempts were crushed. Thus, in spite of the Soviet model's participation policy, the two existing models in Eastern Europe remained quite distinct: some autonomy in Yugoslavia, no more than some decentralization in the other countries.

12

Eastern and Western Europe in the 1980s

A second oil crisis, state measures to curb it, and deliberate state interventions changed labor relations in Eastern and Western Europe during the 1980s. Western European models of labor relations were also affected by shifts in the composition of the work force, the Soviet model by *perestroika*.

SOLIDARNOŚĆ

In July 1980 the Polish government took a considerable risk and for the third time since 1970 announced a rise in food prices. Again, a strike wave was the reaction. This time the government and the party leaders immediately stated that they would not budge an inch, a statement that led to another series of strikes. In addition to Warsaw, Lublin became a main center of action, where railway workers were important participants. The main demand was a wage increase to compensate for the rise in prices. Other demands included more equality and an end to the material privileges (for example, special shops) that party and government functionaries enjoyed. The government stimulated enterprise bargaining in order to shift the target of the strikes. The new strategy seemed successful because a number of collective agreements were reached, most of them providing for wage increases. The wave of strikes slowly came to an end.

Suddenly, there was a new outburst of strike activity toward the end of July, affecting almost all industrial areas. The movement gained momentum when it was joined by dockworkers in the main Baltic ports in mid-August. The key demand now was the right to set up free unions, independent of the Communist party. The demand was voiced most ardently at the Lenin shipyards of Gdańsk, the major scene of the 1970 revolt. The strike in Gdańsk was organized to some extent by the successors to the 1970 strike committee. This time it was better able to coordinate the action through an interenterprise strike committee.

The committee's twenty-one claims included the right to organize free unions. The Polish government offered the strikers free elections within the existing and official unions instead of free unions, but this concession failed to stop the strikes from spreading. In a state of disarray, the party and the government changed leadership and engaged in talks with the Gdańsk strike committee. On August 31, after several days of negotiations, the Agreement of Gdańsk was signed. The agreement contained twenty-one points, matching the list of demands. The core of the agreement was that the Polish government recognized the need for independent, self-managing unions because the old unions had failed to meet the workers' expectations. Moreover, strikes would be legalized. A second issue concerned censorship. Though it was not abolished, the mass media would henceforth be allowed to express a multitude of opinions, and a Catholic mass would be broadcast every Sunday. A third issue involved a number of social and economic reforms, including automatic wage adaptation to price increases, a five-day work week, increases in old age pensions, and an end to the privileges enjoyed by party functionaries.

Autonomous organizations were thus allowed for the first time since Communism came to power in Eastern Europe, an important deviation from the Soviet model. The changes were a concession to an organization of relatively well-paid workers, which had already accomplished some de facto autonomy. In September many independent unions were formed, and some old unions (including the dockers' union) reverted entirely to independent unionism. A National Committee of Solidarity, Solidarnošč, was established to coordinate the movement. The leadership of this movement was entrusted to the dockworker Lech Walesa, who had also signed the Agreement of Gdańsk for the strike committee. The situation resulted in dual power, in which the new union could wrest almost any concession from government by threatening to call a strike. Party and government paralysis, visible in the frequent changes in top leaders, reached its zenith in 1981. The process was followed with great interest and anxiety throughout Europe. The rest of Eastern Europe rejected the "antisocialist" forces embodied in Solidarnošč. On several occasions, Poland (and Western Europe) feared a Soviet invasion of the country. Meanwhile, the Polish economy faced disaster. Worker absenteeism soared, productivity fell sharply, and lines outside of stores grew to previously unknown lengths.

Three problems dominated the relationship between the government and the new union movement: first, the implementation of improvements in labor conditions that were stipulated in the Gdańsk agreement; second the official recognition of the new union organizations at the local and national levels; and third, the publication of news in the mass media about union activities. The common trend was that Solidarnošč would call a general strike in order to enforce one or more of the twenty-one points and that the government would subsequently announce its almost total compliance. Next, the union would cancel the general strike but also demand (and receive) full pay for workers who had already started some strike activity on a local scale. After some time government inactivity would again lead to a new round of developments, characterized by the same sequence of events. In this way, the union movement increasingly took the initiative while further paralyzing a government caught between various tugging forces: a drop in production, a growing foreign debt, Soviet pressure against making concessions, and internal pressure in favor of them.

The official promise, broadcast on television, to pay the wage increase that had been agreed upon only partly prevented a first general strike. A second general strike was called to protest against the judicial refusal to approve the statutes of *Solidarność*. The refusal related to the fact that the statutes did not refer to the leading role of the party. A footnote added to the statutes solved the problem, and the strike was canceled again. Toward the end of 1980 the union had managed to bolster its membership to more than 9 million, making it the second largest autonomous union organization in Europe (after the TUC). Moreover, it had been officially recognized, a totally new feature in the Soviet model. The union was even able to enforce the construction of a monument in Gdańsk commemorating the victims of 1970.

The promised five-day work week became a new issue in 1981. The work week was eventually reduced to forty-two hours after abortive talks and two partial general strikes. It was also agreed that a full five-day work week would be introduced in 1982. A next issue was the recognition of a peasant trade union. When talks with the government failed again to bring results, more than 10 million people participated in a four-hour general protest strike, constituting the largest action since the rise of the protest movement. The government complied. The introduction of self-management became a relatively new issue during the summer of 1981, at least with respect to the hiring and firing of enterprise management. Cabinet ministers were present at *Solidarność*'s first congress and reached a compromise regarding self-management. The approaching winter was also a major theme, in light of the economic crisis. Some union members pleaded for the adoption of an anti-crisis agreement with the government, while others argued for increasing the pace of political reforms. When the government, under military leadership by now, spoke in favor of full powers, the union called for a general protest strike on December 17. The government declared a state of martial law a few days before that and arrested a number of union leaders. They were released soon afterwards, but *Solidarność* was outlawed. Nevertheless, Communist rule in Poland remained rather relaxed, and Walesa was not sentenced.

STATE DEFICITS AND UNEMPLOYMENT IN WESTERN EUROPE

In part, the Polish economic problem had been caused by the second oil crisis of 1979, which raised oil prices to new heights. Apart from encouraging the shift to nuclear power, the rise caused a new wave of trade deficits and currency problems. It also raised inflation and unemployment in a number of Western European countries. As was the case during the 1930s government policies were aimed at curbing the crisis. A series of devaluations solved the currency problems, but employment policy posed a volatile problem in Western Europe. In combination with a rapidly growing budget deficit, these policies provided a new source of friction between the political Left and Right, and between unions and employers.

State spending during the 1970s, including social welfare payments, had increased rapidly to over 50 percent of national income. Social security transfers were the main contributor to this growth, due to the extension of benefit rights. Unemployment became a growing source of social security spending during the crisis of the early 1980s. Even discounting social security, state spending continued, while the amount of incurred taxes decreased. To the conservatives and the Christian democrats, and also to employers, the increase in state spending not only reduced the maneuvering room for the private sector, but it also interfered with private initiative and the spirit of enterprise. These parties argued that the state should reemphasize and stimulate enterprise rather than hinder it. The promise of tax reductions contributed to the wide appeal of conservative policy suggestions during the early 1980s. Accordingly, there was a general shift to more conservative governments. Their chief priority was to reduce the state deficit in order to restore the economic base of social life. In so doing they would also fight unemployment in the long run. Social democrats, as well as most unions, remained dedicated to the Keynesian strategy of demand management as a solution to the problem of unemployment. They stressed the role of employment policy as a means to improve employment and to reduce the state deficit in the long run.

Great Britain and the Low Countries were the most ardent participants in the fight against public spending. Their policies of austerity contributed to a rise in unemployment to 15 percent or more. British Prime Minister Margaret Thatcher was the most forceful in her policies. Nationalized industries, including public utilities, were reprivatized under Thatcherism. Northern England, dominated by mining and traditional industries, was left to face an uncertain fate. Towns turned into slums of unemployed workers, recalling memories of the crisis during the 1930s. The British unions accused the government of deliberately using unemployment as a means to fight the unions. The counterargument was that unemployment was due mainly to union intransigence. In order to fight union power the government passed a new series of laws, reminiscent of the Industrial Relations Act of 1971. Legislation was directed most of all at the closed shop, but it also prohibited solidarity strikes and imposed secret ballots before a strike could be called. The unions resisted the measures, but the combination of unemployment and more employer determination provided the government with some success in restraining the unions and in curbing the shop stewards. Although other conservative governments in Europe were more sensitive to unemployment, they, too, attacked the continuing rise of public spending. Cuts in spending affected social security, industrial assistance, and the public sector.

The social security system was subject to a variety of measures, such as benefit reductions, the introduction of a first day without pay in sickness insurance, and tighter application rules. The various measures led to protest demonstrations, but except for adjustments in sickness pay, they could be introduced without any real opposition.

Financial assistance to industry was a second target. West Germany and Belgium tried to save money by making such assistance dependent upon wage restraints or wage cuts, in some cases, even requiring the breach of a collective contract. Government decisions to stop subvention often met with strong protest. In Longwy (Lorraine), strikers plundered public buildings when the local steelworks closed in 1984. By far the largest conflict took place in British mining, which was still a sector of considerable importance. Spontaneous strikes broke out in March 1984 against the closure of unprofitable mines. The result was a national strike that lasted almost a year. The miners' union backed the strike but did not recognize it because the union wanted to escape the recently imposed legal obligation to use an official strike ballot. (Its conduct was punished with a fine of £200,000.) The strike led to bloody incidents between picketers and nonstrikers, and also to large numbers of arrests among the strikers. Public transport workers supported the miners by calling strikes aimed at preventing the import of foreign coal. The strike also aroused international solidarity, but the £500,000 pounds given by Soviet unions only added to the government's determination to win the battle. The strike lost momentum in early 1985, creating a source of new conflicts within the mining communities between picketers and those willing to resume work. It ended without any concessions from the government.

The rising costs of health care and social services made governments look for viable options and cutbacks. State services were reorganized and reduced in size. In spite of various protest strikes, governments also imposed wage cuts in the public sector. Examples were the British National Health Service, French health and education, and public services in the Low Countries. All took place between 1982 and 1984. In the course of such strikes, specific complaints often extended to more general demands involving employment policy with respect to the public sector.

These conservative and Christian democrat state policies differed from those of the few socialist cabinets that remained. The most conspicuous example was France. After a victory in 1981 the socialist government, the first since the popular front, nationalized large banks and monopoly firms in industry and raised social security benefits such as old age pensions and family allowances, as well as the minimum wage (SMIG). It also increased the number of jobs in the public sector and especially in public utilities like energy as more direct measures to cope with unemployment. The work week was reduced to thirty-nine hours, signaling a first step in a gradual transition to thirty-five hours. Within a year, however, several developments forced the socialists to give up Keynesian demand management: the deterioration of the balance of payments, a large capital flight, and the continuing growth of unemployment to over 2 million people. There was a complete turn to a program of austerity, including a tax increase, a wage freeze, and restrictions on the amount of money that could be spent abroad. The new measures gave rise to two major protest strikes in the public sector against the decline in real wages. A new conservative government reversed the nationalizations; the turn to the Left had been even shorter than in 1936. Like the Popular Front, the socialist government had been forced to cancel a series of reforms due to serious economic problems and capital flight. Nevertheless, the socialist government was able to extend employer-union and employer–work force negotiations. In 1982 three Auroux laws (named after the minister responsible) strengthened the position of works councils and designed new procedures to handle complaints and protest. The third law provided for annual negotiations for wages and work time.

The Swedish social democrats were more successful in keeping down unemployment and in carrying through reforms. In 1983 they introduced the Meidner plan, placing investment funds under union control. The goal of the funds was to compensate workers for wage moderations. The funds were financed out of a 0.2 percent tax on the payroll and a 20 percent tax on exceptional profits. Despite vigorous employer resistance (employers even organized a demonstration in Stockholm), five regional investment funds were set up. The unions elected five out of nine board members. However, the funds were not allowed to purchase more than 8 percent of the shares in any enterprise, to prevent a complete union takeover of enterprises. In other countries ideas were put forth to use individual shares to compensate wage restraints, but they rarely resulted in effective measures.

The different forms of social and economic policy had a strong impact on labor relations. They placed limits on bargaining and gave rise to protest demonstrations and strikes. Disappointed by the resulting conflicts, some longed to see a return to corporatism, which in retrospect, seemed more harmonious than it had been in reality. Only one example of this system remained in the early 1980s, and that was Austria. This country's continuation of corporatism not only reduced the amount of conflict, but it also limited increases in wages and unemployment.

Changes in economic conditions also made governments look for other ways to influence or even control wage bargaining more directly. A popular (at least among governments) and immediate response to the rise of oil prices was to render wage indexing inoperative. Wage adaptation was either skipped or postponed, constituting a change from synchronism to heterochronism (as it was called in Greece). Such interventions called forth protest demonstrations everywhere, and in Greece even a short protest strike involving 1 million workers, but most governments were able to impose their will. They also pressed for a more lasting moderation in wages and work-time reduction, and repeatedly appealed to the two parties to refrain from creating labor conflicts during these hard times. In West Germany, where the government was not allowed to interfere directly, the government influenced bargaining by making unemployment policy dependent upon the outcome of labor negotiations.

In general, the unions complied. Because they were eager to retain some freedom to operate, they hastily gave in when governments threatened to interfere. This led unions to concede part of the wage indexing in Italy (in 1983), in exchange for a reduction in work time. A similar path was followed in Holland and Belgium, where agreements prevented stricter state measures. Nevertheless, wage increases were not ruled out and remained a source of conflict. The decade even started with a very large labor conflict involving wages in Sweden. The unions first proclaimed a ban on overtime work, followed by a strike and a general lockout in 1980 that lasted more than a week and affected most sectors of the national economy. The conservative government became involved because the unions expected new tax concessions to compensate for wage restraints, by that time a usual procedure. It was not the employers or unions but the government that gave in. The Italian unions could mobilize 10 million workers in 1982 for a one-day protest strike against the employers' refusal to raise wages.

Conditions improved during the second half of the 1980s, but wage moderation remained a government concern, and employment policy remained a bone of contention. Governments continued to be targets of protest action, especially in the French model. Retrenchments and work schedule changes were the issues in French public transport. Concerns led to a three-week general railway strike in December 1986 and a number of actions in Parisian transport services in November 1988. In December 1988, 5 million Spanish workers staged a one-day protest strike organized by the socialist and Communist unions and aimed at the socialist government's employment policy.

Socialist governments in both France and Spain took a very cautious stance indeed. In addition to perpetuating protest strikes, this stance also provided a base for the depoliticization of labor relations and the spread of collective bargaining. Employers were appeased rather than alienated, which reduced the traditional partisanship of the state in the French model; and in France the Auroux reforms seemed to have some effect. Moreover, the Communist parties were only able to secure very low turnouts in elections and, like the CGT, they were forced to reassess their own position. France and Spain followed Italy's example of depoliticization. The Italian historic compromise and the unions' unity-in-action approach during the 1970s had encouraged such a development. What Margaret Thatcher had done to the British model, the soft approach had done to the French model: produced a trend toward more formal bargaining. Meanwhile, the German model was undergoing change too. Apart from the state intervention dating back to the oil crisis, a further shift to the enterprise level constituted the main trend in Western Europe as work time became more flexible and the work force become more dominated by clerical occupations.

WORK TIME AND FLEXIBILITY

Because of the recession, the main issue in employer-union negotiations became work time. Unions underscored the need to fight unemployment. The other argument, that employees needed more time off to compensate for an increasing work load, was also voiced from time to time, however. The most general demand was a reduction of the work week to thirty-five or thirty-six hours, or at least to thirty-eight hours as a first step. Employers and the government preferred early retirement schemes as tools to fight unemployment. Pre-pension plans would have less lasting effect on labor costs and more direct effect on employment. Often, the government was invited to contribute financially to early retirement provisions. When it refused, the outcome of collective bargaining was mostly limited to extending holidays, without having any effect on employment. The absence of such effects led the unions to stress the work-load argument even more and argue for a shorter work week rather than a shorter working life. Their first success was in France. The official proclamation of the thirty-nine-hour work week in 1981 had been preceded by an agreement in which employers, fearful that the socialist government would go further, conceded the thirty-nine-hour work week and five weeks of holidays. The CGT, awaiting in vain government intervention on the issue of work time, remained aloof. The West German government promised to pay a portion of early retirement provisions if the unions would shift their demands in that direction, but the metal union continued to push for a thirty-five-hour work week. In 1984 it called a strike in Stuttgart's metal industry, a popular target. Employers responded with a lockout. It took a month before an agreement was reached to institute a thirty-eight-and-a-half-hour work week. The rest of the country and other industries followed this example. Since the average work week remained approximately forty hours, part of such a reduction was actually given as a hidden wage increase in the form of overtime pay. Given the economic conditions, employers preferred paying overtime to hiring new personnel.They were also able to shift part of their burden to the workers. In contrast to previous work-time reductions, unions had to make explicit concessions in wage payments this time.

The employers replied more offensively as well, by making work time more flexible. This "flexi-time" could take three forms. It could involve a change in the traditional organization of the work week (five days of eight hours each, or 5 × 8). Work time would no longer be limited to the time between 8 A.M. and 5 or 6 P.M. In order to exploit high technology and large capital investments fully, employers advocated spreading work across more hours of the day and the week, including Saturday or even Sunday. They also advocated allowing workers within the same enterprise section to work different schedules. Such work weeks could consist of 3 × 12 hours, 4 × 9, or 6 × 6. The application of these formulas was not very widespread, however. Some of them required a change in labor legislation, and they met with union opposition. Unions feared a return to long workdays with a concomitant negative impact on workers' social contacts and family life.

Employers also promoted a second and more important form of flexibility, part-time work. Their reasoning was motivated by the revolution taking place in information technology, which supplied rapid and detailed knowledge of product demand. Like overtime, part-time work facilitated a smooth adaptation of production to changes in demand. It had the advantage of concentrating employment during peak hours and busy periods, and reducing it during slow periods. To the employers, it represented a means to fight worker indifference and to reduce costs. As a consequence, it would also reduce unemployment in their view. For the workers, part-time work met the needs of married women, who were increasingly participating in the labor market, as well as increasingly falling victim to unemployment. Indeed, many more women than men were involved in part-time work. The conditions ranged from uniform working times throughout the year to complete flexibility without any guarantee of work. The third form of flexi-time was the shift from life-long employment toward temporary contracts. This third form also affected women more than men.

The unions tried to stem the tide in the direction of part-time work and temporary contracts. They feared a reinforcement of the divisions already existing in the labor market between well-paid men and a category of mainly female second-rate workers with low pay and unstable working times. Such workers might be less subject to labor protection and simultaneously less eager to defend their own rights and less interested in unionism. Union fears were intensified because flexi-time had to be developed for each enterprise separately. Especially to the German-model unions with their tradition of central and industrial bargaining was the combination of growing numbers of part-time workers and enterprise-level decisionmaking an added threat. The trend toward enterprise-level decisionmaking and the stress on unions were also expressions of a more general change in the nature of the Western European economy and labor force.

LABOR RELATIONS AND THE RISE OF CLERICAL WORKERS

The composition of the work force changed dramatically in Western Europe during the 1970s and 1980s. Rationalization and automatization had already reduced the proportion of production workers, but this development had been compensated by the continuing growth of industry. However, the former trend exceeded the latter in the 1970s. Manual (blue-collar) production workers became clerical (white-collar) office workers, employed in the service industry rather than in manufacturing. In combination with the expansion of services, this made clerical workers a majority group within the work force of the richer part of Western Europe. This trend deeply affected labor relations during the 1970s and 1980s. Not only the third sector (commercial services) increased rapidly in the new postindustrial society; the fourth sector (state services and nonprofit organizations) expanded too. This shift from commercial to nonprofit and public employment continued during the 1980s, despite cuts in state budgets. The proportion of women rose, but they still occupied less rewarding jobs as secretaries, typists, and assistants to professionals or senior staff.

New forms of high technology and data processing in particular accelerated the process of automatization and rationalization in production as well as in office work during the 1980s. Advanced technologies were no longer dependent on traditional surface connections, so enterprises settled near airports, large cities, and in "sun belts" like southwestern Germany and southeastern England. Traditional industrial areas like northern England and even the Ruhr area were left with industries in decline and high unemployment rates.

The new middle class of qualified workers continued their defense of clerical privileges. Nevertheless, several factors reduced the social separation, including converging levels of education, patterns of mass consumption and mass media exposure, and a general shift from manual to clerical work. The growing scale of economic life reduced the clerical workers' loyalty to the firm and increased mobility. Not surprisingly the change in the composition of the work force affected the trade unions. In addition to students, young professionals and other young members of the new middle class had joined the protest movement of the late 1960s. Rationalization threatened career patterns and traditional working methods. Company closures threatened employment even if manual workers were laid off more easily. The attempt by unions to synchronize bargaining and to coordinate demands for manual and clerical workers occurred especially in sectors in trouble. Common demands sometimes paved the way to common agreements. At the same time, clerical workers were anxious to protect the privileges that they held in working conditions. They dissociated themselves as often from manual workers' representatives as they did from management.

Their rate of organization also remained low compared to that of manual workers, although it increased. Staff members and higher qualified echelons of administrative and technical workers had their own growing organizations, which quite often operated outside the main union federations. Lower-paid office workers were hardly organized. The situation reflected the rise of unions representing manual workers, which had started among skilled workers. Sweden was the only country where unions organized more than a minority of clerical workers. The success of its *tjänstemännen* federation was partly due to the recruitment of women, who comprised a majority of its membership. However, in many countries the increase in clerical workers and the growth of the public sector allowed the unions involved to overtake industrial unions in size. The organization of clerical workers became the largest union in Austria and in the Catholic Belgian federation, overtaking the unions representing the construction industry and metallurgy respectively. The unions of state employees also increased their membership.

This change affected the union federations in three ways. First, the numbers of clerical workers who joined did not make up for the losses in traditional industries, still the backbone of trade unionism. In combination with the recession of the late 1970s and 1980s overall membership and the rate of organization dropped, except in the Scandinavian countries and Belgium. Here, union involvement in social security provisions kept their membership stable. Second, the growth of independent clerical workers' organizations allowed them to de-

demand a seat in consultative agencies. Despite heavy resistance by the major federations, cadre organizations in the Low Countries succeeded in enforcing this kind of recognition.

Third, the shift in membership affected not only union size, but also union ability to mobilize workers. The traditional core of the unions, skilled workers in industry, tended to be more strike-prone than other members. Despite a growing willingness to express concern or protest, clerical workers lacked the solidarity and the combativeness of their manual counterparts, and thus the unions lost at least one of their traditional functions. The drop in membership during the 1980s made them search for new functions. The goal was to attract clerical workers, but this caused a predicament that was not easily solved. Unions sometimes stressed their nature as service institutions that assist people in matters involving dismissal, career, and social problems. Most clerical workers, however, rarely needed such advice. At the same time, the emphasis on services alienated the more militant manual workers from the unions and served to accelerate the loss of membership. The large numbers of female clerical workers exacerbated the problem of uniting the union members. Women's work outside the home hardly changed traditional family life, in which women continued to do most of the household work. This reinforced their low level of interest in labor conditions or a professional career. The spread of part-time work, usually involving women, in the 1980s buttressed this lack of interest and kept their rate of organization low.

The changes in the nature of labor and unionism affected labor relations deeply. Their main effect was a partial shift from the industry to the enterprise level. This process especially challenged the German model of industry bargaining, but also affected the other models, in particular the informal part of British-model relations and the rate of conflict in the French model. The shift tended to imply two related trends: a change in the nature of enterprise bargaining and in shop floor decisionmaking.

The first trend represented a direct effect of the increasing numbers of clerical workers. An interest in pursuing a career made clerical workers more concerned about enterprise labor conditions than about industry bargaining. They felt that labor relations should be a joint affair of enterprise or plant management and the enterprise work force. This implied the need to improve the status of the works council and concurrently a loss of function for the union or the union's representatives. Rather than getting involved in bargaining on behalf of their membership, unions were to assist clerical workers in negotiating enterprise agreements or in workers' council consultation. The unions regretted the loss of function this entailed and also the decline of sectoral and central coordination and solidarity. To the workers involved, it was less a loss of solidarity than a sign of worker liberation. At last workers seemed able to do their own bargaining and reach important agreements without much outside assistance. This constituted a logical sequel to the extension of workers' rights during the 1970s in the areas of labor conditions, employment, and safety.

Among employers, American high-technology firms, accustomed to enterprise negotiations or consultation, especially favored this development. Indeed, the trend from collective bargaining between employers and unions toward works council negotiations or consultation was practiced first in the European plants and offices of American companies like IBM, with highly qualified personnel. Because of its origins, this was called the Americanization of labor relations. The employers involved not only advocated Americanization, but were often able to impose it because of the very low rate of organization within the enterprise work force. Although high wages facilitated this company policy, the lack of protection against arbitrary dismissals was one of its effects.

The second trend also concerned the interests of clerical workers and employers. Clerical workers were willing to share management functions in defining targets, allocating tasks, and evaluating work performance. The involvement of workers in lower-level management and control had been a characteristic of the continuous line of authority in the clerical workers' bureaucracy and was extended in scope and degree of autonomy during the 1970s. Employers also introduced it in traditional industry and among manual workers. To employers it constituted a device to fight indifference and absenteeism, to raise worker responsibility, and of course to raise productivity. Apart from the Norwegian experiments with self-governing groups and their spread to other countries, the main trend came from Japan. The rise of that country as a major industrial power had aroused European interest in the strong ties between Japanese workers and their companies. A specific form of decentralization and worker involvement gained some popularity toward the end of the 1970s, as it seemed to be one of the keys to Japan's success. This type of decentralization consisted of quality circles, in which enterprise sections were made responsible for the quality of their production. They were first introduced in European plants affiliated with Japanese companies and later imitated by other industrial enterprises. Quality circles were intended not only to improve worker integration, but also to facilitate the introduction of new technology and raise its effectiveness.

Group responsibility was only one aspect of the "Japanization" of labor relations. A second feature was the spread of extensive networks of company facilities, covering social and family life. Initially, such provisions were considered to call for a return to a paternalistic past that did not fit present-day European conditions. Nevertheless, employers who visited Japan were impressed by the sense of community the provisions created in Japanese enterprises and workers eagerly accepted such provisions as fringe benefits.

In both aspects, Japanization reinforced worker integration into the enterprise. This turned it into an even greater challenge to the unions than Americanization. Unions risked being regarded as a threat to group cohesion in those places where not all workers were organized. Like Americanization, Japanization had the potential to bring about a conflict between workers' rights and union rights. Like traditional Fordism, it could even imply a return to more employer domination, through negotiated settlements with the enterprise work force and not with the unions. After the extension or recognition of union activities at the enterprise level in the 1970s, the new trend partially separated the various levels of unionism. In the French and German models, the enterprise activities were cut off from the industrial and central levels. Shop-level activities in the British model were downgraded in favor of a formalization of enterprise level contacts. Such developments could imply a de-unionization of the enterprise and a pacification of employer–work force contacts in all models. To the Western European unions, these trends were deliberate employer strategies in that direction, facilitated by the recession and unemployment. Employers stressed the need to fight absenteeism and indifference rather than industrial dispute.

Even more than in private industry and services, the rise of clerical workers took place in the fourth sector of nonprofit services and especially the public sector. This development reinforced the position of the government as an employer; it was already by far the largest employer in most countries. It also continued to recruit new workers at a time when industry was more preoccupied with dismissing them. The state retrenchments during the 1980s did not reverse this process. With the growth of unemployment in the mid–1970s the public sector unions could bargain more offensively than those in the private sector. They succeeded in transforming the public sector into the leading sector, setting an example for the rest of the economy. This turned traditional relations upside down, with a public sector that had mostly adopted changes in labor conditions originating in the private sector. On the other hand, in the 1980s the public sector unions were also confronted with the governments' determination to lower the budget and to impose wage restraints in the public sector as a model for private industry and services. These stances functioned as a double example: one of union power for the unions, and one of wage restraints for the government. This clearly affected labor relations during the 1970s and 1980s. Many members of the growing public sector unions were clerical workers. Nevertheless, public sector clerical workers were more militant and willing to express protest than their counterparts in the private sector, despite the fact that they often had only a limited right to strike. The growth of public sector unions and their militancy at a time when industrial unions were forced to be moderate caused some tension between the public and private sector unions.

The more prominent position of the public sector also affected the employers' organizations. Their members employed a decreasing proportion of the work force, and they came to represent an ever smaller part of economic life. More often than before, they felt unable to bargain autonomously and awaited the outcome of public sector bargaining, cherishing the hope that it might lead to restraint. Occasionally, they exerted pressure on the government to remain firm in its stand, because employers feared that higher wages in the public sector would raise private sector wages as well as taxes. In this way, the importance of the public sector in the economy during the 1980s enhanced the role of government in labor relations even further. The determination of some governments to cut public spending and public sector wages added to their importance.

WOMEN WORKERS: FROM PROTECTION TO POSITIVE ACTION

The rise of clerical work in the public sector contributed to a growth in the participation of women in the Western European work force. The proportion of women in the work force had already increased since the war, most markedly in Sweden where almost 80 percent of all women were employed in the mid–1980s, more than double the rate of 1950. This more equal representation did not mean full equality, however. Women were not only overrepresented in low-paying functions, both in industry and services, but also in part-time employment. Even if they performed the same kind of work, they were still often paid less than men. Equality between men and women increasingly became a matter of discussion and state concern during the 1970s and 1980s, due not only to the growing participation rate of women but also to the rise of the feminist movement.

As part of the general protest movement that arose during the late 1960s and early 1970s, a second feminist wave came to influence political and social life. Initially, this movement continued to voice demands that had already been expressed by the first wave at the end of the nineteenth century: equal rights and nondiscrimination. After several years the movement radicalized and, partly under the influence of "women's lib" in the United States, changed its aim to liberation from oppression. The position of women was no longer perceived as being victims of discrimination, to be removed by parliamentary pressure, but of oppression. Militant women organized a women's liberation movement to fight this oppression. A main issue was the continuing separation between male-dominated public life and female activities in private or family life. Women should not only be able to engage in all kinds of economic and social activities, as the first wave had demanded, but also be represented equally in economic and social life. The second wave shared the first wave's rejection of the idea that women need to be protected. This idea was perceived to represent a barrier to full participation in the economy. The movement was successful in directing attention not only to legal barriers, but also to the possibilities of affirmative action, or positive action, within enterprises.

Instead of national governments, whatever their composition, international organizations became a major forum of discussion and major agents of change. The United Nations proclaimed 1975 as the International Women's Year and in the same year the ILO changed its interest from protection to equal opportunities. The European Community also became active in this area. In 1972 government leaders mapped out a course of action in social policy, in line with the extension of social policies in the member states in addition to economic policy, which had enjoyed priority until then. In the mid–1970s the community put the ideas on equality into practice and issued a series of legally binding directives. The first related to wage equality and to a certain degree borrowed the broad definition of wage equality for work of equal value from ILO Convention No. 100. The second directive focused on equal opportunities to enter the labor process, equal opportunities of vocational training, and equal treatment in labor conditions. The third directive provided for equal treatment in social security.

The directives included a deadline for their incorporation into national legislation. Since the community was ahead of most member states in the areas the directives covered, the deadline forced these nations into compliance. Indeed, the members of the community changed their legislation accordingly, but only after recurrent delaying of the term set by the community and in some cases only after binding intervention by the European Court of Justice. The member states themselves also became more active in this area. Some of them established specific councils or committees to advise the government and change public opinion. A number of countries added a minister of emancipation to the cabinet.

In the early 1980s the community encouraged affirmative action to promote a more equal position for women, though more legally binding activities had to wait until 1986. A fourth directive was issued in that year, dealing with equal treatment in enterprise or sectoral social security provisions. It was followed by a fifth directive pertaining to the position of independent female workers. Although the interest in positive action was not confirmed in a directive, several nations started experiments in this direction. The European experiments were influenced by the United States, where affirmative action had a longer history. A major aim was not just equal treatment, but equal representative of women in all kinds of economic activity, especially in higher management and public sector functions. Positive action included a great variety of measures, some directed at the work force in general, such as information on female employment and heightening the awareness of formal or informal discrimination and inequality. Other measures aimed at increasing the number of women occupying male-dominated positions, mostly through indirect means such as vocational training, promotion measures, and childcare facilities. More exceptional were direct measures intended to bring about more equality in higher-echelon functions. Such forms of preferential treatment or "positive discrimination" ranged from hiring female applicants when they were as qualified as male applicants to a total exclusion of men during the application process. The latter measure often included a floor quota, for instance that at least 40 percent of all positions involved were to be occupied by women. The public sector was ahead of private enterprise in most forms of positive action because it was subject to less employer resistance and the public sector served as a role model for the rest of society. However, such direct measures (and quotas in particular) were rather exceptional and met with male opposition, even in the public sector. Change was slow indeed, but the issue remained on the agenda.

As it did in most issues, Scandinavia remained ahead of the rest of Western Europe with respect to the measures taken against inequality and in provisions for working women. In other countries the stronger position of conservatives and Christian democrats (in the Low Countries) or the relative absence of the state as a bargaining party in labor conditions (in Great Britain) retarded progress.

1992—THE WESTERN EUROPEAN CATCHWORD IN THE EARLY 1990s

The European Community will remove the internal trade barriers and become one large market in 1992. Toward the close of the 1980s this transition became a popular topic of discussion. Employers welcomed the opportunity to expand exports, while the unions were concerned about the social face of Europe. They feared a loss of function for the central and sectoral-level employer-union contacts and a growing weakness vis-à-vis the large multinationals. The failure of the European Community's efforts to impose standards of conduct upon multinationals added to the unions' doubts. Examples were statutes for European companies and the Vredeling directives, named for the responsible member of the European Committee, that provided for worker consultation in multinationals. In the richer countries the unions also feared a leveling down of labor and living conditions to the level of southern Europe or Great Britain. On the other hand, some forecast a bright future of Europe-wide negotiations, which would help the poorer countries to catch up with the rest of the community.

Indeed, 1992 might have an influence on labor relations. Given the existing cultural, social, economic, and political differences between the twelve member states, however, this influence would probably be limited and indirect at most. The main effect would be that it would accelerate the current trends in the nature of the enterprise and of labor, and in government involvement.

Automation, the shift from manufacturing to service industries, and the computerization of office work were prominent developments in the nature of the enterprise. Although small and medium-sized enterprises seemed the most flexible response, they were attractive prey for multinationals, which were engaged in expansion to survive 1992. The resulting process of growing scale increased the frequency and the extent of enterprise bargaining (though increasing subunit autonomy within larger companies partly compensated for the trend). Large enterprises pressed for such contacts. They attempted to bypass sectoral bargaining, in order to take into account differences in technology and productivity within their sectors.

The increasing numbers of clerical workers in the labor force and flexi-time were major forces affecting the nature of labor. Throughout Europe the gap widened between Europeans employed in office work and immigrants from outside Europe who were employed in manual work or were unemployed. Unions tried to continue or reinforce the tradition of sectoral bargaining where they had such a tradition, but they had to recognize the changes in organization rate and propensity in action. The changes favored enterprise-level activities rather than sectoral bargaining.

Government intervention had opposite effects. Not only in the British model, but also on the continent, national governments promoted a formalization of bargaining at the sectoral rather than at the enterprise level.

The changes in the nature of enterprises and of labor affected especially the

German model through the partial shift from sectoral to enterprise-level bargaining. The combination of forces pointed to a certain amount of convergence in the direction of sectoral bargaining as the Western European standard, complemented or even challenged by enterprise-level bargaining.

National politics also affected labor relations in another way. The rise of state intervention in the German and British model during the 1970s and 1980s had called forth a reaction in the form of political actions and a politicization of labor relations, reducing the difference with the French model. The state role as an arbiter or an outsider changed to some extent to a role as a party involved, obliged to take sides. Changes in economic and social conditions, whether due to 1992 or not, might lead to repeated government intervention or to claims of state action. This could even apply to the European Commission, since the commission has already been active in the area of social policy and the Western European unions have made demands to the European Community in relation to 1992. The demands include employment policy and worker participation in enterprise making. Unions and employers' organizations are still weakly developed at the European level, however, and especially the British Conservative government resists any further development of European social policies. Thus, convergence not only concerns the form and the level of bargaining, but also the degree of politicization. However, the models are still far from uniform in this respect.

Economic and social conditions, notably the high unemployment level, reinforces the role of the national government in a number of countries. Though there has been a return to economic growth in the mid–1980s, in several countries unemployment hardly declines. (Spain even has the highest rates in Europe of both economic growth and unemployment.) In the early 1990s the combination of growth and unemployment determines the issues as well as the degree of state involvement in Western Europe.

PERESTROIKA—THE EASTERN EUROPEAN CATCHWORD IN THE EARLY 1990s

Any Western European changes were overshadowed by developments in the Soviet Union, where a new course changed the face of the nation. Several years of piecemeal reform in Eastern Europe preceded this new course.

The rise of autonomous unionism in Poland in the early 1980s had caused a brief spurt in worker participation. The actual importance of developments outside Poland had been limited, however. The Soviet Union introduced labor collectives in 1983, which consisted of the enterprise work force (without management). The collectives were to meet regularly to express their views on enterprise trends. They had a consultative role in the appointment and dismissal of managerial personnel. They were not allowed to set up a standing committee, however, or engage in other activities between their meetings, since that would interfere with the activities of party and trade unions. Apart from Yugoslavia, the only country that proceeded in the direction of more self-management or workers' control was Hungary. Managers were no longer appointed for life, but were elected for a fixed period of five years. The enterprise council could then reelect them or elect others from a list of candidates. Its influence compared favorably with that of its Soviet counterpart, though it met less frequently. The composition of the Hungarian councils was changed as well to one of parity between workers and management.

Hungary also experimented with new forms of private enterprise. Within enterprises small groups of workers (economic work collectives) were allowed to contract work during their spare hours and allocate the proceeds among the members. The unions at first opposed this new form of group competition, believing it would affect the interest in socialist competition, increase wage differentiation, and reduce union influence. Indeed, the system did undermine the role of voluntary socialist brigades to some extent. It also caused more wage variation and affected the unions' tasks. Collective agreements at the regional and branch levels lost part of their function, as they did not cover the work collectives. Hungary was also the first country in Eastern Europe to introduce the forty-hour work week officially, but this reduction in work time was compensated by an increase in overtime work in the economic work collectives.

The new Soviet leader, Mikhail Gorbachev, introduced a number of sweeping reforms during the second half of the 1980s. A very ambitious campaign of *perestroika* radically changed economic and political institutions and processes and even introduced elements of parliamentary democracy. Part of the campaign was directed at *glasnost*, allowing overt and spontaneous criticism of Soviet politics and even of Soviet leaders. In combination, the reforms were intended to transform Soviet society from a closed bureaucracy into a more open workshop bursting with activity. *Perestroika* included three changes in economic structure and labor relations. First was a further decentralization of the economic structure. Henceforth, enterprises were to have full autonomy in decisions on the size of their work force and wages. This shift in influence implied a greater role for union activities within the enterprise, if only to keep wage differentiation in check. Second, small private enterprises were allowed more room to operate, especially in the areas of construction, repair workshops, transport, and other services. In practice, these reforms mainly legalized existing forms of private economic activity, comparable to the grey or black circuit in Western Europe. A third change consisted of provisions for the election of enterprise directors by their work force. Related changes in the party and the unions also raised the importance of popular elections at the expense of party nominations and elections. The measures were intended to make the economy function better and to increase worker interest and motivation. Although the reforms resembled earlier efforts, especially the Khrushchev reforms, they went far beyond those of the previous periods. They aroused interest and even admiration throughout Europe.

By the end of the 1980s economic reforms had failed to materialize, but social life was undergoing great change. Apart from the position of the party, every aspect of society had become the object of a rather open discussion, in which even top leaders were criticized publicly. Food supply shortages were a major topic of criticism. Within the enterprises, managers were pressed to encourage further contacts on the shop floor. Management and workers' meetings became a forum of lively discussion and criticism. The Soviet Union even experienced strike waves, especially among ethnic minorities and miners. The strikes of ethnic minorities were part of more encompassing protest actions against Russian domination but also against oppression by other minorities, especially in the Transcaucasian republics. The actions challenged the party leadership and *perestroika*. The strike wave in mining in 1989 spread from Siberia to the Ukraine and involved several hundred thousands of workers. They demanded not only better labor conditions, but also more autonomy for their mines in matters of labor conditions. This allowed the party leadership to treat these actions as supportive of the policy of decentralization and enterprise autonomy.

The reforms aroused widespread enthusiasm throughout the rest of Eastern Europe, but the introduction of similar reforms was delayed in a number of countries because *perestroika* threatened vested interests in centralized and bureaucratic control of economic and social life. Moreover, the start of the Soviet campaign almost coincided with an accident at the Chernobyl nuclear power station, north of Kiev. A direct effect of the accident was not so much a change in energy policy, but a serious decline (because of contamination) in agricultural exports from Eastern Europe. To make up for this loss, the imports of new technologies had to be reduced, and new austerity measures were imposed.

In Romania these difficulties were added to problems caused by a too rapid growth of petrochemistry in the 1970s and its collapse in the early 1980s. As part of a renewed austerity program, restrictions were imposed on private consumption, including the heating of private homes. In combination with a work week that continued to exceed forty-five hours, this made the country the most austere in Europe, with the exception of Albania. In November 1987 wage cuts resulted in a local revolt in Brasov. The wage reductions were justified as an adaptation of wages to the degree of plan fulfillment. Though this adaptation was basically an enterprise-related task, it reduced enterprise autonomy because it made wages dependent on central planning decisions. Until then few enterprises had dared to effectuate such a measure because the nonfulfillment of planning quotas was the rule rather than an exception. The uprising started after the announcement, on pay day, that wages were to be cut by 45 percent. It spread from one factory to another, until strikers and rioters met police forces, leading to the arrest of large numbers of workers.

In Yugoslavia, official wage freezes in 1986 and 1987 gave rise to a number of strikes. Though the protests did not result in a nationwide movement, tension increased because of the sheer number of strikes and their duration. In contrast to previous protest actions, which had hardly lasted more than a couple of hours, some of the strikes went on for weeks. Moreover, the unions supported the workers' demands for wage increases. The government gave in in 1986, and in

1987 it threatened to commit troops in case of an emergency. Toward the end of the 1980s, strikes increasingly concerned the nationality question, especially the position of the Albanian-speaking population in the Kosovo region.

Although strikes were still rather exceptional, they became a major topic of discussion and also a major concern to Eastern European governments. To prevent another wave of labor unrest, the Polish government even legalized *Solidarnosc* in exchange for support for the government's economic policy and the pledge not to support strikes. A few months later *Solidarnosc* had won partially free elections and found itself leading a new government with total responsibility for social and economic policy. Hungary moved even further in the direction of parliamentary democracy and also pioneered in the official tolerance of strikes. The Hungarian parliament even rejected a bill on the right to strike because it contained too many restrictions. A second draft was accepted in 1989, with fewer restrictions.

In sum, the Polish movement for autonomous unionism in the early 1980s had challenged the Soviet model and failed in its efforts. Toward the close of the 1980s the Soviet Union itself was in ferment, changing the nature of command in the Soviet model, if not the very nature of the model. The Eastern European changes affected labor relations at various levels. First, Yugoslavia still allowed more worker participation in enterprise decisionmaking than the rest of Eastern Europe. The gap was reduced, however, by the developments in Hungary and even in the Soviet Union. Second, Hungary and Poland from 1989 on were ahead of Yugoslavia with respect to trade union autonomy vis-à-vis the Communist party at the central and the sectoral levels. The developments in these countries challenged the leading role of the Communist party, the core of the Soviet model and an important part of the Yugoslav model. This increased the variety of labor relations within the Soviet model and reduced or even removed the differences with the Yugoslav model. Some countries, such as Romania, stuck to the traditional Soviet model, with its very rigid party control. The Soviet Union moved in the direction of more worker participation, in which Yugoslavia had a long tradition. Hungary and Poland moved even further, becoming the autonomous wing of Eastern Europe. Labor relations in these countries are highly explosive, however. The communist-dominated unions have lost their authority, even though they try to keep pace with their members and support strikes or other protest actions. New organizations have not yet been created, with the exception of *Solidarnosc*, but that movement's participation in government still leaves workers without any formal device to channel demands. If the trend toward parliamentary democracy continues, labor relations could move toward a combination of politicization, including union involvement in political conflict, a high degree of enterprise activism, and a labor culture of protest and spontaneous strikes, as in the French model. The developments in East Germany and Czeckoslovakia at the end of 1989 might even give the German model a chance.

Bibliography

COMPARATIVE/INTERNATIONAL

Aaron, Benjamin, and K. W. Wedderburn, eds. *Industrial Conflict*. London: Longman, 1972.

Abendroth, Wolfgang. *Sozialgeschichte der europäischen Arbeiterbewegung*. Frankfurt am Main: Suhrkamp, 1965.

Alber, Jens. *Vom Armenhaus zum Wohlfahrtsstaat*. Frankfurt am Main: Campus, 1982.

Albers, Detlev, et al. *Klassenkämpfe in Westeuropa*. Reinbek: Rowohlt, 1972.

Alcock, Anthony. *History of the International Labour Organization*. London: Macmillan, 1971.

Barbash, Jack, ed. *Trade Unions and National Economic Policy*. Baltimore: Johns Hopkins University Press, 1972.

Barkin, Solomon. *Worker Militancy and Its Consequences, 1965–75*. New York: Praeger, 1975.

Bean, R. *Comparative Industrial Relations*. London: Croom Helm, 1985.

Bendix, Reinhard. *Work and Authority in Industry: Ideologies of Management in the Course of Industrialization*. New York: John Wiley, 1956.

Berger, Gerhard, ed. *Handbuch der Arbeitsbeziehungen: Deutschland, Österreich, Schweiz*. Berlin: De Gruyter, 1985.

Beyme, Klaus. *Challenge to Power*. London: Sage, 1977.

Blanpain, Roger, ed. *Comparative Labour Law and Industrial Relations*. Deventer: Kluwer, 1985.

Blum, Albert A., ed. *International Handbook of Industrial Relations*. London: Aldwych, 1981.

Bomers, Gerard B. J. *Multinational Corporations and Industrial Relations*. Assen: Van Gorcum, 1976.

Braunthal, Julius. *Geschichte der Internationale*, 2 Vols. Berlin: Dietz, 1974.

Bruin, T. de, and A. Peper, eds. *Arbeidsverhoudingen in Europa*. Alphen a/d Rijn: Samson, 1981.

Carew, Anthony. *Democracy and Government in European Trade Unions*. London: Allen and Unwin, 1976.

Castles, Stephen, and Godula Kosack. *Immigrant Workers and Class Structure in Western Europe*. London: Oxford University Press, 1973.

Clegg, H. A. *Trade Unionism under Collective Bargaining*. Oxford: Basil Blackwell, 1976.

Cronin, James E., and Carmen Sirianni, eds. *Work, Community and Power*. Philadelphia: Temple University Press, 1983.

Crossick, Geoffrey, and Heinz-Gerhard Haupt, eds. *Shopkeepers and Master Artisans in Nineteenth-Century Europe*. London: Methuen, 1984.

Crouch, Colin, and Alessandro Pissorno, eds. *The Resurgence of Class Conflict in Western Europe since 1968*, 2 vols. London: Macmillan, 1978.

Delamotte, Yves. *The Social Partners Face the Problems of Productivity and Employment*. Paris: OECD, 1971.

Dlugoborski, Waclaw. *Zweiter Weltkrieg und sozialer Wandel*. Göttingen: Vandenhoeck und Ruprecht, 1981.

Dubois, Pierre. "Niveaux de main d'oeuvre et organisation du travail ouvrier. Etude de cas français et anglais," *Sociologie du Travail* 22 (1980): 257–274.

Dunlop, John T. *Industrial Relations Systems*. New York: Henry Holt, 1958.

European Trade Union Institute. *Research Report* 1–35. Brussels: ETUI, 1979–1987.

————. *Info* 1–25. Brussels: ETUI, 1982–1987.

Europese Gemeenschap. *Georganiseerd overleg in de Lidstaten van de Gemeenschap, Het*. Brussels: EG, 1980.

Europese Gemeenschap voor Kolen en Staal. *Loonontwikkeling en de loonpolitek in de Industrieën der Gemeenschap, 1945–1956, De*. Luxemburg: EGKS, 1960.

Friedman, Robert R., et al., eds. *Modern Welfare States*. Brighton, England: Wheatsheaf, 1987.

Garson, G. David. *Worker Self-Management in Industry*. London: Praeger, 1977.

Geary, Dick. *European Labour Protest, 1848–1939*. London: Croom Helm, 1981.

"Gewerkschaftsbewegung am Ende," *Prokla*. 1984, nr. 5.

Gourevitch, Peter, et al. *Unions and Economic Crisis: Britain, West Germany and Sweden*. London: Allen and Unwin, 1985.

Hayward, Jack, ed. *Trade Unions and Politics in Western Europe*. London: Frank Cass, 1980.

Heitlinger, Alena. *Women and State Socialism*. London: Macmillan, 1979.

Hörnig, Karl H., ed. *Der "neue" Arbeiter*. Frankfurt am Main: Fischer, 1971.

Hyman, R. *Industrial Relations: A Marxist Introduction*. London: Macmillan, 1975.

Ingham, Geoffrey K. *Strikes and Industrial Conflict: Britain and Scandinavia*. London: Macmillan, 1974.

International Labour Organization, *Collective Bargaining: A Response to the Recession in Industrialised Market Economies*. Geneva: ILO, 1984.

————. *Collective Bargaining in Industrial Market Economies*. Geneva: ILO, 1978.

Jacobi, Otto, et al., eds. *Economic Crisis, Trade Unions and the State*. London: Croom Helm, 1986.

————. *Technological Change, Rationalisation and Industrial Relations*. London: Croom Helm, 1986.

Jenson, Jane A. O., ed. *Feminization of the Labour Force*. Cambridge, England: Policy Press, 1988.

Kassalow, Everett M. *Trade Unions and Industrial Relations*. New York: Random House, 1969.

Katznelson, Ira, and Aristide R. Zolberg, eds. *Working Class Formation*. Princeton, N.J.: Princeton University Press, 1986.

Kendall, Walter. *The Labour Movement in Europe*. London: Allen Lane, 1975.

Kennedy, Thomas. *European Labor Relations*. Lexington, Mass.: D.C. Heath, 1984.

Kjellberg, Anders. *Facklig organisering i tolv länder*. Lund: Arkiv, 1983.

Kocka, Jürgen, ed. *Europäische Arbeiterbewegungen im 19. Jahrhundert*. Göttingen: Vandenhoeck and Ruprecht, 1983.

Köhler, Peter A., and Hans F. Zacher, eds. *Ein Jahrhundert Sozialversicherung*. Berlin: Duncker und Humblot, 1981.

Korpi, Walter, and Michael Shalev. "Strikes, Industrial Relations and Class Conflict in Capitalist Societies," *The British Journal of Sociology* 30 (1979): 164–187.

Kunz, Andreas. "Arbeitsbeziehungen und Arbeitskonflikte im öffentlichen Sektor, Deutschland und Grossbritannien im Vergleich." *Geschichte und Gesellsschaft* 12 (1986): 34–62.

Lange, Peter, et al. *Unions, Change and Crisis: French and Italian Union Strategy and the Political Economy 1945–1980*. London: Allen and Unwin, 1982.

Lehmbruch, Gerhard, and Philippe C. Schmitter, eds. *Patterns of Corporatist Policy-Making*. London: Sage, 1982.

Liebhaberg, Bruno. *Industrial Relations and Multinational Corporations in Europe*. Westmead, England: Gower, 1980.

Littler, Craig R. *The Development of the Labour Process in Capitalist Societies*. London: Heinemann, 1982.

Maier, Charles S. "Between Taylorism and Technocracy: European Ideologies and the Vision of Productivity in the 1920s," *Journal of Contemporary History* 5 (1970): 27–62.

Maurice, Marc, et al. *The Social Foundations of Industrial Power*. Cambridge, Mass.: MIT Press, 1986.

Michel, Joël. "L'échec de la grève générale des mineurs européens avant 1914," *Revue d'histoire moderne et contemporaine* 29 (1982): 214–234.

Mielke, Siegfried, ed. *Internationales Gewerkschaftshandbuch*. Opladen: Leske, 1983.

Mouvements ouvriers et dépression économique de 1929 à 1939. Assen: Van Gorcum, 1966.

Müller-Jentsch, Walther. "Versuch über die Tarifautonomie. Entstehung und Funktionen kollektiver Verhandlungsysteme in Grossbritannien und Deutschland," *Leviathan* 11 (1983): 118–150.

Niethammer, Lutz. "Das Scheitern der einheitsgewerkschaftlichen Bewegung nach 1945 in Westeuropa," *Aus Politik und Zeitgeschichte No. 16* (1975): 34–63.

Organization for Economic Cooperation and Development, *Collective Bargaining and Government Policies*. Paris: OECD, 1979.

——. *Wage Politics and Collective Bargaining. Developments in Finland, Ireland and Norway*. Paris: OECD, 1979.

Pelinka, Anton. *Gewerkschaften im Parteienstaat*. Berlin: Duncker und Humblot, 1980.

Poole, Michael. *Industrial Relations*. London: Routledge and Kegan Paul, 1986.

Reinalda, Bob, and Natascha Verhaaren. *Vrouwenbeweging en internationale organisaties 1868–1986*. De Krimpe: Ariadne 1989.

Ruggie, Mary. *The State and Working Women*. Princeton, N.J.: Princeton University Press, 1984.

Sabel, Charles F. *Work and Politics*. Cambridge: Cambridge University Press, 1982.

Schmitter, Philippe C., and Gerhard Lehmbruch, eds. *Trends towards Corporatist Intermediation*. London: Sage, 1979.

Scholl, S. H., ed. *150 jaar Katholieke Arbeidersbeweging in West-Europa 1789–1939*. Hilversum: Paul Brand, 1961.

Shalev, Michael. "Industrial Relations Theory and the Comparative Study of Industrial Relations and Industrial Conflict," *British Journal of Industrial Relations* 18 (1980): 26–43.

Sisson, Keith. *The Management of Collective Bargaining*. Oxford: Basil Blackwell, 1987.

Spyropoulos, Georges, ed. *Trade Unions Today and Tomorrow*, 2 vols. Maastricht: Presses Interuniversitaires européennes, 1986.

Stearns, Peter N., and Daniel Walkowitz, eds. *Workers in the Industrial Revolution*. New Brunswick, N.J.: Transaction Books, 1974.

Sturmthal, Adolf. *White Collar Trade Unions*. Urbana, Ill.: University of Illinois Press, 1966.

Sullerot, Evelyne. *Histoire et sociologie du travail féminin*. Paris: Gonthier 1968.

Tilly, Louise A,. and Joan W. Scott. *Women, Work and Family*. New York: Holt, Rinehart and Winston, 1978.

Torington, Derek, ed. *Comparative Industrial Relations in Europe*. Westport, Conn.: Greenwood Press, 1978.

Treiman, Donald J., and Patricia A. Roos. "Sex and Earnings in Industrial Society: A Nine-Nation Comparison," *American Journal of Sociology* 89 (1984): 612–643.

Tudyka, Kurt P., ed. *Multinationale Konzerne und Gewerkschaftsstrategie*. Hamburg: Hoffmann und Campe, 1974.

Ulman, Lloyd, and Robert J. Flanagan. *Wage Restraint*. Berkeley, Calif.: University of California Press, 1971.

Verleisdonk, F.A.H. *Stakingen tegen de overheid*. Assen: Van Gorcum, 1965.

Verstraelen, J. *Geschiedenis van de Westeuropese arbeidersbeweging 1789–1914*. Brussels, 1954.

Vilmar, Fritz. *Industrielle Demokratie in Westeuropa*. Reinbek: Rowohlt, 1975.

Wilczynski, J. *Comparative Industrial Relations*. Basingstoke: Macmillan, 1985.

Windmuller, J. P. and A. Gladstone, eds. *Employers' Associations and Industrial Relations*. Oxford: Clarendon, 1984.

———. *The International Trade Union Movement*. Deventer: Kluwer, 1980.

Winkelhof, L. H. van. *De Normaalarbeidsdag*. Rotterdam, 1916.

AUSTRIA

Deutsch, Julius. *Geschichte der österreichischen Gewerkschaftsbewegung*, 2 vols. Vienna: Volksbuchhandlung, 1975.

Gerlich, Peter, et al., eds. *Sozialpartnerschaft in der Krise*. Vienna: Böhlau, 1985.

Hautmann, Hans, and Rudolph Kropf. *Die österreichische Arbeiterbewegung vom Vormärz bis 1945*. Vienna: Europa, 1974.

Hindels, Josef. *Osterreichs Gewerkschaften im Widerstand 1934–1945*. Vienna: Europa, 1976.

Martinek, Oswin, et al., eds. *Arbeitswelt und Sozialstaat*. Vienna: Europa, 1980.

Prader, Hans. *Die Angst der Gewerkschaften vor 'm Klassenkampf.* Vienna: Arbeitsgem. f. Sozialw. Publizistik, 1975.

Talos, Emmerich. *Staatliche Sozialpolitik in Österreich.* Vienna: Verlag f. Gesellschaftskritik, 1981.

BELGIUM

Berghman, J. *Arbeidsverhoudingen in het bankwezen.* Louvain: University of Louvain, 1971.

Blanpain, R. *De collectieve arbeidsovereenkomst in de bedrijfstak naar Belgisch recht.* Louvain: University of Louvain, 1961.

Bondas, J. *Een halve eeuw syndicale actie 1898–1948.* Brussels: N.p., n.d.

Brouwers, L. *Vijftig jaar christelijke werkgeversbeweging in België.* 2 vols. Brussels: Uniapac, 1974.

Chlepner, B. S. *Cent ans d'histoire sociale en Belgique.* Brussels: Université de Bruxelles, 1974.

Dechèsne, L. *L'avènement du régime syndical à Verviers.* Paris, 1908.

Delperée, A. *La reglementation conventionelle des conditions de travail en Belgique.* Paris: Recueil Sirey, 1938.

Delsinne, L. *Le mouvement syndical en Belgique.* Brussels, 1936.

Demaret, M. *Les accords collectifs du travail dans quelques secteurs professionels.* Gembloux, 1966.

Dhondt, J. *Geschiedenis van de socialistische arbeidersbeweging in België.* Antwerpen: S. M. Ontwikkeling, 1955.

Joye, Piere, and Rosine Lewin. *Voor's werkmans recht.* Louvain: Kritak, 1980.

Klein-Beaupain, Thérèse. *Deux systèmes de relations industrielles en Belgique.* Brussels: Université de Bruxelles, 1979.

Liebman, Marcel. *Les socialistes belges 1885–1914.* Brussels: Vie ouvrière, 1979.

Mineur, J. *La reglementation conventionelle des salaires en Belgique.* Gembloux: Duculot, 1936.

Moden, Jacques, and Jean Sloover. *Le patronat belge.* Brussels: Crisp, 1980.

Neuville, J. *La condition ouvrière au XIX Siècle,* 2 vols. Brussels: Vie ouvrière, 1976–1977.

———. *L'evolution des relations industrielles,* 3 vols. Brussels: Vie ouvrière 1976–1981.

———. *Naissance et croissance du syndicalisme.* Brussels: Vie ouvrière, 1979.

Slomp, H. "Tien jaar loonbeleid in België," *Economisch-Statistische Berichten* 70 (1985): 501–502.

———. and Tj. van Mierlo. *Arbeidsverhoudingen in België,* 2 vols. Utrecht: Het Spectrum, 1984.

Verbond van Belgische Ondernemingen. *Sociaal overleg op interprofessioneel vlak 1936–1974, Het.* Brussels: VBO, 1974.

Wat zoudt gij zonder 't werkvolk zijn, 2 vols. Louvain: Kritak, 1977.

EASTERN EUROPE (EXCLUDING SOVIET UNION)

Adam, Jan. *Wage, Price and Taxation Policy in Czechoslovakia 1948–1970.* Berlin: Duncker and Humblot, 1974.

Babeau, André. *Les conseils ouvriers en Pologne*. Paris: Colin, 1960.

Bloomfield, John. *Passive Revolution: Politics and the Czechoslovak Working Class 1945–1948*. London: Allison and Busby, 1979.

Broekmeyer, M. J. *De arbeidersraad in Zuidslavië*. Meppel: Boom, 1970.

Evanson, Robert K. "Regime and Working Class in Czechoslovakia 1948–1968." *Soviet Studies* 37 (1985): 248–268.

Fisera, Vladimir. *Workers' Councils in Czechoslovakia 1968–9*. London: Allison and Busky, 1978.

Kolaja, Jiri. *A Polish Factory*. Lexington: University of Kentucky Press, 1960.

———. *Workers' Councils*. London: Tavistock, 1965.

Kovanda, Karel. "Works Councils in Czechoslovakia, 1945–1947." *Soviet Studies* 29 (1977): 255–269.

Mellis-Bihler, Ruth. *Die Mitwirkung der Werktätigen im Wirtschaftssystem der DDR*. Bamberg: Schmacht, 1977.

Montias, J. M. "Economic Conditions and Political Instability in Communist Countries," *Studies in Comparative Communism* 13 (1980): 283–299.

Nelson, Daniel N. "Workers in a Workers' State: Participation in Rumania," *Soviet Studies* 32 (1980): 542–560.

Pravda, Alex. "Trade Unions in East European Communist Systems: Towards Corporatism?" *International Political Science Review* 4 (1983): 242–260.

Racz, Barnabas A. "Recent Developments in Hungarian Enterprise Democracy," *Soviet Studies* 36 (1984): 544–559.

Reynolds, Jaime. "Communists, Socialists and Workers: Poland 1944–1948," *Soviet Studies* 30 (1978): 516–539.

Roggemann, Hedwig. *Das Modell der Arbeiterselbstverwaltung in Jugoslavien*. Frankfurt am Main: Europäische Verlagsanstalt, 1970.

Ruane, Kevin. *The Polish Challenge*. London: BBC, 1982.

Staniszkis, Jadwiga. "The Evolution of Forms of Working-Class Protest in Poland: Sociological Reflections on the Gdansk-Szczecin Case, August 1980," *Soviet Studies* 33 (1981): 204–231.

Triska, Jan, and Charles Gati, eds. *Blue-Collar Workers in Eastern Europe*. London: Allen and Unwin, 1981.

Wachtel, Howard M. *Workers' Management and Workers' Wages in Yugoslavia*. Ithaca, N.Y.: Cornell University Press, 1973.

Weydenthal, Jan B. de, et al. *The Polish Drama 1980–1982*. Lexington, Mass.: D.C. Heath, 1983.

FRANCE

Adam, Gérard, et al. *La négociation collective en France*. Paris: Editions Ouvrières, 1972.

Aminzade, R. "Capitalist Industrialization and Patterns of Industrial Protest," *American Sociological Review* 49 (1984): 437–453.

Bergonnioux, Alain. *Force Ouvrière*. Paris: Seuil, 1975.

Berlanstein, Lenard R. *The Working People of Paris 1871–1914*. Baltimore, Md.: Johns Hopkins University Press, 1984.

Bezucha, Robert J., "The Pre-Industrial Worker Movement. The *Canuts* of Lyon," in

Robert J. Bezucha, ed., *Modern European Social History*. Lexington, Mass: D.C. Heath, 1972, pp. 93–123.

Bouvier-Ajan, M. *Histoire du travail en France depuis la Révolution*. Paris: Librairie Générale de Droit, 1969.

Brizay, Bernard. *Le patronat, histoire, structure, stratégie du CNPF*. Paris: Seuil, 1976.

Bron, Jean. *Histoire du mouvement ouvrier français*, 3 vols. Paris: Editions Ouvrières, 1970–1973.

Dassa, Sam. "Conflit ou négociation. Les grèves, leurs résultats et la taille des enterprises," *Sociologie du Travail* 25 (1983): 32–44.

Descostes, Marc, and Jean Louis Robert. *Clefs pour un syndicalisme du cadre*. Paris: Editions Ouvrières, 1984.

Eyraud, François. "La négociation salariale dans la métallurgie," *Sociologie du Travail* 25 (1983): 295–312.

————, and Robert Tchobanian. "The Auroux Reforms and Company Level Industrial Relations in France," *British Journal of Industrial Relations* 23 (1985): 241–259.

Fine, M. *Towards Corporatism: The Movement for Capital-Labor Collaboration in France 1914–1936*. Madison, Wis.: University of Wisconsin Press, 1971.

Fridenson, Patrick. "Les premiers ouvriers français de l'automobile (1890–1914)," *Sociologie du Travail* 21 (1979): 297–325.

Hanagan, Michael P. *The Logic of Solidarity: Artisans and Industrial Workers in Three French Towns 1871–1914*. Urbana, Ill.: University of Illinois Press, 1980.

Labi, Maurice. *La grande division de travailleurs*. Paris: Editions Ouvrières, 1964.

Lebovics, Herman. "Protection Against Labor Troubles: The Campaign of the *Association de l'Industrie française* for Economic Stability and Social Peace During the Great Depression 1880–96," *International Review of Social History* 31 (1981): 147–165.

Lefranc, Georges. *Le mouvement syndical de la libération aux évenements de mai-juin 1968*. Paris: Payot, 1969.

Leguin, Yves. *Les ouvriers de la region lyonnaise (1848–1914)*, 2 vols. Lyon: Presses Universitaires de Lyon, 1977.

Loubère, Leo. "Coal Miners, Strikes and Politics in the Lower Languedoc, 1880–1914," *Journal of Social History* 2 (1968): 25–50.

Mallet, Serge. *La nouvelle classe ouvrière*. Paris: Seuil, 1969.

Merriman, John M., ed. *Consciousness and Class Experience in Nineteenth Century Europe*. New York: Holmes and Meier, 1980.

Moss, Bernard H. *The Origins of the French Labor Movement 1830–1914*. Berkeley: University of California Press, 1976.

Mouriaux, René. *La CGT*. Paris: Seuil, 1982.

Rahm, Peter Carl. *Die Gewerkschaftsbewegung in Frankreich*. Heidelberg: University of Heidelberg, 1980.

Reynaud, Jean-Daniel. *Les syndicats en France*, 2 vols. Paris: Seuil, 1975.

Sewell, William H. *Work and Revolution in France*. Cambridge: Cambridge University Press, 1980.

Shorter, Edward, and Charles Tilly. *Strikes in France 1830–1968*. New York: Cambridge University Press, 1974.

Smith, W. Rand. *Crisis in the French Labour Movement*. London: Macmillan, 1987.

Stearns, Peter N. *Paths to Authority: The Middle Class and the Industrial Labor Force in France 1820–48*. Urbana, Ill.: University of Illinois Press, 1978.

————. *Revolutionary Syndicalism and French Labor*. New Brunswick, N.J.: Rutgers University Press, 1971.

Wiardi Beckman, H. B. *Het syndicalisme in Frankrijk*. Amsterdam, Querido, 1931.

GERMANY (WEST)

Adam, Hermann. "Zur Problematik der konzertierten Aktion," *Aus Politik und Zeitgeschichte*, No. 39 (1973): 3–15.

Alemann, Ulrich von, ed. *Partizipation-Demokratisierung-Mitbestimmung*. Opladen: Westdeutscher Verlag, 1978.

Beier, Gerhard. *Der Demonstrations- und Generalstreik vom 12. November 1948*. Frankfurt am Main: Europäische Verlagsanstalt, 1975.

Bergmann, Joachim, et al. *Gewerkschaften in der Bundesrepublik I*, Frankfurt am Main: Aspekte, 1976.

Deppe, Frank, et al. *Geschichte der deutschen Gewerkschaftsbewegung*. Cologne: Pahl-Rugenstein, 1977.

Dombois, Rainer. "Stammarbeiter und Krisenbetroffenheit," *Prokla*, No. 36 (1979): 161–187.

Erd, Rainer, and Walter Müller-Jentsch. "Ende der Arbeiteraristokratie? Technologische Veränderungen, Qualifikationsstruktur und Tarifbeziehungen in der Druckindustrie," *Prokla*, no. 35 (1979): 17–47.

Feldman, Gerald D., and Irmgard Steinisch. *Industrie und Gewerkschaften 1918–1924: die überforderte Zentralarbeitsgemeinschaft*. Stuttgart: Deutsche Verlags Anstalt, 1985.

Glovka, Spencer E. "Between Capital and Labour: Supervisory Personnel in Ruhr Heavy Industry before 1914," *Journal of Social History* 9 (1975): 178–192.

Grebing, Helfa. *Geschichte der deutschen Arbeiterbewegung*. Munich: Nymphenburger, 1966.

————. "Politische und soziale Probleme der Arbeiterklasse am Ende des Zweiten Weltkrieges und in der unmittelbaren Nachkriegszeit," *Intern. Wissensch. Korrsepondenz zur Geschichte der deutschen Arbeiterbewegung* 22 (1986): 1–6.

Homburg, Heidrun. "Anfänge des Taylorsystems in Deutschland vor dem Ersten Weltkrieg," *Geschichte und Gesellschaft* 4 (1978): 170–194.

Kocka, Jürgen. *Unternehmensverwaltung und Angestelltenschaft am Beispiel Siemens 1847–1914*. Stuttgart: Ernst Klett, 1969.

Kruschke, Reinhard. *Betriebliche Gewerkschaftsorgane und Interessenvertretung*. Berlin: Arbeitswelt, 1975.

Mason, Timothey. *Sozialpolitik im Dritten Reich*. Opladen: Westdeutscher, 1977.

Mattheier, Klaus. *Die Gelben. Nationale Arbeiter zwischen Wirtschaftsfrieden und Streik*. Düssesldorf: Schwamm, 1973.

Moses, John A. *Trade Unionism in Germany from Bismarck to Hitler, 1869–1933*, 2 vols. London: Prior 1982.

Pinl, Claudia. *Das Arbeitnehmerproletariat*. Cologne: Kiepenheuer und Witsch, 1977.

Renzsch, Wolfgang. *Handwerker und Lohnarbeiter in der frühen Arbeiterbewegung*. Göttingen: Vandenhoeck und Ruprecht, 1980.

Reulecke, Jürgen, ed. *Arbeiterbewegung am Rhein und Ruhr*. Wuppertal: Hammer, 1974.

Schäfer, Hermann P. "Die 'Gelben Gewerkschaften' am Beispiel des Unterstützungsvereins der Siemens-Werke Berlin,'' *Vierteljahresschrift für Sozial- und Wirtschaftsgeschichte* 59 (1972): 41–76.

Schneider, Michael. *Die Christlichen Gewerkschaften 1894–1933*. Bonn: Neue Gesellschaft, 1982.

Stolla, Uta. *Arbeiterpolitik im Betrieb*. Frankfurt am Main: Campus, 1980.

Vetterli, Rudolf. *Industriearbeit, Arbeiterbewusstsein und gewerkschaftliche Organisation*. Göttingen: Vandenhoeck und Ruprecht, 1978.

Wachenheim, Hedwig. *Die deutsche Arbeiterbewegung 1844 bis 1914*. Cologne: Westdeutscher, 1967.

Waline, Pierre. *Cinquante ans de rapports entre patrons et ouvriers en Allemagne 1918–1968*, 2 vols. Paris: Colin, 1970.

Wendt, Bernd-Jürgen. ''Mitbestimmung und Sozialpartnerschaft in der Weimarer Republik,'' *Aus Politik und Zeitgeschichte*, No. 26 (1969): 27–46.

GREAT BRITAIN

Alderman, Geoffrey. ''The National Free Labour Association. A Case Study of Organised Strike Breaking in the Late Nineteenth and Early Twentieth Centuries,'' *International Review of Social History* 21 (1976): 309–336.

Bain, Georges Sayers. *The Growth of White-Collar Unionism*. Oxford: Oxford University Press, 1972.

———, ed. *Industrial Relations in Britain*. Oxford: Basil Blackwell, 1983.

Barnes, Denis. *Governments and Trade Unions: The British Experience, 1964–79*. London: Heinemann, 1980.

Batstone, Eric, et al. *Shop Stewards in Action: The Organization of Workplace Conflict and Accommodation*. Oxford: Basil Blackwell, 1970.

Bauman, Zygmunt. *Between Class and Elite: The Evolution of the British Labour Movement*. Manchester: Manchester University Press, 1972.

Beynon, Huw. *Working for Ford*. London: Allen Lane, 1973.

Booth, Alan. ''Corporatism, Capitalism and Depression in 20th-Century Britain,'' *The British Journal of Sociology* 33 (1982): 200–223.

Brown, Kenneth D., *The English Labour Movement 1700–1951*. Dublin: Gill and Macmillan, 1982.

Burgess, Keith. *The Challenge of Labour*. London: Croom Helm. 1980.

Carpenter, L. P. ''Corporatism in Britain 1930–45,'' *Journal of Contemporary History* 11 (1976): 3–25.

Clegg, Hugh Armstrong. *The Changing System of Industrial Relations in Great Britain*. Oxford: Basil Blackwell, 1983.

Cole, G.H.D. *A Short History of the British Working-Class Movement: 1789–1947*. London: Allen and Unwin, 1948.

Crompton, Rosemary. ''Trade Unionism and the Insurance Clerks,'' *Sociology* 13 (1979): 403–426.

Crossick, Geoffrey. *The Lower Middle Class in Britain*. London: Croom Helm, 1977.

Crouch, Colin. *Class Conflict and the Industrial Relations Crisis*. London: Humanities Press, 1977.

Dorfman, Gerald A. *Wage Politics in Britain 1945–1967*. Ames, Iowa: Iowa University Press, 1973.

Flanders, Alan. *Management and Unions*. London: Faber and Faber, 1970.

Fraser, Derek. *The Evolution of the British Welfare State*. London: Macmillan, 1984.
Gospel, Howard F. "Employers' Labour Policy: A Study of the Mond-Turner Talks 1927–33," *Business History* 21 (1979): 180–197.
Gray, Robert. *The Aristocracy of Labour in Nineteenth-Century Britain in 1850–1914*. London: Macmillan, 1981.
Hammond, J. L., and Barbara Hammond. *The Town Labourer*. London: Longman, 1978.
Hinton, James. *The First Shop Stewards Movement*. London: Allen and Unwin, 1973.
Hobsbawn, Eric J. *Labouring Men*. London: Weidenfeld and Nicolson, 1974.
Huiskamp, M. J. *Shop stewards and arbeiderszeggenschap*. Alphen a/d Rijn: Samson, 1976.
Hunt, E. H. *British Labour History: 1815–1914*. London: Weidenfeld and Nicolson, 1981.
Lovell, John. *British Trade Unions 1875–1933*. London: Macmillan, 1977.
Melling, Joseph. " 'Non-Commissioned Officers': British Employers and Their Supervisory Workers 1880–1920," *Social History* 5 (1980): 183–221.
Ogden, S. G. "Trade Unions, Industrial Democracy and Collective Bargaining," *Sociology* 16 (1982): 544–563.
Pelling, Henry. *A History of British Trade Unionism*. Hammondsworth: Penguin, 1979.
Penn, Roger. "Trade Union Organization and Skill in the Cotton and Engineering Industries in Britain 1850–1960," *Social History* 8 (1983): 37–55.
Thompson, E. P. *The Making of the English Working Class*. Harmondsworth: Penguin, 1974.
Ward, J. T., and W. Hamish Fraser. *Workers and Employers*. London: Macmillan, 1980.
Webb, Sidney, and Beatrice Webb. *The History of Trade Unionism*. London: Longmans, Green and Co., 1920.
Wendt, Bernd-Jürgen. "Industrial Democracy: Zur Struktur der englischen Sozialbeziehungen," *Aus Politik und Zeitgeschichte*, No. 46 (1975): 3–48.
Wigham, Eric. *Strikes and Government 1893–1974*. London: Macmillan, 1976.
Wrigley, Chris, ed. *A History of British Industrial Relations 1875–1914*. Brighton, England: Harvester, 1982.
Yarmie, Andrew H. "Employers' Organizations in Mid-Victorian England," *International Review of Social History* 25 (1980): 209–235.
Zeitlin, J. "Crafts Control and the Division of Labour: Engineers and Compositors in Britain 1890–1930," *Cambridge Journal of Economics* 3 (1979): 263–274.

HOLLAND

Bölger, B. *Organisatorische verhoudingen tusschen werkgevers en arbeiders*. Haarlem: Tjeenk Willink, 1929.
Brugmans, L. J. *De arbeidende klasse in Nederland in de negentiende eeuw 1813–1870*. Utrecht: Het Spectrum, 1975.
Coomans, Paul, et al. *De Eenheidsvakcentrale (EVC) 1943–1948*. Groningen: Tjeenk Willink, 1976.
Doorn, Kees van, et al. *De beheerste vakbeweging*. Amsterdam: Van Gennep, 1976.
Fase, W.J.P.M. *Vijfendertig jaar loonbeleid in Nederland*. Alphen a/d Rijn: Samson, 1980.

Frenkel, B. S., et al. *De structuur van het c.a.o.-overleg*. Alphen a/d Rijn: Samson, 1980.

Hagoort, R. *De christelijk-sociale beweging*. Hoorn: Edeca, 1933.

Harmsen, Ger, and Bob Reinalda. *Voor de bevrijding van de arbeid*. Nijmegen: SUN, 1975.

Hoeven, P.J.A. ter. *Breukvlakken in het arbeidsbestel*. Alphen a/d Rijn: Samson, 1972.

Huiskamp, M. J. "De cao-structuur in de Nederlandse industrie," *Economisch-Statistische Berichten* (1983): 131–137, 154–158, 180–194.

Jong Edz, F. de. *Om de plaats van de arbeid*. Amsterdam: Arbeiderspers, 1956.

Nobelen, P.W.M. *Ondernemers georganiseerd*. Rotterdam: University of Rotterdam, 1987.

Oudegeest, J. *De geschiedenis van de zelfstandige vakbeweging*, 2 vols. Amsterdam: NVV, 1926.

Reinalda, Bob. *Bedienden georganiseerd*. Nijmegen: SUN, 1981.

Reynaerts, W.H.J., and A. G. Nagelkerke. *Arbeidsverhoudingen, theorie en praktijk*, 2 vols. Leiden: Stenfert Kroese, 1982.

Roes, J., ed. *Katholieke arbeidersbeweging*. Baarn: Ambo, 1985.

Roland Holst, Henriëtte. *Kapitaal en Arbeid in Nederland*, 2 vols. Nijmegen: SUN, 1971.

Slomp, H. *De cao in Nederland tot 1907*. Nijmegen: Universiteit van Nijmegen, 1981.

Tempel, Jan van der. *De Nederlandse vakbeweging en haar toekomst*. Amsterdam: Ontwikkeling, 1920.

Teulings, Ad, et al. *De nieuwe vakbondsstrategie*. Alphen a/d Rijn: Samson, 1981.

Voorden, W. van, ed. *Arbeidsverhoudingen uit model*. Alphen a/d Rijn: Samson, 1981.

Weggemans, J. H., ed. *Arbeidsverhoudingen bij de overheid*. Deventer: Kluwer, 1985.

Windmuller, John P. *Labor Relations in the Netherlands*. Ithaca, N.Y.: Cornell University Press, 1969.

IRELAND

Nevin, Donald, ed. *Trade Unions and Change in Irish Society*. Dublin: Mercier, 1980.

O'Brien, James. *A Study of National Wage Agreements in Ireland*. Dublin: Economic and Social Research Institute, 1981.

Pollock, Hugh M., ed. *Industrial Relations in Practice*. Dublin: O'Brien, 1981.

ITALY

Agócs, Sandor. "The Road of Charity Leads to the Picket Lines: The Neo-Thomistic Revival and the Italian Catholic Labor Movement," *International Review of Social History* 23 (1973): 28–50.

Ball, Donald H. "Worker Culture and Worker Politics: The Experience of an Italian Town 1880–1915," *Social History* 3 (1978): 1–21.

Barkan, Joanne. *Visions of Emancipation: The Italian Workers' Movement since 1945*. New York: Praeger, 1984.

Horowitz, Daniel L. *The Italian Labor Movement*. Cambridge, Mass.: Harvard University Press, 1963.

Hunecke, Volker. *Arbeiterschaft und industrielle Revolution in Mailand 1859–1892*. Göttingen: Vandenhoeck und Ruprecht, 1978.

Neufeld, Maurice F. *Labor Unions and National Politics in Italian Industrial plants.* Ithaca, N.Y.: Cornell University Press, 1954.

Tilly, Louise A. "I Fatti di Maggio: The Working Class of Milan and the Rebellion of 1898," in Robert J. Bezucha, ed., *Modern European Social History.* Lexington, Mass: D.C. Heath, 1972, pp. 124–158.

MALTA

Kester, Gerard. *Transition to Workers' Self-Mangament.* The Hague: Institute of Social Studies, 1980.

PORTUGAL

Wiarda, Howard J., *Corporatism and Development.* Amherst, Mass.: University of Massachusetts Press, 1977.

SCANDINAVIA

Bull, Edvard. "Industrial Workers and Their Employers in Norway, circa 1900," *The Scandinavian Economic History Review* 3 (1955): 64–84.

Evander, Nils. "Collective Bargaining and Incomes Policy in the Nordic Countries: A Comparative Analysis," *British Journal of Industrial Relations* 12 (1974): 417–437.

Ferraton, Hubert. *Syndicalisme ouvrier et social-democratie en Norvège.* Paris: Colin, 1960.

Galenson, W. *The Danish System of Labor Relations.* Cambridge, Mass.: Harvard University Press, 1952.

Korpi, Walter. *The Working Class in Welfare Capitalism: Work, Unions and Politics in Sweden.* London: Routledge and Kegan Paul, 1980.

Lafferty, W. M. *Economic Development and the Response of Labor in Scandinavia.* Oslo: Universitetsforlaget, 1971.

Lash, Scott. "The End of Neo-corporatism? The Breakdown of Centralized Bargaining in Sweden," *British Journal of Industrial Relations* 23 (1985): 215–238.

Leiserson, Mark W. *Wages and Economic Control in Norway 1945–1957.* Cambridge, Mass.: Harvard University Press, 1959.

Michels, Ank. *Labour Relations in Denmark.* Copenhagen: Unpublished paper, 1986.

Peterson, Richard B. "Swedish Collective Bargaining—A Changing Scene," *British Journal of Industrial Relations* 25 (1987): 31–48.

Philip, David. *Le mouvement ouvrier en Norvège.* Paris: Editions Ouvrières, 1958.

Therborn, Göran. *The Swedish Class and the Welfare State: A Historical-Analytical Overview and a Little Swedish Monograph.* Nijmegen: Institute of Political Science, 1983.

SOVIET UNION

Becker, A. *Sowjetische Lohnpolitik zwischen Ideologie und Wirtschaftsgesetz.* Berlin: Duncker und Humblot, 1965.

Brown, Emily Clark. *Soviet Trade Unions and Labor Relations*. Cambridge, Mass.: Harvard University Press, 1966.

Brügmann, Uwe. *Die russische Gewerkschaften in Revolution und Bürgerkrieg 1917– 1919*. Frankfurt am Main: Europäische Verlaganstalt, 1972.

Conquest, Robert. *Industrial Workers in the USSR*. London: Bodley Head, 1967.

Dewar, Margaret. *Labour Policy in the USSR, 1917–1928*. London: Royal Institute of International Affairs, 1956.

Johnson, Robert Eugene. *Peasant and Proletarian. The Working Class of Moscow in the Late Nineteenth Century*. Brunswick, N. J.: Rutgers University Press, 1979.

Koenker, Diane, and William G. Rosenberg. "Skilled Workers and the Strike Movement in Revolutionary Russia," *Journal of Social History* 19 (1986): 605–629.

Lane, David, ed. *Labour and Employment in the USSR*. Brighton, England: Harvester, 1986.

Lane, David, and Felicity O'Dell. *The Soviet Industrial Worker*. Oxford: Cowley, 1978.

Moskoff, William. *Labour and Leisure in the Soviet Union*. London: Macmillan, 1984.

Ruble, Blair A. *Soviet Trade Unions*. Cambridge: Cambridge University Press, 1981.

Rutland, Peter. "The Shchekino Method and the Struggle to Raise Labour Productivity in Soviet Industry," *Soviet Studies* 36 (1984): 345–365.

Schapiro, Leonard, and Joseph Godson, eds. *The Soviet Worker*. London: Macmillan, 1982.

Schwarz, Solomon M. *Labor in the Soviet Union*. New York: Praeger, 1951.

Slider, Darrell. "Worker Participation in Socialist Systems: The Soviet Case," *Comparative Politics* 18 (1986): 401–418.

Ziegler, Charles E. "Worker Participation and Worker Discontent in the Soviet Union," *Political Science Quarterly* 98 (1983): 235–253.

SPAIN

Almendros Morcillo, F., et al. *El sindicalismo de clase en España (1939–1977)*. Madrid: Península, 1978.

Barcells, Albert. *Trabajo industrial y organización obrera en la Cataluña contemporánea (1900–1936)*. Barcelona: Laia, 1974.

Fernanda, Romeu-Alfaro. *Las clases trabajadores en España (1898–1930)*. Madrid: Taurus

Seidman, Michael. "Work and Revolution: Workers' Control in Barcelona in the Spanish Civil War 1936–38," *Journal of Contemporary History* 17 (1982): 409–433.

Shubert, A. Revolution in Self-Defence: The Radicalization of the Asturian Coal-Miners 1921–34," *Social History* 7 (1982): 265–282.

Tunon de Lara, Manuel. *El movimiento obrero en la historia de España (1823–1936)*. Madrid: Taurus, 1972.

SWITZERLAND

Kämpgen, Jürgen. *Die Zusammenarbeit der Sozialpartner*. Bern: Herbert Lang 1976.

Schweizerische Arbeiterbewegung. Zürich: Lünmatt, 1975.

Index

About the Author

HANS SLOMP is a Universitair Docent (Lecturer) in the Institute of Political Science at the University of Nijmegen, Holland. He is the author of a number of publications on labor relations in Holland and Belgium including a monograph, *Arbeidsverhoudingen in Belgie* (Labor Relations in Belgium), and *Utrecht: Het Spectrum 1984*.